THE MOTIVATION HANDBOOK

Sarah Hollyforde, MCIPD, MBA, is a professionally qualified human resources (HR) manager. With 20 years' experience in both the private and public sector, her background has been in many differing areas including technology, operations and interim management. She has been involved in a wide range of HR applications, specialising in recruitment, selection, and learning. Having managed teams of all sizes, permanent and temporary, Sarah brings the benefit of her experiences in people management to the subject of motivation.

Steve Whiddett, BSc (Hons), MSc, C.Psychol., is a chartered occupational psychologist. He is the founder of ProLibra, an organisation specialising in work-based holistic personal development. Until 2002 he was a partner at Pearn Kandola where he specialised in assessment and development. Before that, he was a senior psychologist with one of the world's leading test publishers, where he was responsible for development, training and consultancy in job analysis techniques. Steve brings a wealth of practical experience to his field, having applied psychology in a wide range of multinational and national private and public sector organisations.

Steve Whiddett and Sarah Hollyforde co-wrote *The Competencies Handbook*, published by the CIPD in 1999.

The Chartered Institute of Personnel and Development is the leading publisher of books and reports for personnel and training professionals, students, and for all those concerned with the effective management and development of people at work. For details of all our titles, please contact the Publishing Department:

tel. 020 8263 3387

fax 020 8263 3850

e-mail publish@cipd.co.uk

The catalogue of all CIPD titles can be viewed on the CIPD website:
www.cipd.co.uk/publications

THE
MOTIVATION
HANDBOOK

Sarah Hollyforde
and
Steve Whiddett

Chartered Institute of Personnel and Development

Design by Paperweight
Typesetting by Intype London Ltd
Printed in Great Britain by The Cromwell Press,
Trowbridge, Wiltshire

British Library Cataloguing in Publication Data
A catalogue record for this book is available from the British Library

ISBN 0–85292–925–0

The views expressed in this book are the authors' own and
may not necessarily reflect those of the CIPD.

Chartered Institute of Personnel and Development. CIPD House,
Camp Road, London SW19 4UX
Tel: 020 8971 9000   Fax: 020 8263 3333
E-mail: cipd@cipd.co.uk Website: www.cipd.co.uk
Incorporated by Royal Charter. Registered charity no. 1079797

CONTENTS

ACKNOWLEDGEMENTS

We would like to thank all those people who have helped us write this book. In particular we would like to mention Mike Dudley, Alison Tennant, Andrew Stephens and John Christie, who kindly spent time giving us feedback. We would also like to thank Anne Cordwent, our editor, who was the key driving force ensuring that we met our (tight) deadline!

There are also many others without whom we would not have been able to complete the task. These include colleagues, clients, teachers and the researchers in the field of motivation whose valuable contributions have helped shape our views and given us the rich material that enabled us to produce this book.

1   INTRODUCTION

All authors sincerely wish that their readers are motivated to read their books. But books with a long introduction or prologue, especially when combined with an entreaty to read it all first, can put people off – especially when the reader has limited time and just wants to 'get stuck in' to the main text. So, for those readers who wish to get stuck in, we have a message

YOU DON'T HAVE TO READ THE INTRODUCTION FIRST!
– just read the notes in the box below.

Readers can leap straight in to the book. We think it is self-explanatory so you should be able to find your way around quite easily. All the same, there are some points we would like to make first.

READ THESE NOTES IF YOU ARE NOT GOING TO READ THE REST OF THE INTRODUCTION

About the book

- ☐ This book is written for anyone involved in people management. It will be of specific interest to those studying for formal qualifications, such as those following the CIPD's Professional Qualification Scheme, an MBA or other business courses.

- ☐ The motivation theories outlined in this book are those most commonly referred to in management training.

- ☐ Wherever possible we have reviewed the original text by the key author of each theory.

- ☐ The theories are covered in outline. Readers who would like to study a theory in more depth should refer to the References list at the end of each theory section.

□ The practical sections address a range of motivational issues in work settings. They cover how motivation theory may apply in such situations, illustrated with examples from organisations.

About motivation

□ Motivation is personal and not *created* by another. What organisations and managers can do is provide the environment, support and resources that will influence and effect motivation.

About style of presentation

□ We have used UK English throughout the text, even where original quotes were in American English. However, book and journal titles mentioned in the References/Further Reading are as they appear in the original text.

□ We have used the term 'manager' to describe anyone with responsibility for the management of other people. This term therefore includes team leaders, supervisors, department heads, project leaders, directors, and so on.

□ Whereas we have avoided using 'he', 'him' and 'his' to refer to people in general, we have remained faithful to original quotes, using 'he', 'him' or 'his' when the writer did.

For those readers who wish to read on we have structured the rest of the Introduction as a series of questions about motivation in general and about the book in particular.

What is motivation?

Most people are interested in motivation, even if the interest extends only as far as wondering why someone behaved in a particular way. But what exactly is it?

There are many definitions of motivation. Baron (1991) states that motivation is 'the internal processes that activate, guide, and maintain behaviour (especially goal-directed behaviour)'. Robertson and Smith (1985) agree, declaring that 'motivation is a psychological concept related to the strength and direction of human behaviour'.

Both of the definitions above assume that all behaviour, regardless of how it is instigated, is a consequence of motivation. Kanfer (1998), however, feels that motivation is only about the 'free will' element of behaviour and defines it as 'the psychological mechanisms governing the direction, intensity, and persistence of actions *not* due solely to individual differences in ability or to overwhelming environmental demands that coerce or force action' (her italics).

Herzberg (1987) takes this further. He feels that motivation that is the result of a 'kick in the pants' is not motivation but 'movement'. He describes movement as 'a function of fear of punishment or failure to get extrinsic rewards' and motivation as 'a function of growth from getting intrinsic rewards out of interesting and challenging work'.

To some this is no more than an argument about semantics, and whatever the behaviour, the drive pushing or pulling a person to act in a particular way is 'motivation'. From our research it appears that most researchers consider motivation to represent the drive behind human behaviour. It is this general definition that corresponds to our use of 'motivation' in this book.

One of the challenges facing researchers into motivation is that it cannot be seen. Kanfer (1990) states that what most people see is 'a multidimensional stream of behaviour and the products of those behaviours'. She goes on to say that 'motivational processes can be inferred only from analysis of this continuing stream of behaviour that is determined both by environment and heredity and is observed through their effects on personality, beliefs, knowledge, abilities, and skills'.

The reason motivation is hidden is that it comes from the individual. People cannot be motivated to do something if there is nothing in it for them. Of course, the 'reward' may be instrumental in achieving something else (ie a person may be motivated to do something they don't find rewarding in itself because it will help them get something else they do find rewarding). Also, the 'reward' may be the avoidance of a negative outcome as much as it may be the achievement of a positive outcome.

What does this book contain?

This book outlines the conclusions that the main researchers into the complex area of motivation have reached. We have written this book to cover the major motivation theories and to illustrate how these theories can apply to practical situations.

> **Part I: Motivation theories** outlines the major motivation theories, and some related theories. Each theory chapter has a summary of the theory together with some of the criticisms and/or support the theory has attracted. Wherever possible, we reviewed the original texts. To bring each theory to life, we illustrate it with examples using four fictional characters (see **Character profiles**).

> **Part II: Practical applications** illustrates how motivation theory can apply in work-related situations – at all levels, from setting strategy (organisation level) to applying it in groups and teams, and at individual level. Each chapter uses examples drawn from real organisational experience to bring the situations to life.

The contents have been formatted so that readers who have a particular motivation subject they wish to address can quickly skip to the part of the book most useful to them.

Each chapter of the book is 'free-standing' in that it can be read independently of every other chapter. In order to avoid rewriting the theory sections in the practical chapters (Part II) we have assumed a certain residual knowledge of each theory. Those without such knowledge can refer back to the relevant theory in Part I to get an overview.

How can readers use this book?

We have used a format in this book that allows readers to dip into the chapter they feel will be most useful to them. We envisage that those studying motivation as part of a course are likely to start at the theory sections. Those responsible for the management of a team are more likely to start at the practical sections.

Those wishing to use the book as a self-help guide (ie to resolve queries they have about their own motivation) should start by referring to the **Individual-level section** (Chapters 30 to 33) most pertinent to their own situation. These chapters should spark off ideas that will help resolve, or explain, the reader's own circumstances.

What is a motivation theory?

A theory is 'a collection of assertions, both verbal and symbolic, that identifies what variables are important for what reasons, specifies how they are interrelated and why, and identifies the conditions under which they should be related or not related' (Campbell, 1990).

A motivation theory is therefore one that outlines a researcher's answers to such questions as 'Why do people make the choices they make?' or 'What makes someone persist at one activity and yet quickly give up another?' or 'To what extent is a person's behaviour a free choice?' Weiner (1992) suggests that these researchers have a brief that goes beyond simply providing an answer. Motivational psychologists need to have a *better* answer to motivational questions than the layperson.

Weiner takes this position because, to varying degrees, most people wonder about why they, or others, behave in the way they do, and many arrive at their own conclusions. Motivational psychologists therefore have to arrive at more accurate conclusions that take into account the complexity of human behaviour (a feature that many amateur psychologists and simplistic people management 'solutions' neglect). Moreover, Weiner states that a good theory is one that 'may be applied in different situations to interpret specific actions. That is, a scientific explanation includes general principles that transcends the specific instance' (Weiner, 1992).

Following Weiner's statement, a good motivation theory would be one that applies to all situations. Thierry and Koopman-Iwema (1984) think that such a theory does not exist. They observe that 'We cannot maintain that there exists a widely acknowledged, comprehensive theory on motivation: on the contrary... there is a large number of "partial theories" which differ from one another in various respects.' They go on to point out that 'The great majority of the studies restrict themselves to a few aspects of behaviour, and research programs aiming at a coherence or even integration of theories are rarely taken up.'

What classifications of motivation theory are there?

Many books or articles on motivation classify the core theories in various ways. For example, Kanfer (1990) classifies them as:

☐ *need-motive-value theories* – those that 'emphasise the role of personality, stable dispositions, and values as a basis for behavioural variability' (eg **Existence-relatedness-growth theory** and **Hierarchy of needs theory**)

☐ *cognitive choice theories* – those that 'focus on cognitive processes involved in decision-making and choice (eg **Achievement theory** and **Expectancy theory**).

☐ *self-regulation-metacognition theories* – those that 'focus on the motivational processes underlying goal-directed behaviours (eg **Goal-setting theory**).

Thierry and Koopman-Iwema (1984) classify theories as:

☐ *content theories* – those that 'focus on *what* it is about the individual and/or about his environment that attracts his attention, what incites and sustains behaviour' (eg **Achievement theory**, **Hierarchy of needs theory** and **Internal–external control theory**).

☐ *process theories* – those that are 'related to the question *how* behaviour is energised, how it is channelled, how it is continued or changed' (eg **Drive theory**, **Equity theory** and **Expectancy theory**).

There is also a generally recognised split between theories that suggest behaviour is motivated by a push from the external environment to resolve an imbalance in the *status quo* and theories that suggest behaviour is motivated by a pull from the internal environment to set up an imbalance.

In this book we have chosen to simply list the theories in alphabetical order for easy reference.

What theories are included in this book?

Motivation is a widely researched and reported subject. Many motivation theories exist, so we had to make a choice in what to include. Our criteria for inclusion was based largely on how popular and widely referred to a particular theory is (so theories that appeared once in a journal did not make it into the book) and how applicable to the workplace it is (so theories relating to a specific area, such as sport, were rejected). Motivation theories linking behaviour with early personal development (eg psychoanalytical theories), although popular on psychology courses, we considered beyond the scope of a general management handbook.

There were three main reasons for our selection criteria. Firstly, this book is intended to be a *general* guide to popular motivation theories, not a psychology textbook. Secondly, we focused on motivation in work settings. Lastly, we aimed for the text to be as practical as possible and therefore tipped the balance of the book slightly more in favour of practical applications than theory.

How can organisations and managers motivate their staff?

The short answer to this is that motivation is not something which can be 'imposed' on someone else. Adverts for products to assist in changing a lifestyle (giving up smoking, going on a diet, etc.) claiming that the organisation in question can 'give you the motivation' are not exactly telling the truth! What organisations and managers *can* do is provide the environment, support and resources that impact on the motivation of individuals. This can be in the form of providing the rewards, working conditions, systems and processes, learning opportunities, encouragement, and so on, that maximise the chances that employees will be motivated to give their best to the organisation.

How can motivation theories be applied to practical situations?

Having a 'good motivation theory' is all very well, but why should anybody other than theorists be interested? Can't we all go about our daily business without knowing a single theory? Of course we can. However, a good or powerful theory can help in many ways. Campbell (1990) outlines a list of features of a powerful theory, one of which is that it provides 'useful guidance for how to approach a wide variety of specific problems'.

Motivation theories can therefore offer guidance to anyone with an interest in motivational issues. It is worth noting, however, the word 'guidance'. Motivation theories do not give a definitive answer to all motivation questions. There are many variables (relationships with others, background, personality, financial circumstances, mood, and so on) that work together to create a situation and a person's reaction to it. It is difficult for anybody – even perhaps the person concerned – to fully understand why variables result in particular behaviours.

What motivation theories *can* do is provide frameworks within which those who are interested in motivation (of themselves and/or others) can start to understand why people behave in particular ways in specific circumstances. Motivation theories are therefore useful in that they 'start the ball rolling'.

We can illustrate this point with an organisation that is designing a new job. Motivation theories such as the **Job characteristics theory** and **Equity theory** are useful frameworks to start the design process. However, neither theory can state exactly what that organisation should do within its own environment or situation – that is the role of whoever is in control of the design process.

When dealing with individuals, motivation theories can help managers consider how and why people are motivated. For example, **Hierarchy of needs theory** may help managers figure out where someone is in terms of the satisfaction of his or her short- and long-term needs – which may in turn influence how they seek to create the situations that may be the most motivating. We reiterate the point made previously: motivation theories will not give the answer to how to create the most motivating situation for each individual in a manager's team – that is the role of the manager together with each individual.

How have motivation theories been applied to practical situations in this book?

We have applied the theories in ways we see as being appropriate. However, we are not suggesting that the solutions, or suggestions, offered by the theories are the only ways in which these issues can be tackled. We acknowledge that there may be other interpretations of the theories. Readers should therefore use the practical sections to spark off ideas about how motivation theories could apply in their own situations, rather than trying to use them as the definitive guide to all their motivational issues.

As mentioned above, each practical chapter covers a range of applications for motivation theory in organisations. Not every theory is covered in every practical chapter, firstly because they do not all apply directly to every situation, but also because to have done so would have been impractical.

Some readers may be encountering issues not covered within this book. In this event we recommend that a similar situation that *is* covered may give some insight. Alternatively, a quick read through of the **Key points** of each theory (outlined in each theory chapter) may help. Readers with their own, personal motivation issues to address should read on.

How can readers use this book to deal with their personal motivational issues?

Although we have not included a 'self-help' section, readers who wish to explore their own issues of personal motivation can still use the book to help. The best way to do this, we think, would be to refer to the **Individual-level chapters** (Chapters 30 to 33) first to find the situation most closely resembling their own. For example, if a reader is wondering why his or her motivation for a job has diminished, he or she may refer to the **Managing under-performers chapter** (Chapter 32). If someone is preparing for an objective-setting meeting and wants to ensure that those at the meeting feel motivated by him or her, he or she could refer to the **Objective-setting chapter** (Chapter 30).

Motivation is a complex area. *The Motivation Handbook*

provides a clear and concise framework that covers the major theories and explores how those theories can apply in practical work situations. The *Handbook* has been designed to be easy to use, and has been created to be as relevant as possible to most readers' experiences of motivation at work.

References

BARON R. A. (1991) 'Motivation in work settings: reflections on the core of organizational research'. *Motivation and Emotion*. Vol. 15, No. 1. pp.1–8.

CAMPBELL J. P. (1990) 'The role of theory in industrial and organizational psychology'. In Dunnette M. D. and Hough L. M. (eds) *Handbook of Industrial and Organizational Psychology*. Palo Alto, CA, Consulting Psychologists.

HERZBERG F. A. (1987) 'One more time: how do you motivate employees?'. *Harvard Business Review*. Vol. 46. pp109–20. (Note: This article includes a reprint of an article that appeared in *Harvard Business Review* in Jan–Feb 1968.)

KANFER R. (1998) 'Motivation'. In Nicholson N. (ed.) *Encyclopedic Dictionary of Organizational Behavior*. Oxford, Blackwell Publishers Ltd.

KANFER R. (1990) 'Motivation theory and industrial and organizational psychology'. In Dunnette M. D. and Hough L. M. (eds) *Handbook of Industrial and Organizational Psychology*. Palo Alto, CA, Consulting Psychologists.

ROBERTSON I. T. *and* SMITH M. (1985) *Motivation and Job Design*. London, Institute of Personnel Management.

THIERRY H. *and* KOOPMAN-IWEMA A. M. (1984) 'Motivation and satisfaction'. In Drenth P. J. D., Thierry H., Willems P. J. and de Wolff C. J. (eds) *Handbook of Work and Organizational Psychology*. Chichester, John Wiley & Sons Ltd.

WEINER B. (1992) *Human Motivation. Metaphors, theories and research*. California, Sage Publications.

PART I

MOTIVATION THEORIES

2 INTRODUCTION TO MOTIVATION THEORIES

Part I of the book covers a range of core motivation theories together with some theories related to motivation. Each section is set out in a standard format so that readers can easily find the information they are seeking. This format corresponds to:

Title

This is the most common name for the theory. Theories are listed in alphabetical order.

Core/related theory

A *core theory* is one that is specifically about motivation.

A *related theory* is one that covers issues related to motivation, although it is not itself specifically about motivation.

Also known as

A list of common alternative names for the theory.

Key author(s)

A list of authors most connected with writings on the theory.

Summary of theory

A brief outline of the key points of the theory. Key words are **emboldened** for ease of reference.

Wherever possible, we have reviewed the original texts.

Examples

Illustrations of key points of the theory using fictional characters. Some background to the characters is described in the **Character profiles** just before the Introduction of the book.

Key points

For quick reference, the main points made by the theory are listed.

Commentary   An overview of some of the research sup-
                        porting or criticising the theory, plus
                        comments of our own.

Our aims for the theory chapters are that readers will be able
to understand the key points within each theory and gain a
broad overview of the conclusions reached, and the support
and criticisms attracted by it.

3 ACHIEVEMENT THEORY

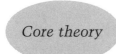

Core theory

Also known as

      Achievement/power theory
      Need for achievement theory
      Theory of needs

Key author(s)

      D. C. McClelland
      J. W. Atkinson

Summary of theory

      Achievement theory is the result of research into behaviour in *achievement-oriented activities*. Such activities are characterised by three factors:

- The individual feels responsible for the outcome (success or failure).
- The individual expects to receive unambiguous feedback on the results of his or her actions.
- There is some degree of uncertainty or risk in the activity.

      The motivation to pursue an achievement-oriented activity is based on three key conditions:

- The activity must be one the individual wants to undertake.
- The outcome of the activity must be one the person thinks he or she can successfully achieve (expectancy).
- The outcome must be one that has value to the person (incentive).

Behaviour in achievement-oriented activities is stated as being based on the need for achievement, (ie the strength of the motive to achieve 'success'). The individual defines 'success'. One person's definition of 'success' could well be different from another's. The more successful someone perceives the outcome of an achievement-oriented activity, the more likely he or she is to enjoy the experience and therefore to strive to build on it or repeat it in the future.

Atkinson (1964) defined the *need for achievement* ('nAch') as a 'capacity to experience pride in accomplishment'. A sense of accomplishment can be recognised in the link between *expectancy* and *incentive* (see above). The more certain someone is that he or she will be successful in an activity, the less likely he or she is to feel a sense of accomplishment in achieving it. This is based on the assumption that there is a greater sense of achievement when someone has successfully completed a difficult task than after completing an easy one. For example, people are more likely to feel a sense of pride in meeting a challenging deadline than they would when achieving an easy one.

Surely, though, challenging tasks also bring with them the eminent possibility of failure? Atkinson (1964) proposes that every achievement-oriented activity has an inherent *'approach-avoidance conflict'*. In other words, there is conflict between working towards a positive sort of outcome (approach) and not doing the activity to avoid a negative outcome (avoidance). Achievement theory is therefore not only about positive success. Someone may be motivated to avoid a situation in which he or she foresees failure more than he or she is motivated to seek a situation in which success is more likely. *Fear of failure* ('fF') is 'a wish to avoid the shame of failure' (Mook, 1987).

Atkinson also suggests that the predicted value ('valence') of the outcome influences even those with high nAch. Such individuals, if they feel the goal or outcome has no valence, are unlikely to strive for success and more likely to take action simply to avoid failure.

Initial research papers concluded the motivation to avoid failure might instigate achievement-oriented behaviour. In other words, a person could be motivated to do something as a way of avoiding failure. Later research stated this was an incorrect interpretation of the data and that the correct interpretation of the motivation to avoid failure corresponds to 'what activities a person is not likely to undertake, not what activities he is likely to undertake' (Atkinson and Feather, 1966).

So, could people with high nAch be described as thrill-seekers, being more motivated the more risky the activity? Not exactly. In fact, people with high nAch are generally most motivated by tasks of *intermediate* difficulty. On the one hand they do not want to undertake tasks so easy that they would feel no sense of pride in achieving them. On the other hand they do not want to undertake tasks so hard that there is a more than average chance of failure. People with fF tend to undertake tasks with more extreme goals – either very easy (to increase the chances of success) or very difficult (so they cannot be expected to achieve them – setting themselves up to fail before they have even begun).

McClelland felt that the need for achievement is influenced heavily by the culture within which people are brought up. In societies where there is a focus on the work ethic people are more likely to work towards achievement, or towards avoiding failure. This is the result of learning what is rewarded within the society as a whole (praising success in the media and folk-tales, for example) and within the immediate family/social group (eg hugs, smiles, family tales).

In addition to achievement, McClelland also suggests that people are motivated by their need for power and their needs for affiliation.

The need for power ('nPow')

When testing his nAch theory, McClelland found there were some managers who, despite being very senior in their organisation, did not have high nAch. McClelland explained their motivation for achieving such success through the construct nPow. This is a person's need to have an impact on other people. McClelland suggests that there are three ways in which nPow can manifest itself:

☐ through *strong actions* – these include:

- assault and aggression
- giving help or assistance
- controlling others
- influencing or persuading others
- trying to impress someone

☐ through *action that produces strong emotions in others* – this is regardless of whether or not the act, in itself, seems to be strong

☐ through *actions that would enhance or preserve a person's reputation.*

People who are high-nPow tend to have some particular characteristics:

☐ They accumulate prestige possessions.

☐ They play competitive sports which are one-to-one (eg football or tennis) rather than one-against-nature or against-the-clock (eg swimming or golf).

☐ They like belonging to organisations and holding office in them.

☐ They satisfy their power motive through thought and feeling (eg reading sports magazines or watching violent TV shows).

People who are high-nPow tend to demonstrate their need in either of two ways:

☐ *Personalised power* ('pPow') describes people who see their relationships with others as 'personal' – a competitive situation in which they use their power to strive to be the winner. They are usually low on inhibition. McClelland describes their style as involving a kind of one-to-one competitiveness in which they want most of all to dominate or win out over someone else.

☐ *Socialised power* ('sPow') describes people who see relationships with others as impersonal. They prefer to use their power for the general good of the group. Conflict with others is not necessarily avoided, but it is carefully planned in advance because sPow people recognise that for every win there is a loss. Such people are usually self-disciplined.

The need for affiliation ('nAff')

This describes the need for creating and maintaining positive relationships with others. Those high in nAff tend to like being around people and avoid conflict situations because they have a fear of rejection. High-nAff people work hard to achieve acceptance and may also be high-nAch if they think that this will improve their chances of acceptance by others.

Examples (see **Character profiles**)

Mandy could be described as being motivated by the achievement of success in management development. Success to Mandy includes the publication of articles, speaking at conferences, and so on. She is striving for this as the result of positive feedback about an article she wrote for her company journal and a talk she gave to the executive team last year. Mandy has recently been motivated by the opportunity to speak at a conference next year. She is working hard on preparing for this, spending some of her own time on it as well as the time she was given at work.

Neil could be described as having a motivation to avoid failure. When applying for jobs recently (the result of which is his current job) his then manager wanted him to apply for a secondment position to a high-profile senior position in another part of the organisation. Although Neil acknowledged that the job would give him good experience and a pay rise, he did not want to apply for it because he felt he would almost certainly not get it. Despite regular encouragement from his boss, Neil always found reasons not to submit his application. In the end, the closing date went by and Neil had still not applied. Although Neil felt a stab of disappointment, he was mostly pleased he had not set himself up to fail. As he said to his partner, 'I can't fail at something I didn't try, can I?'

Key points

- [ ] Where there is an 'achievement-oriented activity', behaviour is based on the need for achievement (nAch).
- [ ] Achievement-oriented activities are those where the person is responsible for the outcome, where the person

can expect unambiguous feedback on his or her actions, and where there is some uncertainty or risk.

☐ Need for achievement (nAch) is the capacity to experience pride in accomplishment. A sense of accomplishment is recognised in the link between expectancy and incentive.

☐ Each person has his or her own definition of what success is.

☐ Achievement-oriented activities involve an inherent 'approach-avoidance conflict' – ie a conflict between achieving a positive outcome or avoiding a negative outcome.

☐ People with high nAch tend to be motivated by tasks of intermediate difficulty. People with a high need to avoid failure (fF) tend to set themselves extreme goals.

☐ Need for power (nPow) is a person's need to have an impact on other people through personalised power (pPow) or socialised power (sPow).

☐ Need for affiliation (nAff) corresponds to a need for creating and maintaining positive relationships with others.

Commentary

Early on, Achievement theory was not specifically about work. It was later tested out on a wide range of people, including businesspeople. McClelland's research was focused more on population-wide outcomes, Atkinson's more on how the theory applied to individuals.

Achievement theory has evolved and been refined over the years. Indeed, McClelland *et al* (1953) state that 'the data came first and the theory second'. They also state that if they had had the theory when they started, it 'would have led to the design of "cleaner" experiences'. Still, they had high hopes for the theory, declaring that further research might result in a theory that would be 'general enough to handle simple animal drives on the one hand or complex human motives involving belief systems on the other'.

Some writers see the achievement motives for success and for failure-avoidance working hand in hand. A person might thus be motivated by goals that not only increase the chance of success but, at the same time, diminish the chance of failure (Thierry and Koopman-Iwema). It is difficult to deduce from this theory how much of a person's motivation is inspired by the probability of success and how much by the incentive to achieve. Even the person concerned probably could not explain the ratios.

Achievement theory deals with a specific area of motivation given an 'all things being equal' situation. The effects on the motivation to achieve within situations in which all things are *not* equal have not been explored in depth. For example, the theory does not address how high-nAch people would deal with a situation in which they were offered a very attractive reward to undertake a task with a high probability of failure or how feelings of security and confidence may affect the need for achievement.

Weiner suggests that Achievement theory does not consider how the *causes* of success or failure affect feelings of pride or shame. He feels that it is people's perception of *why* something was successful or not which dictates how they feel about the outcome as much as the outcome itself. See **Attribution theory** (Chapter 5) for further information.

Achievement theory does not explore *why* some people relish a challenge and others fear failure. For example, when dealing with people with high fF, if a manager knew *why* it was that failure was feared, perhaps he or she could support the individual in dealing with the situation when such fear was evidently causing problems.

Achievement theory does not explain how managers can identify whether people are high-nAch or high-fF. A person who sets a very stretching goal may be someone who is high-nAch and has overestimated the probability of success or high-fF and is setting up a 'no-win' situation. Knowing which it is would help managers and their reports to agree more realistic goals and would also assist in analysing past failures or successes.

This theory also suggests that people with high nAch and who see effort as the primary element of successfully completing goals, may take on tasks beyond their capability because they believe that if they try hard enough, they will succeed. It may be a successful strategy to achieve longer-term goals. However, in the short term, this may be counter-productive.

It would be easy to think that a challenge is something that is considered technically difficult. Yet there may be non-technical elements of a task which give people a sense of attainment. Even a routine task may give accomplished individuals satisfaction if they set themselves challenging goals for the task. For example, an experienced employee may find satisfaction in a simple filing task if he or she establishes sub-goals such as completing the task within a tight time-deadline or faster than someone else.

Achievement theory is useful when considering why people react differently to achieving challenging goals and why they react to failure in individual ways. However, it is limited in that it offers no accurate way to measure levels of nAch, nPow or nAff and does not explain underlying reasons for motivations.

References

ATKINSON J. W. (1964) *An Introduction to Motivation.* Princeton, Van Nostrand.

ATKINSON J. W. (1974) 'The mainsprings of achievement-oriented activity'. In ATKINSON J. W. and RAYNOR J. O. (eds) *Motivation and Achievement.* New York, Wiley.

ATKINSON J. W. *and* FEATHER N. T. (1966) *A Theory of Achievement Motivation.* New York, John Wiley.

MCCLELLAND D. C. (1951) *Personality.* New York, Holt, Rinehart & Winston.

MCCLELLAND D. C., ATKINSON J. W., CLARK R. A. *and* POWELL E. L. (1953) *The Achievement Motive.* New York, Appleton-Century-Crofts.

MCCLELLAND D. C. (1961) *The Achieving Society.* Princeton, Van Nostrand.

MCCLELLAND D. C. (1965) 'Toward a theory of motive acquisition'. *American Psychologist.* Vol. 25. pp321–3.

MCCLELLAND D. C. (1971) *Assessing Human Motivation.* New York, General Learning Press.

McClelland D. C. (1975) *Power: The inner experience.* New York, Irvington.

Mook D. G. (1987) *Motivation: The organization of action.* New York, W. W. Norton & Company.

Thierry H. *and* Koopman-Iwema A. M. (1984) 'Motivation and satisfaction'. In Drenth P. J. D., Thierry H., Willems P. J. and de Wolff C. J. (eds) *Handbook of Work and Organizational Psychology.* Chichester, John Wiley & Sons.

Weiner B. (ed.) (1974) *Achievement Motivation and Attribution Theory.* Morristown, NJ, General Learning Press.

Weiner B. (1980) *Human Motivation.* New York, Holt, Rinehart & Winston.

4   ACTIVATION THEORY

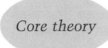

Core theory

Also known as
> Arousal theory

Key author(s)
> D. E. Berlyne
> W. E. Scott

Summary of theory
> Activation theory is primarily a physiological theory of motivation, based on studies of the effects of heightened and depressed levels of activation or arousal on the brains and bodies of organisms. Berlyne and Scott were among the first to apply Activation theory to a work setting. The theory is based on the premise that people strive to maintain a certain balance of activation. If a person is over- or under-activated, he or she will seek activities to redress the situation. Another key premise of Activation theory is the *Yerkes-Dodson law*. This states that people work at their best when they are moderately aroused (rather than over- or under-aroused).
>
> Revealing its physiological background, one definition of *activation* is 'the degree of excitation of the brain stem reticular formation' (Berlyne, 1967). For those of us who are not neurophysiologists it is perhaps more helpful to think of activation as 'the extent of release of stored energy through physical activity' (based on Duffy, 1962). Activation might therefore be seen as a range of 'activity' from comatose (in which state stored energy is hardly being released at all) to

hyperactive (in which stored energy is released at a rate too fast for the body to cope with effectively).

The *optimum level of arousal* is not so clearly defined. The original theory defines it in terms of physical stimulation but behavioural theorists include elements of perception. It is reasonable therefore to conclude that optimum levels are a combination of physical and psychological needs and as individual as fingerprints.

Research of Activation theory in work settings concentrates on what happens when people are *under-activated* in their jobs. Jobs that result in *over*-activation are largely ignored in the research 'perhaps because few such jobs exist for rank-and-file workers in contemporary organisations' (Hackman and Oldham, 1976). Over-activation is explored only in general terms.

Jobs in which people are under-activated tend to be routine jobs. It is the repetitive nature of the job that leads to problems in motivation rather than the routine *per se*. This is demonstrated by the observation that people tend to feel more activated at the start of the day or when starting a new task.

Any new job tends to engage interest early on. Not only do new job-holders have to learn the job (for even if they have done it before elsewhere, there will be differences), they also need to become familiar with their new environment. Activation levels at this stage are likely to be high. However, the longer a person does a routine job, the more likely activation levels are to decrease. Performance may then decline, and continue to do so, unless the person can be 're-activated'.

Low activation is particularly important in organisations. Research shows that at low activation levels, performance is decreased due to three key factors.

□ a lack of alertness
□ a dulling of the senses
□ a lack of muscular co-ordination.

Such physical reactions are likely to impact on productivity. Outcomes might include some or all of:

□ an increase in errors
□ an increase in the time taken to complete a task

□ a greater variability in performance
□ an increase in the likelihood of accidents.

In situations of under-activation, people seek *activities to increase their stimulation*. In a work situation they may do this in a number of ways.

□ They may leave the situation, temporarily (eg physically moving about) or permanently (eg resigning from the job).
□ They may think of an anticipated or past event that stimulates them (ie daydream).
□ They may undertake social activity (eg conversation with colleagues, horseplay).
□ They may introduce variation within the job (ie change the process to make it more interesting).

There is potential in the activities listed above for behaviour that managers do not want to see! This theory could explain why some people in routine, repetitive jobs may be happy at work but not perform particularly well. Individuals who love their jobs because they have fun with the people they work with may well fall into this category.

External variation to try to deal with low levels of activation (eg formal rest periods, systems for employees to monitor their own progress, and – the most effective external activator – monetary reward) often focuses on the processes around the work, rather than on the job itself. Most change of this type results in an increase in activation simply because of the novelty. Berlyne (1967) pointed out, however, that even where external variation is initially successful in increasing activation, its effects are short-lived.

It should be possible to make most routine jobs stimulating by changing the job itself. Berlyne (1967) suggests that we could introduce a number of *different types of stimulation*, including:

□ novelty
□ complexity
□ variation
□ intensity

☐ uncertainty.

Berlyne also accepts, however, that there is little evidence that any one of these in particular will change levels of activation – not least because it is difficult to separate them. For example, introducing task complexity is likely *also* to introduce variation and novelty. This poses problems for researchers, but the above list does suggest ways in which managers may try to increase activation levels of jobs if under-activation is an issue.

Examples (see **Character profiles**)

When Rachel was at college she worked in a shop stacking shelves to earn some extra money. The job was thus very repetitive, even if well paid (for a student, anyway), and friends often expressed surprise that she stuck at the job for so long. They thought she would have preferred to work on the tills, or at least in a job they considered challenging. Rachel, however, found the job almost therapeutic. She was working very hard at college and there was a lot to take on board, so she was actually glad her job did not require too much thinking.

Frank's first job was on a production line producing car components. The job was repetitive, involving no variety at all. The only decision operatives on the shop floor had to make was when to ask managers for a decision! In the early days Frank did not mind this, not least because he was working with a bunch of great people. They had quite a laugh – often playing practical jokes on other teams. Their supervisor could hardly approve that they wasted operational time, but Frank and his pals felt that having a laugh at work made the days go more quickly.

Key points

☐ Activation (or arousal) is a description of energy released through activity. It can be seen as a range of states of activity from comatose to hyperactive.

☐ People strive to maintain a certain balance of activation, and they work at their best when they are moderately aroused (the Yerkes-Dodson law).

☐ Each person has his or her 'optimum' level of arousal based on physical and mental stimulation.

☐ Jobs considered under-activating tend to be repetitive. Such jobs can have mental and physical effects that can be detrimental to performance at work.

☐ Actions taken by job-holders to bring activation up to the optimum level include leaving the situation (temporarily or permanently), daydreaming, social activity, and creating variety within the job.

☐ External variation, introduced by the employer, may work for a while, but the effects tend to be short-lived.

☐ Ways of changing the job to make it more stimulating include introducing novelty, complexity, variation, intensity, and uncertainty.

Commentary

Activation theory is similar to **Drive theory** (see Chapter 8) in that both work on the premise that people are motivated to redress an imbalance. However, in Drive theory, motivation is to reduce a drive/stimulus to a 'zero' state. In Activation theory, motivation is to keep drive at an 'optimum' state.

The main criticism of Activation theory is that a good deal more research is needed to test its validity in a work setting. If nothing else, a way should be found to measure the elements that go towards making an activity more or less stimulating. Even Berlyne (1967) accepts that it is difficult to establish how much external factors (in the job itself) affect stimulation and how much personal factors (eg mood) affect it.

A logical conclusion from Activation theory is that in order for productivity to increase, jobs should be enriched and enlarged to match activation levels preferred by a job-holder. However, this theory does not illuminate how to assess someone's 'optimum' activation level. In fact, Berlyne acknowledges that direct measurement of activation level is problematic – not least because most people are fairly reluctant to have electrodes implanted in their brains! Thankfully, he suggests that less direct means of measurement – such as physiological tests of arousal (eg pupil size) or psychometric tests – could be developed.

Berlyne admits that it is difficult to identify what it is about a stimulus that creates change in activation levels. As noted above, although there is a range of possibilities it may be hard to separate them enough to conduct worthwhile research. But Berlyne suggests variation is the key. He feels that simply increasing the number of tasks is unlikely to increase activation except in the short term. Yet even increasing the variety of tasks is likely to be successful only if the tasks require sufficiently different responses to make them interesting. Consider, for instance, a job that involves inputting data onto a PC from standard forms. If the organisation decides to introduce 'variety' simply by increasing the range of forms from which data has to be input, the job is unlikely to become more interesting for the new forms will essentially require the same operative functions as previous forms.

Hackman and Oldham feel that Activation theory offers useful insights into the design of jobs. However, for the reasons outlined above, they feel that until there is a reliable and valid way to assess the optimum activation levels of people at work, the best an organisation can do with this theory is apply it crudely – for example, 'in situations where it is clear that most employees are enormously over- or under-stimulated by their jobs' (Hackman and Oldham, 1976).

Individual, optimum levels of arousal are reached not only through work. Although the time-scale over which arousal can be averaged out is likely to be relatively short, it is not unreasonable to conclude that someone with an extremely stimulating life outside work may be satisfied with a comparatively unstimulating job. Likewise, someone with a very stimulating job may find that he or she prefers the quiet life at home.

Although the state of over-arousal in a work setting was not explored specifically by Berlyne and Scott, it is logical to conclude that people who feel over-stimulated in their jobs will seek ways of redressing that situation. It is logical also to assume that in the face of an over-stimulating situation people would take similar actions to those they would take to deal with an under-stimulating one (although reducing rather than increasing variation). This implies that over-stimulation can be as counter-productive to an organisation as its opposite.

Activation theory seems to make sense when thinking about the behaviour of people in boring jobs, and to some extent that of people in jobs that are extremely busy. It can also help managers understand why people react differently to the same job. The effects of under-stimulation seems to ring true in organisations with routine and repetitive jobs (production lines, call centres, and so on). Yet managers should not assume that the theory applies to all individuals in the same way. Individual optimum levels of activation are not easy to measure: the theory should therefore not be applied to individuals without close contact at work with each one to understand the situation from his or her viewpoint.

References

BERLYNE D. E. (1967) 'Arousal and reinforcement'. *Nebraska Symposium on Motivation.* Vol. 15. pp1–110.

DUFFY E. (1962) *Activation and Behavior.* New York, Wiley.

HACKMAN J. R. *and* OLDHAM G. R. (1976) 'Motivation through the design of work: test of a theory'. *Behavior and Human Performance.* Vol. 16. pp250–79.

SCOTT W. E. (1966) 'Activation theory and task design'. *Organizational Behavior and Human Performance.* Vol. 1. pp3–30.

5   ATTRIBUTION THEORY

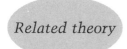

Related theory

Also known as

Key author(s)

F. Heider

B. Weiner

Summary of theory

Attribution theory, first proposed by Heider, is not strictly a theory of motivation. Whereas motivation describes the *direction* of behaviour, Attribution theory describes the beliefs people have about *why* they behave in the way they do. One definition stresses this. 'Attribution theory concerns the processes by which an individual interprets events as being caused by a particular part of a relatively stable environment' (Kelly, 1967).

Weiner found close links between Attribution theory and **Achievement theory** (see Chapter 3). Achievement theory suggests that people seek pride in accomplishment or avoid the shame of failure. Weiner feels it is not just the success or failure of activities that engender pride or shame but also the explanations the person attributes to the *causes* of success or failure. For example, Achievement theory suggests that failure for high-nAch individuals should demotivate them – because the probability of future success has been lowered by the recent failure. Later research showed, however, that people with high nAch were *more* motivated to carry on when they failed to achieve a goal. Weiner suggests this is because high-nAch people view the cause of failure to be lack of effort rather than lack of competence. So when a high-nAch person fails in a task, he or she ascribes it to not working hard enough and will continue to want to succeed, at least for a time. See **Achievement theory** (Chapter 3) for further information.

People with a high need to avoid failure (high fF) are more likely to attribute failure to their own lack of ability (rather than effort) or to situational factors outside their control. This means that they are likely to give up on the task at the first setback. Such a passive response to failure is often referred to as *learned helplessness*. There is an element of self-fulfilment in this attitude, for the greater the expectancy individuals have that they are going to fail, the more likely it is that they will, because they do not contemplate persevering.

Heider suggests that attribution of success or failure at a task is linked to *the perceived skill of the person in relation to the complexity of the activity*. Complexity is measured by how likely people think it is that others could do the same thing. 'If we know that only one person succeeded or only one person failed out of a large number in a certain endeavour, then we shall ascribe success or failure to this person. . . . On the other hand, if we know that practically everyone who tries succeeds, we shall attribute success to the task' (Heider, 1958).

Attribution theory also applies to how people deal with the performance of other people. The cause to which a manager ascribes another's success or failure at a task influences how that manager deals with the other. A manager who attributes the outcome to the person's skills is likely to deal with it differently from how he or she would deal with it if the outcome was attributed simply to the situation.

Individuals may attribute unexpected successes or failures to *luck* or *opportunity*. Both have to do with favourable or unfavourable environmental conditions. Luck centres on an element of chance (eg winning the lottery) and does not depend on the efforts, skills or abilities of the individual. Opportunity is when circumstances allow a person to take advantage of the situation to undertake an activity he or she would not otherwise have been able to. For example, a person might well believe that he or she achieved promotion at work only because the opportunity presented itself.

Attribution theory is also linked to **Internal–external control theory** ('I-E theory'). I-E theory proposes that not everyone in the same situation will attribute the same outcomes to the same causes. It goes on to state that an individual with an internal locus of control (see **Glossary**) is likely to attribute the cause of any outcomes to his or her own efforts (or lack of them). An individual with an external locus of control is likely to attribute the cause of any outcome to the environment. See **Internal–external control theory** (Chapter 15) for further information.

Examples (see **Character profiles**)

Rachel and her fellow students sat a short test at the outset of their course. Although Rachel passed the test with high marks, she felt that this was more to do with the test than her skills because everyone else on the course passed with similar marks. When she achieved a distinction for the whole course, however, she did feel it was to do with her efforts and skills because she was only one of two in her year to get such a mark.

Neil really wanted to learn how to play golf, in particular because he thought that it would improve his business network. He took lessons and practised regularly. There were many times when he failed to hit the ball even in the right direction – he just could not get the hang of how to swing the golf club. Yet he persevered although some of his friends thought he should call it a day and accept that he was never going to be much good. Neil felt his failures were far more to do with his lack of effort than with any lack of skill on his part. To this day Neil is not a good golfer, but he is always striving to improve (and has gained some good business leads at the golf club!).

Key points

☐ Attribution theory is an explanation of the beliefs people have about *why* they behave in the way they do.

☐ It is not just the success or failure of activities that

engender pride or shame but also the explanations that a person attributes to the *causes* of success or failure.

□ Attribution of success or failure at a task is linked to the perceived skill of the person in relation to the complexity of the activity.

□ Unexpected successes or failures may be attributed to luck or opportunity. Luck is chance that is not dependent on the effort, skills or abilities of an individual. Opportunity is when circumstances allow a person to take advantage of the situation to undertake an activity positively.

□ Attribution theory is linked to Internal–external control theory.

Commentary

Although Attribution theory is not a theory of motivation, it is included because it can help understanding about how people might interpret success and failure. It can help managers gain some insight into the reasons people behave in the way they do – what underpins their motivations and drives.

Generally, research has supported Attribution theory. In particular, links between expectancy and the way in which people attribute the cause of actions have been strongly supported. However, it is a theory that is not as clearly defined as our simple explanation may make it appear. For example, locus of control depends on a number of variables – what an individual may feel in control of on one day, he or she may not feel so well in control of on another. This means managers cannot assume that a person with high nAch will always attribute causality to his or her own efforts, or lack of them, or that those with high fF will always attribute causality to their own skill, or lack of it.

Attribution theory suggests that to change motivation, if appropriate, it would first be necessary to change someone's belief as to the cause of his or her successes and failures. This is a challenging situation, not least because the manager has to be as objective as possible (ie not put his or her own interpretation on events) and it requires staff members to be able to articulate their perceptions clearly and accurately.

Observer bias (eg to what factors a manager ascribes an

employee's success or failure during performance reviews) is a key issue when applying Attribution theory in a work setting because it is not easy to remove. This *fundamental attribution error* is the 'tendency of observers to underestimate the importance of situational factors and overestimate the influence of internal dispositions and traits . . . as the cause of actor behavior and outcomes' (Martinko, 1998). Managers may in this way ignore the situational factors that surround an employee's performance, good or bad, ascribing the cause of success or failure to the employee rather more than perhaps they should.

Although Attribution theory offers an explanation for how people think of success or failure, this explanation may not be easily understood by the people themselves. Their emotions may cloud the issue even more. Of course, they may also find it difficult to be honest about their perceptions of causality if they think it will cause conflict. For example, if a manager is discussing the reasons for a failure to achieve a goal with an individual who thinks that it was due to the manager's lack of support, the person may feel unable to say that. The implication of this for managers is that it may be difficult to establish what a person does attribute his or her success or failure to, even when discussing it together personally.

Attribution theory helps managers understand why it is that some people are motivated to try despite failure whereas others give up at the first hurdle. It is a key theory underpinning many motivation and behavioural theories, which is why we include it in the book. However, as outlined above, it is also a more complex theory than it may at first appear. This is not to suggest abandoning it as an aid to managing motivation. It is to suggest that managers should not assume that a basic knowledge of the theory is enough to make decisions about other people's motivations. Explore, and proceed with caution!

References

HEIDER F. (1958) *The Psychology of Interpersonal Relations.* New York, Wiley.

KELLY H. H. (1967) 'Attribution theory in social psychology'. In Levine D. (ed.) *Nebraska Symposium on Motivation*. Vol. 15. pp192–237.

MARTINKO M. J. (1998) 'Fundamental attribution error'. In Nicholson N. (ed.) *Encyclopedic Dictionary of Organizational Behavior*. Oxford, Blackwell Publishers.

WEINER B. (ed.) (1974) *Achievement Motivation and Attribution Theory*. Morristown, NJ, General Learning Press.

WEINER B. (1980) *Human Motivation*. New York, Holt, Rinehart & Winston.

6 COGNITIVE EVALUATION THEORY

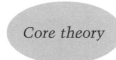

Also known as
  CET

Key author(s)
  E. L. Deci

Summary of theory

The basis of Cognitive evaluation theory (CET) is that an activity which is satisfying in itself (ie intrinsically motivating) becomes more extrinsically motivating when other people link external rewards to the outcomes of that activity. This is because a key part of this theory is about the locus of causality, or locus of control (see **Glossary**). There are two extremes of locus of control:

☐ the *internal locus of control*, where the individual feels his or her behaviour is self-directed

☐ the *external locus of control*, where the individual feels his or her behaviour is directed by others or by the environment.

Locus of control can be illustrated using a simple example in which two people explain their exam success. The person with an internal locus of control credits his or her own hard work. The person with an external locus of control credits luck on the day, easy questions, and so on. Likewise, in the case of failure the first person would put it down to lack of preparation, the second to bad luck, the poor weather, a stressful journey to the exam, or similar. See **Internal–external control theory** (Chapter 15) for further information.

When someone is intrinsically motivated to undertake an activity, he or she generally feels an internal locus of control. If someone else attaches a reward to the activity, CET suggests that the individual will begin to feel that it is the environment that controls the activity and thus their behaviour – external locus of control. CET thus supposes that people in this situation will change their view of the activity and their actions. As a result they become less intrinsically motivated to undertake the activity. This point can be interpreted as a shift of obligation. For example, when someone turns a hobby into his or her job it often means less enjoyment for him or her in doing it. The theory suggests that this is because the activity has changed from something he or she wanted to do for the pleasure of it to something he or she feels obliged to do for the rewards others bestow for it.

Intrinsically motivated behaviours are defined as being 'behaviours which a person engages in to feel competent and self-determining' (Deci, 1975). Intrinsic motivation is assumed to be better than extrinsic only in as much as people are likely to sustain activities they are intrinsically motivated to do for longer periods of time than those they feel extrinsically motivated to do. They are also more likely to derive pleasure from intrinsically motivated activities.

Reward is 'the internal condition brought about by the attainment of the goal (ie the satisfaction)' (Deci, 1975). Goals are not necessarily all 'positive'. 'Reward' can be as much to do with the satisfaction felt from avoiding a negative situation (punishment, shame, etc) as it is to do with the satisfaction felt from achieving a positive situation (pride, approval, etc).

Deci felt that the link between external rewards and their effects (see **Glossary**) on intrinsic motivation highlighted two important implications:

☐ Extrinsic rewards have a stronger impact than intrinsic rewards because people shift from being intrinsically motivated to extrinsically motivated rather more quickly than the other way around.

☐ If people think they are undertaking an activity because of an extrinsic reward, they will only continue to undertake that activity as long as the reward evidently continues to be on offer.

Deci outlines two key elements of the reward, as experienced by its recipient:

☐ the degree to which the person perceives the reward as *controlling* his or her behaviour – Deci contends that rewards given extrinsically are generally used as a control. For example, an employee gets paid because he or she does what the organisation wants; a child gets praise for doing what the parent wants. In these cases, the aim of the rewarder is 'to control the person's behaviour – to make him continue to engage in acceptable behaviours' (Deci 1975)

☐ the degree to which the recipient perceives the reward as being *informational* – Rewards that reinforce feelings of competence and self-determination (the behaviours associated with intrinsic motivation) are comprehended as informational.

Every reward has these two elements. For example, positive feedback given to an individual is part controlling (because it is being given to endorse a behaviour desired by the rewarder) and part informational (because it is reinforcing the person's own satisfaction/reward for doing a good job). However, the balance varies, and it is the element that is perceived to be the greater that influences how the recipient feels about the reward. If a reward is considered primarily controlling, CET suggests a person considers his or her behaviour is motivated by the reward – ie their motivation is extrinsic. If a reward is considered primarily informational, CET suggests a person considers his or her behaviour is motivated by the desire to undertake the task for the satisfaction of the task itself (ie that the motivation is intrinsic) and that the reward is feedback on his or her performance.

Deci proposes that the controlling element applies

particularly when the extrinsic reward is money. In other words, people are likely to find an activity less intrinsically motivating when others link a financial reward directly to it. Non-contingent financial rewards do not affect motivation as much because there is no link between the activity and the reward. Other types of reward (eg praise), however, seem to bear more on the informational element. When rewards are considered informational there seems to be no reduction in intrinsic motivation.

Managers should be careful not to assume that all contingent rewards have a negative effect on intrinsic motivation and that all non-contingent rewards do not (or have a lesser effect). Deci states that 'the simple fact of a contingent-versus-noncontingent situation is not the critical variable, in and of itself, for determining whether or not extrinsic rewards will decrease intrinsic motivation. The important factor is whether or not the *controlling* aspect of the reward is salient' (Deci, 1975 – our italics). For example, consider the extremely contingent financial reward of piece rate pay. Individuals who feel that they are the best-paid operatives in the company because they work hard to earn that amount are likely to feel that the reward is controlling, and they are therefore likely to be extrinsically motivated. Individuals who feel that they are the quickest and best operatives in the company, as reflected in the good pay that they get, are likely to feel that the reward is informational, and they are therefore more likely to be intrinsically motivated.

Would the effect of the reward be the same regardless of how much it is valued? What if an individual thinks the reward is not worthwhile? Deci suggests it is not the 'salience of the reward, *per se*, but rather the salience of the controlling aspect of the reward that is critical' (Deci, 1975). For example, if someone is given praise (reward) for a job well done, it is not the praise itself that is important but how much that praise is comprehended as being controlling.

Negative feedback was shown to cause a decrease in intrinsic motivation. In one experiment, negative feedback included such comments as 'Although you did solve that one, you took longer than average', and 'Well, most people were able to solve that one – but let's go on to the next' (Deci,

1975). In other words, seemingly 'innocuous' phrases were used, but were enough to undermine confidence.

A final point about rewards. Intrinsic motivation is most adversely affected by external rewards when those rewards are expected before the activity is undertaken. External rewards given after the event, but not expected beforehand, still affect intrinsic motivation (mostly because people then re-evaluate the activity in light of the reward) but not as much.

Deci outlines the implications of this theory in the world of work, and in particular how it impacts on job design. The impact is dictated largely by how the organisation thinks people will be motivated in their jobs, extrinsically or intrinsically.

Organisations that assume people will be motivated extrinsically in their jobs are simultaneously assuming that employees will perform effectively in their jobs only to the extent that the rewards they receive are contingent on effective performance. In such organisations jobs should be designed to closely link reward and performance. Deci outlines several factors which may contribute to making such schemes successful:

☐ control mechanisms that effectively link performance with reward
☐ carefully developed standards of performance communicated to workers
☐ clear standards for payment communicated to participants
☐ monitoring of workers' behaviour – although not always the case, it is likely that most workers in such a system will have to follow strict guidelines on *how* to do their jobs as well as being told what outputs are expected
☐ supervisors who support teams through detailed planning and direction
☐ a system for administering rewards in accordance with set standards
☐ rewards seen to be administered fairly.

The limitations to such a scheme include:

□ Controls must be operative at all times to keep people motivated.

□ People tend to do whatever they can to minimise the effort they put in to achieve rewards – this is unlikely to be what the management team intends.

□ Sabotage of the system is likely because people generally dislike control (as opposed to information).

Organisations that assume people will be motivated intrinsically in their jobs are simultaneously assuming that employees will perform effectively if their job is structured in such a way that they will motivate themselves. In such organisations jobs should be designed to allow each person to feel competent and self-determining. Deci suggests that to be successful such situations should take into account several specific factors:

□ People should be given broad objectives and be allowed discretion in how objectives are to be achieved.

□ There should be minimal extrinsic controls.

□ Supervisors should support teams through consultation.

□ Employees should be encouraged to participate in decisions that affect them.

□ The scope of a person's responsibility should take in a complete process (rather than just one small part of it).

The benefits of such a scheme include:

□ Controls are minimal and are more likely to be on outputs rather than inputs (on end results rather than on the means of getting there).

□ People take pride in their work and therefore strive to maximise their effort.

□ Employees are more satisfied and more productive.

Deci declares that 'I am not asserting that people should not be paid. All that I mean to imply is that while contingent rewards can motivate a person extrinsically, they appear to be doing so at the expense of intrinsic motivation' (Deci, 1975). It is unlikely that organisations would keep many employees, if any, if they chose not to pay them. However,

CET suggests, the more closely organisations link rewards to performance, the more they are working to a model of extrinsically motivated staff and all that that entails. Deci accepts that there may be jobs which no one would find intrinsically interesting and it may therefore be appropriate that organisations work on the extrinsic motivation model. However, he also suggests that such organisations should perhaps first look to see if such jobs could be redesigned to make them more interesting.

One final point on money and motivation. Deci feels that managers should distinguish between rewards to keep a person on the job and rewards to motivate people to perform satisfactorily once in the job. As he says, 'Paying workers is necessary to attract them to jobs and keep them satisfied with those jobs. However, if money is to be used as a motivator of performance, the performance has to be perceived by the worker as being instrumental to his receiving the money' (Deci, 1975). (See **Expectancy theory** – Chapter 11 – for more information on instrumentality.) This is a reiteration of the point made above about the value of the reward. In this case 'it is not the money *per se* which motivates performance, but rather it is the way that it is administered' (*ibid.*). If an organisation aims to use money to motivate, it will be an extrinsic motivator and one that will be seen as more controlling than informational. If an organisation's aim is to intrinsically motivate staff, wages should be paid non-contingently to attract people to the job and keep them satisfied but no more.

Examples (see **Character profiles**)

Rachel joined the social committee at work. It was a role that she took on voluntarily because she thought she would meet people from across the organisation and because she wanted experience of working on a committee. For the first six months she enjoyed the role, although it was hard work and took up an amount of her spare time. Rachel did not mind putting in several hours over weekends and evenings because she found the experience satisfying and enjoyable. People often thanked committee members for their hard work, and Rachel was glad her efforts were acknowledged.

Last year the senior management team acknowledged that the role deserved recognition because social activities were a good way of encouraging teamwork. To enthuse people to join the social committee a financial reward was attached to the job. The amount people received varied depending on their contribution to the committee – as decided by the chair. Rachel was grateful for the extra money, but it started to change how she felt about the role. For example, she spent less time on activities she felt were not 'valued' by the chair.

This year the company changed the policy on rewards for the social committee. The net effect of the changes were that the financial rewards were reduced. Rachel felt demotivated by this and decided to resign from the committee. She felt that the role had been devalued by the decision to decrease the pay for it, even though she had been happy to fulfil the role for nothing in the early days.

Key points

☐ Cognitive evaluation theory (CET) supposes that people want to feel in control of their behaviour and to be the 'cause' of it – ie internal 'locus of causality'.

☐ If others link an activity that is intrinsically motivating to extrinsic rewards, an employee is likely to feel that his or her behaviour is controlled by the environment – ie external 'locus of causality'.

☐ Reward can be the satisfaction felt from avoiding a negative situation as well as the satisfaction from reaching a positive situation.

☐ Reward has two key elements – the degree to which it is considered controlling and the degree to which it is considered informational. The element perceived to be the greater influences how the recipient feels about the reward.

☐ Activities with contingent externally-granted rewards that are regarded as controlling are likely to result in employees who undertake the activity feeling less intrinsically motivated and more extrinsically motivated.

☐ Contingent financial rewards have a greater detrimental

effect on intrinsic motivation than either non-contingent financial rewards or contingent non-financial rewards.

☐ Pay is a prerequisite for most jobs, without which most employees would not start, or stay at, work. However, if money is to be used as a motivator, performance has to be perceived as being instrumental to receiving the money.

☐ Negative feedback generally causes a decrease in intrinsic motivation.

☐ Intrinsic motivation is most adversely affected by external rewards when those rewards are expected before the activity is undertaken.

☐ Organisations which assume that people will be motivated extrinsically in their jobs should design jobs that closely link reward and performance. This requires detailed systems and management procedures.

☐ Organisations which assume that people will be motivated intrinsically in their jobs should design jobs to allow individuals to feel competent and self-determining. This requires broad systems and management procedures.

Commentary

Some research into Cognitive evaluation theory (CET) reveals that the link between intrinsic motivation and extrinsic rewards is not as straightforward as Deci proposed. One report showed that financial rewards affected intrinsic motivation far less than was originally supposed if the situation was accepted as typical in that environment. In other words, if someone undertakes an activity that has a financial reward attached to it that everyone gets, the reward in itself affects intrinsic motivation less than Deci's original research suggested (Fisher, 1978).

A key criticism is Deci's lack of clarity about the effects of extrinsic rewards. On the one hand he seems to suggest they have a negative effect on intrinsic motivation, but on the other he states that they will not have such an effect if the recipient perceives them as informational. This controlling-versus-informational element of reward seems to have been overlooked by some critics. For example, consider the following criticisms:

☐ Carver and Scheier question the suggested automatically-negative relationship between intrinsic motivation and contingent extrinsic rewards, stating that some people find a task *more* intrinsically motivating if others have attached a reward to the outcome. They say that 'When such rewards are perceived as reflecting personal competence at the activity, the presence of rewards in greater amounts has been found to produce increases in task interest and task involvement' (Carver and Scheier, 1981).

☐ Manderlink and Harackiewicz (1984) suggest that non-financial contingent rewards vary in their effect on intrinsic motivation. For example, during the stages of learning a new activity feedback may have a positive effect on intrinsic motivation. However, the more experienced a person becomes in the task, the more he or she may find the same feedback is having a negative effect on his or her intrinsic motivation.

Carver and Scheier (1981) point out that psychologists often underplay the informational part of a reward, which may be the issue here. This can be seen in the description of the effects of negative feedback. Deci does not seem to investigate whether recipients of negative feedback would view this 'reward' as informational if they considered it valid. The results of his research therefore suggest that people always consider negative feedback as controlling. In our view, feedback regarding shortfalls in performance does not automatically have to decrease intrinsic motivation if it is valid and well communicated. As Carver and Scheier say, 'It is important to keep in mind that the effect of any reward can be expected to depend upon what information the reward conveys' (Carver and Scheier, 1981).

Clearly this theory has major implications for performance-related pay (PRP) schemes by which organisations quite deliberately link extrinsic reward to a range of activities. If the organisation introduces a PRP scheme because it believes this motivates individuals to perform at their best, there should be some consideration of this theory which suggests that intrinsic motivation is generally adversely affected by extrinsic rewards.

Most rewards in organisations are contingent on performance and therefore more likely to be considered controlling than informational. However, it is the *degree* to which rewards are considered contingent that affects how controlling the reward is viewed. See the chapter on **Reward** (Chapter 23) for further information.

Cognitive evaluation theory is a complex one to apply to a work situation in as much as it does not explain how managers are to know how a person perceives a reward. It also makes the issue of pay a thorny one if organisations wish to encourage intrinsic motivation. However, it does help managers understand why rewards can have a negative effect. It also encourages organisations to think carefully about their reward systems and how close the match is between the features of those systems and the way in which they would prefer people to be motivated.

References

CARVER C. S. *and* SCHEIER M. F. (1981) *Attention and Self-Regulation: A control-theory approach to human behavior.* New York, Springer-Verlag.

DECI E. L. (1975) *Intrinsic Motivation.* New York, Plenum Press.

FISHER C. D. (1978) 'The effects of personal control, competence, and extrinsic reward systems on intrinsic motivation'. *Organizational Behavior and Human Performance.* Vol. 21. pp 273–88.

MANDERLINK G. *and* HARACKIEWICZ J. M. (1984) 'Proximal versus distal goal-setting and intrinsic motivation'. *Journal of Personality and Social Psychology.* Vol. 47. pp 918–28.

7   CONTROL THEORY

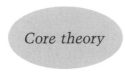

Core theory

Also known as
Negative feedback loop theory

Key author(s)
N. Wiener
G. A. Miller, E. Galanter and I. H. Pribram
H. J. Klein
M. A. Campion and R. G. Lord

Summary of theory
Control theory was originally part of Wiener's study of communication and automatic control systems mainly in machines (cybernetics). It was later adapted for use in explaining human behaviour (Miller, Galanter and Pribram, 1960; Powers, 1973) and applied to work situations (Campion and Lord, 1982). Control theory is based on the premise that human action and motivation is based on a *negative feedback loop*. The negative feedback loop consists of a series of inputs and outcomes that operate on a circular path. These inputs and outcomes may be illustrated by using the classic example – the central heating system:

☐ effector – central heating system
☐ output – hot air that the system produces
☐ detector/sensor – thermometer
☐ comparator – system that compares the current temperature with the standard

- □ standard – temperature setting programmed in to the thermostat
- □ negative feedback – difference between the current temperature and the pre-set temperature
- □ input – message sent to the system as a result of the feedback, which, in this case, will be to take no action if there is no discrepancy, switch off the boiler if the temperature is too high, or switch on the boiler if the temperature is too low.

This loop will continue until a pre-set standard is achieved. At that point, the action will cease, although the loop will continue to check that no new discrepancies have emerged.

As noted above, Control theory was originally part of cybernetics and is therefore largely associated with machine-based systems. However, a number of Control theorists state that the negative feedback loop can be used to explain the motivation behind many human behaviours. The terms of the classic example of the loop (above) can thus be applied to 'human' systems:

- □ effector – the person who takes the action following input
- □ output – the action the person takes in response to negative feedback
- □ detector/sensor – the effector's perception of his or her own actions
- □ comparator – the effector's judgement when assessing performance
- □ standard – the pre-set desired criteria against which performance is assessed
- □ negative feedback – the difference between performance and the standard
- □ input – the judgement that prompts action to resolve the negative feedback.

To many Control theorists this theory seemed to lend itself to motivation because the human drive for competence relies on a control system which checks progress against predetermined standards much like Control theory. However, in its purely 'mechanical' form, Control theory has shortcomings.

This was recognised by one Control theorist who accepted that 'in human systems neither the sensor, standards, nor effector are necessarily fixed quantities' (Klein, 1991). Klein went on to point out that 'feedback involves much more than the mechanical sensing of the environment, goals are not predetermined inflexible standards, and there are several alternatives for reducing discrepancies' (*ibid.*).

To address these deficiencies, Klein renames 'standard' as 'goal' and proposes that several singularly human processes occur between the effector and comparator – such as an individual's change of behaviour or change in the choice of goal. If it is accepted that these additions are not central to the cybernetics approach, the core components of the feedback loop remain. Klein argues that many theories may be adapted to apply to different circumstances – such a change to Control theory, in itself, does not make it an invalid theory.

Negative feedback loops operate at a number of different levels, and goals set in a higher order will influence lower-order goals. For example, if a person has to produce on average 2,000 units of work per month, this goal will inform the lower-order goals of how many units he or she has to produce, on average, in one day or one week. Likewise, producing 2,000 units per month may contribute to the higher-order goal of earning a bonus that may, in turn, contribute to the higher-order goal of maintaining a certain lifestyle. The highest order of goal is likely to be an abstract perception such as logic or moral principles (Carver and Scheier, 1981).

Lower-order goals are usually pursued only as long as their ability to contribute to higher-order goals continues. *Lower-order goals stop contributing* in either of two situations:

☐ if an alternative, more attractive, way of achieving a higher order presents itself – To continue the example above, if a more attractive, alternative, way of achieving this same lifestyle came along (eg a better paid job), the lower-order goal is likely to be supplanted.

☐ if it seems highly unlikely that it will in fact contribute to achieving the higher-order goal – Again using the previous example, if before the end of the month a person is so short of the target that, whatever he or she does, the higher-order goal has become impossible to achieve, he or she may abandon or re-set the lower-order goal.

Some view Control theory as a good way of integrating many other theories of motivation (eg Klein, 1991). In particular, it is considered one of the few theories that focuses on self-regulation in response to external influences such as goals and incentives. Many motivation theories focus on the effects of external influences as if those influences are unchangeable, and they therefore fall short of explaining how people change their responses to those influences.

Control theory links to **Goal-setting theory** (see Chapter 12) in that it is based on standards, or goals, against which behaviour is compared. It is perceived by some as more flexible than Goal-setting theory, however, because it recognises that people have multiple goals at any one point in time, and that these goals will be modified over time.

Examples (see **Character profiles**)

Rachel set herself a goal of getting a distinction on her course. Throughout the course she received feedback on her progress towards this goal. For example, Rachel's tutor knew of her ambition and would give her feedback on her performance at tutorials to help her develop her thinking beyond what was needed simply for a pass. The marked elements of the course also gave Rachel information on how she was doing. Rachel's first assignment did not receive the rating she had been hoping for, and that made her work harder on the next one to compensate. At the end of the course Rachel was one of only two students in her year to get a distinction.

In a previous job, Neil had been a sales consultant for an office supplies company. He was very ambitious and aimed to be the top sales person in his division. During his first year he privately set himself the goal of achieving 50 per cent more sales than the target agreed with his manager. He worked out how much he would need to sell each month in order to achieve this. Each month that went by, however, although he always exceeded his agreed target, he always fell short of the extra needed to achieve his private goal. Eventually, Neil perceived that the 50 per cent was not realistic, and he decided to drop his private goal altogether and just concentrate on the agreed target. On reflection, Neil realised that his private goal had always been far too ambitious, and he now sets himself more realistic private goals and adjusts them if necessary rather than abandoning them all together.

Key points

☐ Control theory is based on the premise that human action and motivation stems from a negative feedback loop. This loop is the system in which performance against a set standard is monitored. Perceived deviation from the standard (negative feedback) results in the system working to bring performance back to the standard.

☐ The system is self-regulating: monitoring and corrective action is therefore carried out as part of the system itself.

☐ Control theory was originally focused on machine-based systems but has been adapted to be applicable to human systems of motivation.

☐ Negative feedback loops operate at a number of different levels. Goals set in a higher order influence lower-order goals.

☐ Lower-order goals are usually pursued only as long as their ability to contribute to a higher order goal continues. They stop contributing if an alternative, more attractive way of achieving a higher order presents itself or if it looks highly unlikely that it will in fact contribute to the higher-order goal.

☐ Control theory would seem to be one of the few theories that focuses on a person's self-regulation in response to external influences such as goals and incentives.

Commentary

Control theory was originally part of the science of machine-related system regulation (cybernetics) and, as such, has attracted most of its criticism from those who feel that it has limited application to the human condition. Locke argues that human beings 'have the capacity to focus (or not focus) their attention on their output, to change or not change their goals, to acknowledge or not acknowledge discrepancies between output and goals, to process this information in many different ways, and to act or not act on the basis of this knowledge' (Locke, 1991) – all of which makes people different from machines.

Human behaviour involves many processes not available to machines. For example, people set their own standard against which outcomes are measured and that standard can be changed by the effector. Clearly, this is not the case with machines. As Locke points out, 'systems have no goals of their own' and therefore rely on humans' installing them (Locke, 1991). Although Control theorists claim to have dealt with this by adding in a range of cognitive processes, many critics feel this is merely a convenience and moves too far away from the original theory to make it justifiable to keep calling it Control theory.

The ability on the part of the effector to set, and change, his or her own goals gives rise to a major criticism of this theory. Control theory relies on the premise that behaviour is the result of a desire to reduce discrepancy – very similar to **Drive theory** (see Chapter 8). Locke and others claim that behaviour is actually motivated by discrepancy *creation*. In other words, because people set their own goals they are creating discrepancy. After all, Locke *et al* claim, if discrepancy removal was the motivating factor, the most effective action would be to adjust the standard to fit the situation. Discrepancy removal is thus a *consequence* of setting standards rather than the *cause*. See **Drive theory** (Chapter 8) for further information.

Control theory implies that people know what to do when there is negative feedback. There may, however, be situations in which people are aware of a shortfall but not sure how to deal with it. For example, when people are new to a job, or are learning, they may be aware of the standards they have to achieve – and may be getting the necessary feedback to realise they are not meeting those standards. Lack of experience, though, may mean that they do not know what to do to redress the situation. Again, this is a fundamental difference between the machine-based Control theory, in which corrective actions have to be programmed in before the system can work (or the system fails), and human Control theory, in which corrective actions may have to be learned along the way.

To pursue this point: the theory implies that actions eventually close the negative feedback loop – by successfully meeting the standard, by changing the standard, or by abandoning it altogether. This suggests that people dislike 'unfinished tasks' and will finish them or render the tasks unnecessary.

The debate between whether Control theory, once adapted to apply to humans, is still Control theory or not is an issue hardly relevant to the manager trying to deal with the motivation of his or her staff. Whatever it is called, unless managers have a good grasp of other motivational theories, Control theory seems somewhat limited in helping them understand behaviour in the workplace. Although it describes how people work towards dynamic goals, it does not help managers understand how those goals are set. Also, although the theory outlines in what circumstances some goals may change, it falls short of explaining the *process* by which people make decisions to change goals. Why is it, for example, that some people continue working towards goals they do not seem to be getting nearer to achieving, or goals that seem to have been met in other ways?

Whatever the theory is called, and whatever its shortcomings, Control theory can help managers understand why people have goals they are motivated to achieve, and why these goals are not always set in stone. Indeed, managers could play an important role in helping their team members set goals and monitor progress towards them.

References

CAMPION M. A. *and* LORD R. G. (1982) 'A control systems conceptualisation of the goal-setting and changing process'. *Organizational Behavior and Human Performance*. Vol. 30. pp265–87.

CARVER C. S. *and* SCHEIER M. F. (1981) *Attention and Self-regulation: A control theory approach to human behavior*. New York, Springer-Verlag.

CARVER C. S. *and* SCHEIER M. F. (1982) 'Control theory: a useful conceptual framework for personality, social, clinical and health psychology'. *Psychological Bulletin*. Vol. 92. pp111–35.

KLEIN H. J. (1989) 'An integrated control theory model of work motivation'. *Academy of Management Review*. Vol. 14. pp150–72.

KLEIN H. J. (1991) 'Control theory and understanding motivated behavior: a different conclusion'. *Motivation and Emotion*. Vol. 15, No. 1.

LOCKE E. A. (1991) 'Goal theory versus Control theory: contrasting approaches to understanding work motivation'. *Motivation and Emotion*. Vol. 15, No. 1.

MILLER G. A., GALANTER E. *and* PRIBRAM I. H. (1960) *Plans and the Structure of Behavior*. New York, Henry Holt.

POWERS W. T. (1973) 'Feedback: Beyond behaviorism'. *Science*. Vol. 179. pp351–6.

WIENER N. (1948) *Cybernetics: Control and communication in the animal and the machine*. Cambridge, Mass., MIT Press.

8   DRIVE THEORY

Core theory

Also known as

Drive reduction theory

Key author(s)

C. L. Hull

Summary of theory

Drive theory seeks to explain why people are driven (motivated) to satisfy their needs, and why such needs elicit certain responses. The theory is based on the premise that people are driven to reduce stimuli, and that the responses they use to reduce those stimuli are those they have learned to be more effective than others. For example, if someone is driven to satisfy the need for food, stimulated by the feeling of hunger, he or she learns that eating food is an effective response because hunger goes away once the food is eaten.

Drives are the result of working to achieve, and/or to maintain, a feeling of balance or satisfaction. Drives are considered either *primary* (relating to physical needs such as for food, drink, rest, nurturing children, etc) or *secondary* (relating to needs such as for relationships, status, etc). Primary drives are the ones considered innate; they are part of a person's makeup and are instinctive. Secondary drives are learned or acquired; they are developed as responses to the environment that a person is surrounded by.

As people experience needs, they learn which behavioural responses are most effective. The more times a particular response satisfies a need, the more that response is reinforced as being effective. It follows that the more strongly a response is reinforced, the higher the likelihood that it will be used again in similar circumstances. See **Reinforcement theories** (Chapter 17) for further information.

If there is a *direct* link between the behaviour and the stimulus, there is *primary reinforcement*. This would apply in the hunger example given above. Eating satisfies the hunger stimulus – there is a direct link between the two. Sometimes people relate outcomes with events that are *indirectly* linked to the key event – *secondary reinforcement*. The more people associate events with each other, the stronger they assume a relationship between them. Eventually, they need only the associated event to elicit a particular behaviour. An example of this is Professor Pavlov's dogs. Pavlov rang a bell every time he fed the dogs. After a time the sound of the bell alone would result in the dogs salivating in expectancy. Secondary reinforcement can be seen in the connection between money and drive satisfaction. When people work for financial gain, it is not the money itself they want – it is the things they can buy with it.

Habits are the result of reinforced responses (behaviours). The more reinforced a particular response, the stronger the habit. The stronger the habit, the more difficult it is to change.

Behaviour, Hull suggests, is the result of drives (which motivate people to meet a need) and habits (the way people have learned to respond to certain events). Later research suggests that the promise of an effective outcome (an incentive) also influences behaviour (see next paragraph). Behaviour is only likely to change if habits cease to result in drives being satisfied. Habits are difficult to break because to *learn* that the old behaviour no longer satisfies the need requires several 'failed' outcomes.

Initially, Hull's Drive theory did not include any reference to an incentive, so all behaviour was seen as the result of drives and habit. The incentive element was introduced to explain why behaviour could change rapidly. For example, receiving an unexpected and large financial windfall may rapidly change an incentive someone previously had for working, and therefore also change his or her related behaviours.

Drives can be increased by deprivation or anxiety. For example, the hunger drive becomes greater the more an individual is deprived of food, or the more an individual becomes anxious that he or she will not be able to find food in the future. Drive theory contends that there is an incremental relationship between drive and reinforced behaviour. The stronger the drive, the stronger the most reinforced habits become. It follows, then, that deprivation or anxiety will be helpful if it encourages the right response – ie that the strongest habit is the one that is most effective. However, if the strongest habit is not effective, heightened drive will only make matters worse. It also follows that flexibility in behaviour reduces as drive increases – choices of behaviour are reduced as anxiety or deprivation are increased.

Examples (see **Character profiles**)

Mandy's manager expects all consultants to be very well prepared for any meeting he holds. The first few meetings Mandy had with her manager embarrassed her. Although she had prepared, it became obvious during the meeting that she had not done enough preparation. Mandy got to the stage where she could not attend any meeting unless she felt she had fully prepared for it – even when the meeting was with a different manager. Mandy's behaviour was the result of secondary reinforcement linking her drive to meet her need to feel that she was doing a good job and her newly acquired habit of thorough preparation before meetings.

Neil was never the best time manager in the organisation. A couple of years ago he attended a time management course and picked up a number of very helpful hints and tips about how to organise his day. Soon after he got back to work following the course there was a crisis at work when half of his team suddenly went off sick at the same time. Neil's newly acquired skills went by the wayside and he reverted to all his old, bad habits, actually making things worse! Nowadays Neil feels that many of the techniques he picked up on the time management course come more naturally to him.

Although some still go by the wayside when he is under stress, many of them have now become habit.

Key points

☐ Drive theory is based on the premise that people learn from previous experience the degree to which their behaviour is effective in meeting their needs.

☐ Primary reinforced behaviour is when a response is directly linked with a stimulus.

☐ Secondary reinforced behaviour is when a response is linked with a stimulus that is connected to, but not actually, the key stimulus.

☐ Primary drives motivate people to meet innate needs such as hunger.

☐ Secondary drives motivate people to meet acquired needs such as status.

☐ The more a response is successful, the more it is reinforced. The more strongly a response is reinforced, the more likely it is that it will be used in similar circumstances in the future.

☐ Habits are the result of reinforced behaviour. The stronger the habit, the more difficult it is to break it.

☐ Behaviour is considered to be the result of drive, habit and incentive. Behaviour usually changes gradually, but there are times when the rapidly changing value of an incentive affects behaviour rapidly.

☐ There is an incremental relationship between drive and reinforced behaviour.

☐ Drives can be increased by deprivation or anxiety. Deprivation or anxiety may be helpful if they encourage the right response but are likely to make matters worse if the strongest habit is not effective.

☐ Flexibility in behaviour reduces as drive increases.

Commentary

Drive theory is based on a physiological premise. It assumes that behaviour is learned subconsciously rather than intellectually. In this sense it is rather simplistic and does not account for people changing behaviour as the result of thinking through an alternative path beforehand. It does not deal with complex activities that have not been experienced before. It does not account for human ability to plan ahead – eg reducing an anticipated drive rather than an actual one. Most of the supporting research is based on animal experiments, not situations in work settings.

Later experiments (still with animals) showed that there does not have to be an effective outcome (a reward) for behaviour to be reinforced. Researchers contended that some learning took place even when there was no reward ('latent learning'). However, even this was refuted. Researchers who disagreed with this contention argued that some reward must have been introduced, even if it was unintentional and through secondary reinforcement. There is some agreement, nonetheless, that it is not the *size* of the reward that matters, just that there is one. Rewards are only considered 'valid' if they are valued by the individual who receives them. This is true for many motivation theories.

Drive theory assumes that behaviour is motivated by the need to reduce a stimulus – that organisms strive to achieve 'zero' stimulation. This clearly does not explain why it is that some people deliberately put themselves into challenging or risky situations. Research into the effect of activity levels on behaviour shows that people do not react well to low levels of stimulation – far from seeking to reduce stimulation to zero, they will seek to *increase* stimulation. Proponents of **Activation theory** (see Chapter 4) suggest that rather than being motivated to reduce stimulation to 'zero', people will try to maintain it at 'optimum'.

Activation theory also challenges Drive theory's contention that there is an incremental relationship between drive and behaviour. Activation theorists would contend that there is actually a law of diminishing returns, and that in such situations people will generally seek to curtail stimulation once the optimum level has been reached. See **Activation theory** (Chapter 4) for further information.

Although it has limitations, Drive theory encourages managers to think about why some behaviours seem ingrained despite being counter-productive. The theory also explains why, when trying to change behaviours, organisations need not only positive rewards to endorse new behaviours (and negative rewards to discourage 'old' behaviours) but also a time of relative calm in which to practise the new behaviours. How often do managers see people revert to their old ways when they feel under pressure, rather than use their newly acquired behaviours?

Drive theory can also help explain why certain behaviours continue despite being contrary to stated policies and procedures. People will learn what is and is not acceptable behaviour in an organisation, and act accordingly, despite what procedures and policies may state. This may well be a consideration when agreeing objectives and managing performance.

We could not find any research to suggest that the validity of this theory has been tested in organisational settings. It is primarily about short-term subconscious drives, and therefore does not address how people are able to deal with things intellectually and for the longer term. However, it may help managers understand that habits are learned responses to drives and are unlikely to be changed if people are not encouraged to learn new behaviours, or allowed the time to do so.

References

HULL C. L. (1943) *Principles of Behavior*. New York, Appleton-Century-Crofts.

HULL C. L. (1951) *Essentials of Behavior*. New Haven, Yale University Press.

WEINER B. (1980) *Human Motivation*. New York, Holt, Rinehart & Winston.

9 EQUITY THEORY

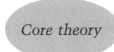

Core theory

Also known as
Inequity theory
Social comparison theory
Social referent theory

Key author(s)
J. S. Adams

Summary of theory
Equity theory is based on the premise that when people enter into an exchange with another (eg the exchange of labour for wages) they compare their situation with that of others around them. The others that are chosen – the 'referent group' – will be people or policies that the person considers to be relevant to him or her. People compare the ratio of their inputs and their outputs with those of their referent group. Using the concept of *'distributive justice'* (the perceived fairness of a distribution of rewards), one or other of the parties in the exchange may feel they are getting short-changed.

In a work setting *inputs* are what people bring to, or put in to, a job; *outputs* are the rewards people get as a result of their inputs.

Inputs include:	*Outputs* include:
☐ experience	☐ pay
☐ skills	☐ benefits
☐ seniority	☐ status

- ☐ intelligence
- ☐ age
- ☐ effort

- ☐ promotion
- ☐ job satisfaction
- ☐ recognition
- ☐ good relationships with others
- ☐ job title

The relevance of inputs and outputs is decided by the individual. This means that the same inputs and/or outputs can be treated as relevant by one party and irrelevant by another. For example, an employee may see service as a relevant input in promotion opportunities, but the employer may not; an employer may see a new computer as a relevant output in lieu of the employee's extra effort, the employee may not. Another feature of inputs and outputs is that they do not have equal weighting. For example, although an employee may see experience as a relevant input to a pay award, he or she might not consider it to be as relevant as the current grade.

Differences in the relevance accorded to inputs and outputs are not the potential nightmare they may sound because social norms provide a framework to which the members of a society can refer for 'accepted' definitions. For example, in a work setting certain inputs (experience, skills, seniority, etc) and outputs (pay, benefits, job satisfaction, etc) are likely to be considered relevant by most people within that setting. It is the importance attributed to these factors that is likely to cause friction, not the factors themselves.

Where people see a favourable comparison between their inputs and outputs and those of others, the situation is perceived as one of equity ('consonance'). Where they see an unfavourable comparison, the situation is perceived as one of inequity ('dissonance'). According to Equity theory, a person generally strives to restore inequitable situations to equitable ones – to move from dissonance to consonance. In a work setting, consonance is likely to lead to job satisfaction. Dissonance generally has a negative effect on morale – although people may be motivated to take action, it will be a motivation that stems from a negative feeling.

Referent groups may not be related to work. They may be family, friends, or even people in the media and not known by the individual. They could include a vision of themselves in the past or how they expect themselves to be in the future. As noted above, they may also be policies that the person feels apply to him or her. The person making the comparison decides who the referent groups are. Consider the example of someone who complains that he or she has not been allocated a car as part of his or her remuneration – even though no one else in the same job in the organisation gets a car. If the referent group the individual is comparing himself or herself with (eg friends) do get cars with their jobs, the individual will experience dissonance.

The key ways in which equity can be restored include:

☐ altering the quantity and/or quality of inputs – eg working less hard to justify being under-compensated

☐ changing outputs – eg negotiating to make the pay structure more equitable

☐ changing the referent group – eg comparing oneself to the work group rather than with friends

☐ trying to change the inputs or outputs of the referent group – eg persuading other people they are not working hard enough.

☐ re-interpreting the situation so as to rationalise any differences – eg coming to think that a task is not as important as was originally thought, and therefore now believing that it is being rewarded fairly

☐ leaving the situation altogether – eg resigning from the job.

What about the 'winners' in unfair exchanges? Equity theory also applies where someone feels that he or she is getting more out of a situation for the same inputs as another. For example, if someone feels he or she is being paid more for a job than someone else (all else being equal), he or she will feel dissonance. The theory suggests that people also try to bring these situations of inequity into equity. Efforts by this group to restore equity could include working harder to justify the higher outcomes, coaching underpaid colleagues so they can improve their inputs, or convincing themselves that they do, in fact, deserve the higher rewards.

Although it is more likely to be an employer who ends the relationship when someone is considered 'over-compensated', there is evidence to suggest that 'when overpaid employees are uncomfortable enough about things they will voluntarily withdraw from an inequitable relationship' (Walster, Walster and Berscheid, 1978).

Examples (see **Character profiles**)

Rachel's department recently took on a new personnel officer (Andrew) at a salary £500 per annum greater than Rachel's. Andrew is two years older than Rachel. He worked in a small manufacturing company as a shift-leader for three years previously, but this is his first job in personnel. Rachel knows Andrew's salary is more than hers. She feels that the situation is inequitable because Andrew is less experienced than her not only in the organisation but also in personnel. Rachel has considered working less hard to justify to herself her lower reward. She has also considered asking for a pay rise to equal or exceed Andrew's, and at one point even thought of leaving. In the end, Rachel asks her boss for an explanation as to why there is a salary difference. She had not realised Andrew in fact had such a lot of relevant experience to bring to the organisation, and eventually feels his extra salary (which after all is not a great deal more than she is earning) is justified.

In the early days in her current job Mandy started to feel uncomfortable with the fact that the partners sought her opinion on complex projects much more often than they sought the views of the other consultants who had been with the partnership for longer. However, she quickly realised that, aside from the partners, she was the most experienced consultant in the organisation. This realisation meant Mandy started to feel fully justified in her involvement in projects and less uncomfortable about it.

Key points

☐ Equity theory contends that the parties in social exchanges will compare the ratio of their inputs and outputs against a referent group. Using the concept of distributive justice, one or other of the parties may feel they are being short-changed.

☐ In a work setting, inputs are what people bring to, or put into, a job. Outputs are the rewards people get as a result of their inputs.

☐ There are social norms that influence which inputs and outputs are considered relevant. However, the relevance and weighting of inputs and outputs are established by each party in the exchange.

☐ The person making comparisons decides on a referent group or policy.

☐ When the ratio of inputs and outputs is deemed equitable with that of the referent group, there is consonance. Where it is deemed inequitable, there is dissonance.

☐ People are motivated to create consonance by removing inequity.

☐ Dissonance may be caused by a person feeling that he or she is receiving outputs of greater value than the referent group for the same inputs. People may strive to create consonance even in this situation.

Commentary

Key author Adams did not suggest that all dissatisfaction and low morale was related to feelings of dissonance – or that all behaviour is the result of trying to address an inequitable situation. However, there is strong support for the notion that people who feel dissonance – especially when they feel they are under-rewarded – will generally strive to achieve consonance. The original research for Equity theory was conducted in business and industrial environments. Later research supports the theory in wider social contexts.

Research also shows that there is more support for the theory when the individual and the referent group have a close relationship than when they are distant. For example, equity is more likely to be sought when comparing against colleagues in the same department than against colleagues in a different office. There is also more support for the seeking of consonance by those who feel under-rewarded than by those who feel over-rewarded.

The theory has been criticised for being unclear about referent groups. Adams did not put forward any ideas about *how* people choose them (see Pritchard, Greenberg, and Adams and Freedman, for example). This makes it difficult to predict how likely it is that someone will experience equity, or inequity, in any specific situation.

Leventhal (1976) questioned why employers felt that equity in pay was important. It was not, he suggests, because they were committed to the ideals of equity and justice but because there were 'pay-offs' such as attracting good workers, believing that it will elicit and sustain high levels of motivation and performance, and avoiding conflict. This implies that for those employers working to achieve a profit, if the 'pay-offs' cease to contribute to profits, equity would cease to be a key issue for them. Interestingly, Leventhal also implies that the wider the gap between individual rewards, even when based on performance, the more conflict there is likely to be.

There is a fundamental discrepancy not addressed by this theory between people's supposed dislike of a feeling of inequity and the capitalist regime in which people create it. For example, in a market economy people are encouraged to win – to be the best. How many organisations have the mission statement 'We want to ensure that we are no better and no worse than the organisations we feel are our equals'? Not many! This is also true, we think, for individuals. Some people do not want to feel they are on a par with their peers, and strive to create a situation of inequity.

Equity theory is particularly relevant when considering diversity in organisations. Grievances raised by minority groups, and actions taken by their members to redress the situation, can in part be explained by this theory. If inequity is highlighted and acknowledged by both parties, this theory suggests that the majority will feel uncomfortable about the situation as well as the minority. However, it is worth remembering that this will not automatically result in a change in the situation because one of the methods by which the majority may deal with their feelings of dissonance is to explain it away – for example, by attributing it to factors outside their control.

Relevance and weighting of inputs and outputs is also important in understanding union-employer relationships. Both parties may consider the ratio of outputs and inputs differently, especially in relation to pay, which may cause conflict when it comes to pay and benefit negotiations. However, research indicates that people generally try to establish a systcm that distributes outcomes in an equitable way within their own frames of reference (Schmitt and Marwell, 1972, for example).

Although this theory may help managers understand that a situation of inequity is likely to motivate people to take action, it is a theory that relies on a negative feeling in the individual to motivate him or her to take action – not a situation that many managers would want to encourage, we suspect. Generalisations can be extrapolated from this theory to the effect that situations which have the potential to be seen as inequitable will almost certainly be seen as such by some of the parties in the exchange. So although it may be impossible to make everyone in the organisation view inputs and outputs in the same way, managers can try to ensure that they minimise the opportunities for dissonance – for example, by involving people in decision-making processes and guaranteeing that communications about reward systems are clear, widespread, and fairly applied.

References

ADAMS J. S. (1963) 'Toward an understanding of equity'. *Journal of Abnormal and Social Psychology*. Vol. 67. pp422–36.

ADAMS J. S. (1965) 'Inequity in social exchange'. In Berkowitz L. (ed.) *Advances in Experimental Social Psychology*. Vol. 2. New York, Academic Press.

ADAMS J. S. *and* FREEDMAN S. (1976) 'Equity theory revisited: Comments and annotated bibliography'. In Berkowitz L. and Walster E. (eds) *Advances in Experimental Social Psychology*. Vol. 9. New York, Academic Press.

ADAMS J. S. *and* ROSENBAUM W. B. (1962) 'The relationship of worker productivity to cognitive dissonance about wage inequities'. *Journal of Applied Psychology*. Vol. 46. pp161–4.

GREENBERG J. (1982) approaching equity and avoiding inequity in groups and organizations'. In Greenberg J. and Cohen R. L. (eds) *Equity and Justice in Social Behavior*. New York, Academic Press.

LEVENTHAL G. S. (1976) 'The distribution of rewards and resources in groups and organizations'. In Berkowitz L. and Walster E. (eds) *Advances in Experimental Social Psychology*. Vol. 9. New York, Academic Press.

PRITCHARD R. D. (1969) 'Equity theory: a review and critique'. *Organizational Behavior and Human Performance*. Vol. 4. pp176–211.

SCHMITT D. R. *and* MARWELL G. (1972) 'The role of attribution processes in mediating the amount of reciprocity for a favor'. *Journal of Experimental Social Psychology*. Vol. 8. pp207–21.

WALSTER E., WALSTER G. W. *and* BERSCHEID E. (1978) *Equity: Theory and research*. Boston, Mass., Allyn & Bacon.

10 EXISTENCE-RELATEDNESS-GROWTH THEORY

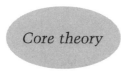

Core theory

Also known as

ERG theory

Key author(s)

C. P. Alderfer

Summary of theory

Existence-relatedness-growth (ERG) theory is a development of Maslow's **Hierarchy of needs theory**. In this theory Alderfer suggests that motivation is the result of people's striving to meet certain basic needs. Whereas Maslow outlined five such needs (see **Hierarchy of needs theory**, Chapter 13), Alderfer suggested these would be better categorised into three core needs.

☐ *Existence needs* are those relating to the various forms of material and physical needs. They include hunger and thirst as well as pay, fringe benefits and physical working conditions. A key characteristic of these needs is 'that they can be divided among people in such a way that one person's gain is another's loss when resources are limited' (Alderfer, 1969). The measurement of how satisfied this need is is therefore mostly stated in terms of what one person has in relation to others.

□ *Relatedness needs* are those experienced in relationships with 'significant others' (eg family, co-workers, friends and enemies). A key characteristic of these needs is 'that their satisfaction depends on a process of sharing or mutuality' (*ibid.*). Acceptance, confirmation, understanding and influence are elements of relatedness needs.

□ *Growth needs* are those relating to personal creativity and productivity. Satisfaction of growth needs comes from people doing things that require them to use their skills to the full, even requiring them to develop new skills. Alderfer (1969) suggests that satisfaction of growth needs 'depends on a person finding the opportunities to be what he is most fully and to become what he can'.

The main benefit of these three distinctions, according to Alderfer, is that they clarify the apparent overlaps between Maslow's five different needs. For example, Alderfer felt it was not clear 'where safety needs depart from physiological needs, on the one hand, and love needs on the other' (Alderfer, 1969). Alderfer states that ERG theory clears up such overlaps as how to categorise different aspects of safety needs or self-esteem. On safety needs, Alderfer states that 'those aspects . . . which deal with physical or material desires belong to the existence category, while those aspects which have to do with interpersonal processes fit the relatedness category'. On self-esteem he states that 'those aspects . . . which depend upon reactions from others fit the relatedness category, while those which represent autonomous self-fulfilling activity belong to growth needs' (*ibid.*).

Alderfer does not suggest that needs are organised in a hierarchy but that they can be regarded as stationed along a *continuum* in terms of their 'concreteness'. Existence needs are at one end, being the most concrete 'due to the fact that their objectives can be reduced to material substances or states' (Alderfer, 1969). Growth needs are at the other end, being the least concrete: 'their specific objectives depend on the uniqueness of each person . . . the actual state of growth of a person can be known only to the person, and it can be known to him only when he is not deluding himself' (*ibid.*). Relatedness is located in the middle of the continuum.

Using this continuum, ERG theory proposes that people move from concrete needs towards the less concrete. So the more existence needs are met, the more relatedness is desired. The more relatedness needs are met, the more growth needs are desired. Growth needs are unlikely ever to be met because the more some growth needs are met, some additional growth needs are desired. The move along thc continuum is the result of 'satisfaction-progression'. That is, the more concrete needs are met, the more energy is released to pursue less concrete goals. For example, once a person has met his or her existence needs, he or she is freer to consider relatedness needs.

Unlike Maslow's **Hierarchy of needs theory** (see Chapter 13), ERG theory addresses the issue of why some people continue to be motivated to meet needs that have apparently been met. Alderfer suggests that when people are frustrated by a lack of progress towards meeting relatedness and growth needs (either because they are being deprived of the means of making such progress or they do not have the capability to make it), lower-level needs may assume greater motivational importance, even if they have already been satisfied. This is referred to as 'frustration-regression' – the idea 'that when a person is not satisfied in attaining less concrete, more uncertain ends, he "regresses" to needs which are somewhat more concrete and less uncertain as to their attainment' (Alderfer, 1969).

ERG theory contains an assumption of the *interchangeability* of various existence needs – lack of satisfaction in one area could be compensated for by an increase in satisfaction in another. For example, extra pay could alleviate poor working conditions (as it often does in extra allowances given to employees in particularly dirty or hazardous jobs). There is also an assumption of *transferability* of relatedness needs. If someone cannot achieve satisfaction in meeting relatedness needs with a particular key person, he or she may transfer the desire to meet this need onto a different person.

Examples (see **Character profiles**)

Rachel's new home has resulted in her being motivated by two levels of need. One is to sort out her finances so she can afford to eat, clothe herself and pay the mortgage without going into debt (existence-level needs), and the other is to build up a new circle of friends (relatedness-level needs). If Rachel chooses to attend evening classes to meet new people, her situation may result in her being very keen to work paid overtime but not on days when she has a class.

Mandy's long-term ambition is to become an expert in her field. Last year she set herself a goal to get an article published. For many months she sent articles to publishers. Every one was rejected and Mandy felt despondent. Her motivation to pursue this goal diminished, and she turned her attention instead to building client relations. She was good at this, was motivated to do it, and knew that she was successful from feedback. So, because her growth needs were being frustrated, Mandy had regressed to the lower-order need of relatedness – one that she knew she could satisfy.

Key points

- [ ] Existence-relatedness-growth (ERG) theory is a development of Maslow's **Hierarchy of needs theory** (see Chapter 13).
- [ ] Alderfer identified three core needs:
  - existence needs relating to basic survival, such as food
  - relatedness needs relating to relationships with others
  - growth needs relating to personal development.
- [ ] Needs relating to growth are said to be never fully satisfied.
- [ ] People may work on one or more of the levels at the same time but will generally move along a continuum from *existence* to *growth* (satisfaction progression).
- [ ] If higher-level needs are not being met, people may well focus on lower-level needs, even if they have been met (frustration-regression).
- [ ] Lack of satisfaction in one area can be compensated for by an increase in satisfaction in another.
- [ ] If someone cannot achieve satisfaction in meeting relatedness needs with a particular key person, he or she may transfer the desire to meet relatedness needs onto a different person.

Commentary

Early research was generally supportive of Existence-related-ness-growth theory, although it has not been fully supported by later research. For example, Alderfer's frustration-regression proposition has not been supported (Rauschenberger, Schmitt and Hunter, 1980).

Alderfer suggested that ERG theory needed further work to test it out. One reason for this is that data were taken from a single organisation (110 employees at several job levels in a bank) and there was 'no way of knowing what special conditions in that organisation may have favoured the particular outcomes observed' (Alderfer, 1969). Also, 'the methodology used here was only one of several possible ways to test the predictions' (*ibid.*) implying that other methodologies might have resulted in different outcomes.

Alderfer's research highlighted limitations with using such broad categories, particularly in the realms of relatedness needs. In his conclusions he suggests that there are some differences in satisfaction depending on who the 'significant other' in the relationship is. In particular, he mentions that dissatisfaction in relationships with co-workers is less likely to lead to frustration-regression than dissatisfaction with 'superiors'. 'If this pattern of results is replicated, it suggests that ERG may have to be modified along the lines that specific relatedness frustrations tend to produce specific existence desires' (Alderfer, 1969).

This theory does not suggest how a person may meet his or her needs – in other words, managers cannot assume that everyone's relatedness needs will be met in the same way. For some it may be close working relationships with colleagues, and for others it may be belonging to a close social group outside work, for example.

ERG theory, with its three broad categories, is perhaps easier to deal with than the five levels of need in **Hierarchy of needs theory**. The suggestion that these categories are not necessarily hierarchical is perhaps more akin to the experience of many managers. As a generalisable framework it may help managers to focus on the needs staff are likely to have at any point in time. For example, when setting up a new team, existence factors may be more motivating than the introduction of a career development programme. However, as with all motivation theories, generalising is exactly that, and individual motivation issues must be addressed with, and for, each individual.

References

ALDERFER C. P. (1969) 'An empirical test of a new theory of human needs'. *Organizational Behavior and Human Performance*. Vol. 4. pp142–75.

ALDERER C. P. (1972) *Existence, Relatedness, and Growth: Human needs in organizational settings*. New York, Free Press.

RAUSCHENBERGER J., SCHMITT N. *and* HUNTER J. E. (1980) 'A test of the need hierarchy concept by a Markov model of change in need strength'. *Administrative Science Quarterly*. Vol. 25. pp654–70.

11 EXPECTANCY THEORY

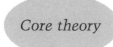

Core theory

Also known as
> VIE theory

Key author(s)
> V. Vroom

Summary of theory
> Vroom drew together the research of others to propose Expectancy theory. His views were based on those of Lewin (1935) and Rotter (1955), among others.
>
> Expectancy theory is based on the premise that people *expect* particular actions to achieve a desired result (have 'expectancy'), and that the desired result is something worth striving for or avoiding (has 'valence'). Vroom (1964) defines these two terms:
>
> ☐ *Expectancy*: 'a momentary belief concerning the likelihood that a particular act will be followed by a particular outcome' – The stronger the certainty that an act will be followed by a particular outcome, the stronger the expectancy is considered to be.
>
> ☐ *Valence*: 'affective orientations toward particular outcomes' – Positive valence is when a person prefers attaining an outcome to not attaining it; negative valence is when a person prefers not attaining an outcome to attaining it. Valence is at zero when the person is indifferent to whether the outcome is attained or not.
>
> Motivation depends on how strong the expectancy is and how

important the goal is to the person. People are likely to be most motivated when expectancy is strong and valence is either positive or negative. (People will be motivated towards obtaining goals worthwhile to them even if that goal is to avoid a situation or outcome.) If valence is neutral (at zero), the theory contends that it is unlikely that someone would be motivated to take a particular action because people are not motivated to work towards something they do not feel is worthwhile.

It is important to distinguish between *valence* and *value*. Vroom states that 'at any given time there may be a substantial discrepancy between the anticipated satisfaction from an outcome (ie its valence) and the actual satisfaction that it provides (ie its value)' (Vroom, 1964). Valence, therefore, is about expectations rather than actual experience. Someone may, for example, find the prospect (valence) of promotion to be something worthwhile striving for, but once promotion has been obtained, may find that it does not live up to those expectations (value).

There is a third, important element to this theory – *instrumentality*. Whereas expectancy is about the perceived likelihood that a particular behaviour will result in a particular outcome, instrumentality is about the perception that an interim outcome will lead to another, important outcome. For example, a person may think that if he or she puts in more effort it will lead to improved job performance that will, in turn, lead to promotion. Assuming that promotion is important (ie it has valence), then improved job performance will be instrumental in achieving it and expectancy will be high if the person thinks there is a high likelihood that increased performance will result in promotion.

Vroom stated that the valence of outcomes is very often a function of the instrumentality of those outcomes to achieve, or avoid, other outcomes. This means that the valence of outcomes which, on their own, would not be considered important, may be increased because of what they lead to. In the example given in the last paragraph, for example, the person might not consider increased job performance had valence if it did not lead to anything that he or she wanted.

However, it has valence because of its instrumental function in achieving the final goal.

There is a *range of instrumentality* from positive to negative (all quotes from Pinder, 1984).

□ *positive* – when 'attainment of the second outcome is certain if the first outcome is achieved'
□ *zero* – when 'there is no likely relationship between the attainment of the first outcome and the attainment of the second'
□ *negative* – when 'attainment of the second outcome is certain without the first, and . . . it is impossible with it'.

Profit-sharing in large organisations, paid as a flat-rate percentage regardless of performance, is likely to have zero instrumentality for increasing individual performance because staff cannot link their individual efforts to the flat-rate profit share. Piece rate pay, however, has positive instrumentality because attainment of pay is certain if performance is achieved. A situation in which a pay rise will be withheld as a result of poor performance is negative instrumentality. Attainment of the pay rise is certain without the poor performance, and impossible with it.

Extrinsic rewards or outcomes are often instrumental in achieving other goals. For example, wages have positive valence because of the positive instrumentality of wages in paying bills. On the other hand, being sacked has negative valence because of its negative instrumentality in maintaining a person's reputation as a good employee.

Vroom found that the extent of job satisfaction (measured as how attractive people find their job) is directly related to the extent to which employees' jobs are instrumental to the attainment of outcomes that are attractive to them. Such outcomes include:

□ pay
□ consideration given to them by supervisors
□ interaction with co-workers
□ the number of different operations they perform.

Vroom also found a link between a lack of some of these

outcomes and turnover and absenteeism. In particular, he found a direct relationship between absenteeism and turnover in people who had little or no opportunity to make decisions, those given little or no opportunity for informal interaction, and those whose supervisors appeared not to be considerate towards them.

Examples (see **Character profiles**)

More money is important to Neil at the moment because he has just become a father for the third time and needs to be able to pay the increased household bills that come with an extra mouth to feed. This means that money has positive valence to Neil. He knows that high sales figures have led to pay rises in the past – so he has great expectancy that more high sales figures will result in another pay rise. Neil also knows that extra effort on his part will be instrumental in achieving high sales figures. Neil is therefore motivated to put in that extra effort because the reward (a pay rise) can be achieved through this effort and extra money is worthwhile to him.

Mandy worked with a consultancy firm in a job she did not enjoy. She was aware that her feelings adversely affected her performance in the job. Mandy expected that by under-performing she would be disciplined (expectancy). The appraisal system was set up for the disciplinary process to be invoked if performance was poor during the first six months of employment (instrumentality). Mandy thought that it was worthwhile avoiding the disciplinary process because she did not want a bad report on her file (valence). Mandy was motivated to try to improve her work because the outcome of not doing so could be avoided through her efforts.

Key points

- ☐ Expectancy theory has two main components:
  - – expectancy: a belief concerning the likelihood that a particular action will be followed by a particular outcome
  - – valence: affective orientations toward particular outcomes.

- ☐ The more certain someone is that an action will be followed by a particular outcome, the stronger is the expectancy.
- ☐ Valence can be seen as positive where outcomes are considered worthwhile obtaining, negative where outcomes are considered worthwhile avoiding, or neutral (at zero) if the outcome is of no importance.
- ☐ The stronger the expectancy, the more likely the person is to be motivated to act to achieve a particular outcome – provided the outcome has positive or negative valence. If the valence of an outcome is neutral, it is unlikely that someone would be motivated to take an action to achieve or avoid it.
- ☐ Valence can be enhanced by the 'instrumentality' of an outcome. This is where attainment of one outcome affects the likelihood of the attainment of a second outcome.
- ☐ Instrumentality ranges from positive to negative.
- ☐ Extrinsic rewards or outcomes are often instrumental in achieving other goals.
- ☐ The extent of someone's job satisfaction is directly related to the extent to which his or her job is instrumental to the attainment of outcomes that are attractive to him or her.

Commentary

Later research generally supports the basic theory of expectancy and valence. Porter and Lawler (1968) undertook some research on Expectancy theory. The outcome of their research supported Vroom's theory that effort depends on the valence placed on certain outcomes and the expectancy that effort will lead to the attainment of those outcomes. However, they felt that such effort does not necessarily lead to better job performance because Vroom's theory neglects to cover ability and role clarity. In other words, a highly motivated person may not be considered successful in his or her job if he or she has neither the ability nor the clear understanding of what it is he or she is supposed to be achieving.

Vroom's work concentrated on extrinsic outcomes rather than intrinsic ones. Extrinsic rewards require others to recognise good performance and to administer the rewards. Intrinsic rewards lead to and constitute an individual's feeling of a job well done: they do not require others to acknowledge them (although that may additionally contribute to intrinsic reward). Porter and Lawler argue that job satisfaction is not necessarily linked with job performance because a job may be intrinsically rewarding (satisfying) but performance may not be recognised as good by others.

Later research has commented on the distinctions between the terms used by Vroom. For example, expectancy and valence are not as distinct from each other as Vroom suggested. When considering expectancy it is inevitable, perhaps, that a person will take into account valence, and vice versa.

Further commentaries on Expectancy theory also distinguish two elements to expectancy. *Expectancy-1* is the belief that effort will result in better performance. *Expectancy-2* is the belief that better performance will lead to the expected rewards. For example, a salesman not only needs to believe that his increased efforts will result in higher sales, but also that his extra sales will be rewarded with higher commission payments.

This last point raises an area of potential confusion – where does instrumentality fit in? If a person expects his or her performance to elicit a particular outcome, is this not the same as saying that performance is instrumental in achieving that outcome? To some extent it is, and the confusion stems from terminology rather than from any problem inherent in the theory. The key difference is that Expectancy-1 relates to effort and performance and is akin to Vroom's expectancy concept. Expectancy-2 relates to performance and outcome, which is akin to Vroom's instrumentality concept.

Campbell and Pritchard (1976) are critical of much of the research that followed Vroom's Expectancy theory on a number of different counts. One of their key criticisms is that the theory was tested as if it was based on behavioural and attitudinal predictions *across*, rather than *within*, individuals. Thus, when the scores of a group of people are collated and used to predict general motivation, the results often show only a moderate level of validity of Vroom's theory. However, this type of research neglects to take into account a whole range of individual differences such as ability, job roles/diffi-culty, different levels of rewards, and so on. It also assumes that people consider valence, instrumentality and expectancy in the same way – which is clearly not the case. Campbell and Pritchard's point is that Expectancy theory should really be considered in terms of the individual, and not in terms of generalisations across a group, if predictions about behaviour are to be considered at all accurate.

Another key criticism of Vroom's theory is that he largely ignores the influence of situational factors. Thierry and Koopman-Iwema, in their summary of criticisms of Expect-ancy theory, state that 'the influence of "other parties" (colleague, superior, quality controller, etc) is taken into account far too little. The respondent has considerably less grip on his own behaviour than is assumed in the theory' (Thierry and Koopman-Iwema, 1984).

Managers attempting to use Expectancy theory as a tool to assist the motivation of their team members should remember that although generalisations can be made from what people may consider a rewarding outcome, the percep-tions of the individual are key. Although any effort put in to explaining how performance links up with outcomes will not be effort wasted, individual differences – such as the desirability of the outcomes – will mean that the effectiveness of the message will vary from person to person.

References

CAMPBELL J. P. and PRITCHARD R. D. (1976) 'Motivation theory in industrial and organizational psychology'. In Dun-nette M. D. (ed.) *Handbook for Industrial and Organizational Psychology*. Chicago, Rand McNally.

GALBRAITH J. and CUMMINGS L. L. (1967) 'An empirical inves-tigation of the motivational determination of task performance'. *Organizational Behavior and Human Perform-ance*. Vol. 2. pp237–57.

LEWIN K. (1935) *A Dynamic Theory of Personality*. New York, McGraw-Hill.

PINDER C. C. (1984) *Work Motivation*. Glenview, Ill., Scott, Forseman.

PORTER L. W. *and* LAWLER E. E. (1968) *Managerial Attitudes and Performance.* Illinois, Dorsey Press.

ROTTER J. B. (1955) 'The role of the psychological situation in determining the direction of human behavior'. In Jones M. R. (ed.) *Nebraska Symposium on Motivation.* Lincoln, University of Nebraska Press. pp245–68.

THIERRY H. *and* KOOPMAN-IWEMA A. M. (1984) 'Motivation and satisfaction'. In Drenth P. J. D., Thierry H., Willems P. J. and de Wolff C. J. (eds) *Handbook of Work and Organizational Psychology.* Chichester, John Wiley & Sons Ltd.

VROOM V. (1964) *Work and Motivation.* New York, Wiley.

12 GOAL-SETTING THEORY

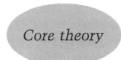

Core theory

Also known as

Task motivation theory

Key author(s)

E. A. Locke.

Summary of theory

Goal-setting theory is based on the premise that people are motivated to achieve the successful attainment of challenging goals. Locke's (1968) studies resulted in three main conclusions:

☐ More difficult goals result in higher levels of performance than easy goals.

☐ Specific goals produce higher levels of performance than general goals (eg 'Do your best!').

☐ Behavioural intentions influence the choices people make.

Levels of performance were defined as a combination of output, reaction time, grades, etc. We look at each of Locke's conclusions in turn.

The first conclusion was that *more difficult goals result in higher levels of performance than easy goals*. The outcomes of a series of experiments (setting tasks such as brainstorming, complex computation, addition, toy construction, and so on) showed that 'although subjects with very hard goals reached their goals far less often than subjects with very easy goals, the former consistently performed at a higher level than the latter' (Locke, 1968). Other studies proved this true even when applied to organisational goals and work settings (for example, Zander and Newcomb, 1967).

The second conclusion was that *specific goals produce higher levels of performance than general goals*. Various studies showed that 'do your best' goals consistently produced lower performance levels than specific goals, even when those specific goals were difficult. In experiments with reasonably long time-scales (up to two hours), performance that might have been expected to fall off actually increased. Locke suggests that one of the features of specific, hard goals is that they 'prolong effort during the latter portions of long work sessions' (Locke, 1968). Locke also reported on a study by Meyer, Kay and French (1965) into goal-setting during appraisal interviews. They found that tasks that were translated into specific goals resulted in greater performance outcomes than tasks that were not. Locke acknowledges that instructions have an impact on the people undertaking tasks. If a goal is set for someone, even if it is agreed with him or her, it has to be clearly translated and understood by the person to make it effective.

The final conclusion was that *behavioural intentions influence the choices people make*. Behavioural intention was defined as 'the intention to make a certain task choice or to respond in a certain way' (Locke, 1968). In other words, Locke concluded that the level of difficulty of a chosen goal depended on what the person undertaking the task was aiming to achieve. For example, Locke reported on an experiment where three groups of participants were asked to choose tasks to try to either (1) 'succeed as much as possible', (2) 'get as great a sense of personal achievement as possible', or (3) 'overcome the greatest possible challenges'. Group (1) chose the easiest tasks; group (3) chose the hardest tasks; and group (2) chose tasks of an intermediate level of difficulty.

The goal has to be something the person accepts is valid, even if validity is reluctantly accepted. For example, a manager sets a difficult goal. The manager's team members may well accept the goal and work towards it, even if they do not like it, simply because of the value they put on the relationship with their boss (whether they like the manager or not). People working in completely different departments may well ignore the challenge because they have no relationship with the manager concerned and therefore do not consider the request to be a valid one.

In setting goals, people are acknowledging that there is something to be gained on successful completion. This could be money, status, satisfaction, or whatever. Locke noted that incentives influence goals as well as levels of performance. So a high-value incentive may encourage people not only to work harder but, if it is linked to a goal, to set harder goals. Locke identified six incentives and researched their effects on goal-setting.

☐ *Money* was found to assist in encouraging commitment to a task that people would perhaps not otherwise have taken on. (Many dissatisfied job-holders would agree!) However, even in situations where there is a direct link between earnings and output (ie piece rate incentives), money *in itself* does not motivate above a certain level of 'safe' income.

☐ *Knowledge of score* (feedback) was found to assist in motivation only where it is considered to be valid and where it can be used to set future goals. If a person receives feedback from someone whom he or she thinks is not in a position to give feedback, it will not be regarded as valid and will not affect motivation. Also, if a person receives valid feedback, but not specific enough to be useful in setting future goals, it is unlikely to affect motivation. Later research shows that self-generated feedback (by which people can keep track of their own progress) is a more effective motivator than feedback given externally (Ivancevich and McMahon, 1982). Locke also states that the level of the standard used in feedback can influence the level of a goal. For example, consider an employee in a call centre. If positive feedback is given once a low-level standard has been achieved (eg answering more calls than the minimum call rate over the past year), the goals that the employee will be motivated to achieve are likely to be lower than in a situation where positive feedback is given once a higher-level standard has been met (eg answering more calls than the maximum call rate over the past year).

□ *Time-limits*, where challenging, tend to have the effect of increasing motivation to achieve a goal. If a time-limit is simply too tight for the task, the task is likely to take longer than if the same task was set on a challenging time-scale.

□ *Participation* in goal-setting was shown, in a number of studies, to increase the motivation of the person to achieve the goal. However, it would also appear that participation in itself is not necessarily motivating. Locke reports on research that found that 'while subordinate participation in the goal-setting process had some effect on improved performance, a much more powerful influence was whether goals were set at all' (Meyer, Kay and French, 1965). Like money, participation may be best thought of as increasing someone's commitment to a goal rather than an end in itself.

□ *Competition* is defined as when another person's or group's performance is the standard by which goals are set and success and failure judged. Motivation to beat a defined benchmark is a key driver for many people and organisations. At an individual level, people are likely to choose benchmarks that are meaningful to them – their own previous performance, the performance of people or groups similar to themselves, and so on. At both organisation and individual level, competition is thought to motivate people to continue to strive to achieve higher standards, especially when the benchmark is set by others. (As Locke says, 'If mile runners only ran against themselves or against a stopwatch, the 4-minute mile might never have been broken.') Competition also motivates people to innovate in areas that assist performance, such as better ways of carrying out a task, better procedures, better products, etc.

□ *Praise or reproof* has a variable effect on motivation. Locke reports that no studies have been made specifically on the effects of praise and reproof in relation to goal-setting. Yet he noted that praise was more effective in improving

performance overall. Reproof seemed to improve performance if feedback was given in relation to a standard.

Locke suggests that the most direct way to encourage goal-
setting – and therefore to increase motivation – is by giving
instructions. As he says, 'One of the most efficient ways to
get somebody to do something is to . . . assign him a goal or
task' (Locke, 1968). Locke accepts, however, that this only
works if the person accepts the instruction as valid and if he
or she is able to do what is asked.

Locke goes on to suggest that the incentives listed above
can be used to encourage goal-setting. But only time-limits
were considered a direct way of influencing goals – again,
provided that the person accepts the limit as valid and that
he or she is able to do the task. Setting a time-limit is a
reasonably clear way of implying a goal – tell someone to do
something by tomorrow, and he or she will have a fairly clear
idea of what the goal should be over the next 24 hours.

Knowledge of the score and providing competition do not,
in themselves, tell people what goals to strive for but could
suggest standards. For example, giving feedback on a specific
aspect of a job (eg financial performance) would suggest that
that element was a key goal. Also, advertising successful
'wins' in relation to the performance of a specific benchmark
(eg providing a league table of team performance) may imply
certain goals.

Money and participation are considered indirect means of
influencing goals. Neither directly suggests that someone
should try to achieve a particular goal. For example, if an
organisation introduces incentive pay on the assumption that
staff will set higher goals to produce more, senior personnel
may be surprised to find they do not get the results they
wanted. This could be because not everyone is motivated by
the promise of more money – some people do not need extra
money; some may use the system to make the same money
as before but in less time; and so on.

Praise and reproof also have an indirect effect on goal-
setting. As Locke points out, they are 'only evaluations of the
subject's past performance and do not imply what *he should
do* in the future' (Locke, 1965 – his italics). There are many

factors that influence how the receiver interprets praise or reproof (whether the comments are regarded as fair, a liking and respect for the giver, and so on).

Robins (2001) outlines four contingent factors that influence the goals–performance relationship. These are:

- □ *goal commitment* – most likely to occur when
  - goals are made public
  - the individual has an internal locus of control (see **Internal–external control theory**, Chapter 15)
  - goals are set by the individual rather than imposed
- □ *adequate self-efficacy* – the more confident people are that they can succeed in the task, the more persistent they will be in trying to achieve it. People with greater self-efficacy also respond more positively to negative feedback than their less confident colleagues in that such feedback is likely to spur them on rather than put them off
- □ *task characteristics* – goals are more motivating when tasks are
  - simple rather than complex
  - familiar rather than novel
  - independent rather than interdependent (although, if interdependent, group goals are better than individual ones)
- □ *national culture* – goal-setting theory works best in cultures where there is
  - a focus on the individual rather than on the group
  - an acceptance of risk-taking
  - a work ethic by which employees believe that striving to achieve at work is an important characteristic.

Examples (see **Character profiles**)

Neil's sales goals are very specific. They all have a time-limit attached to them, he knows what he has to do to achieve them, and he feels they are within his abilities. The sense of competition that he feels has changed since he became the sales manager. Whereas before, when he was a salesman, Neil's competition was mainly with the other sales people in his organisation, the competition is now against his targets.

Although he has agreed some challenging targets, he has privately decided to try to exceed them by at least 10 per cent. Neil finds this very motivating – he knows exactly what he has to do and by when.

Key points

- ☐ Goal-setting theory is based on the premise that people are motivated to achieve successful attainment of challenging goals.
- ☐ Locke's studies resulted in three main conclusions:
  - More difficult goals result in higher levels of performance than easy goals.
  - Specific goals produce higher levels of performance than general goals.
  - Behavioural intentions influence people's choices of goal.
- ☐ Locke identified six key incentives that influence goals:
  - money
  - knowledge of score
  - time-limits
  - participation
  - competition
  - praise and/or reproof.
- ☐ Time-limits are considered a direct way of influencing goals.
- ☐ Money, participation, praise and reproof are considered indirect means of influencing goals.
- ☐ Knowledge of the score and providing competition do not, in themselves, tell people what goals to strive for but could suggest standards.
- ☐ Four contingent factors that influence the goals–performance relationship are:
  - goal commitment
  - adequate self-efficacy
  - task characteristics
  - national culture.

Commentary

Goal-setting theory is useful to many managers because much of people management is specifically about performance against goals. It is also a theory that human resource professionals are likely to be familiar with because it is often used as the basis for performance management schemes that focus on objectives.

Locke pointed out that there are times when an outcome is achieved that is different from the one expected. He accepted that this might have affected the results of some of his experiments (in that an outcome might have come about by accident rather than by design). However, he states that 'No attempt is made in the studies reported to specify the ultimate roots or causes of the particular goals or intentions an individual develops on a task . . . Thus, we are not presenting a complete theory of task performance but only some foundations for a theory' (Locke, 1968).

The use of incentives to help establish goals must be treated with care. For example, asking people to work out a goal on the basis of feedback assumes that they will use the feedback to set goals and that they consider the incentive worth working for. Participation and money have already been mentioned as perhaps better incentives to encourage commitment to a goal than incentives to achieve a higher goal. It would be unwise to assume that praise or reproof alone might motivate someone to set goals.

Although we think it unlikely that many managers would employ such indirect methods to set goals for their teams, how many have done so unwittingly? Readers may recognise the manager who gives a struggling employee positive feedback in the hope that this will encourage him or her to set higher personal goals in the future. Or the manager who sets up a league table of team performance in the hope that those who are not performing well will set themselves goals to achieve more. Such tactics are not uncommon in the workplace – but if managers are using them as a way of setting goals, rather than reinforcing them, they are likely to be confusing their staff at best, and demotivating them at worst.

Although Goal-setting theory specifically states that goals

have to be considered valid for them to be motivating, the theory does not cover the issue of goal *commitment*. People's commitment to a goal is obviously key to anticipating their motivation to succeed at it. Are they likely to persist against all odds or to give up at the first hurdle? Carroll and Tosi (1973) report that self-esteem seems to be an important factor here. For example, managers with high self-esteem reported they were more persistent in meeting their goals than those managers with low self-esteem.

The point raised by Robins (as outlined in the Summary above) implies that Goal-setting theory is limited to those cultures that match the ones in which the research was carried out. In other words, it is more relevant to countries such as the USA and the UK than it is to countries that do not have the features he outlines.

Goal-setting theory is a theory that has great relevance for managers. There are many times in people management when goals are used to motivate. The conclusions of the theory that suggest that the most motivating goals are not only specific but also challenging must ring true for many managers. What is less easy for some managers to remember, however, is that these elements are not enough. People have to accept those goals as valid in order for them to be motivating – and that is the real challenge. Nobody said it would be easy!

References

CARROLL S. J. *and* TOSI H. L. (1973) *Management by Objectives: Applications and research*. New York, Macmillan.

IVANEVICH J. M. *and* MCMAHON J. T. (1982) 'The effects of goal-setting, external feedback and self-generated feedback on outcome variables: a field experiment'. *Academy of Management Journal*. June. pp359–72.

LOCKE E. A. (1968) 'Toward a theory of task motivation and incentives'. *Organizational Behavior and Human Performance*. Vol. 3. pp157–89.

LOCKE E. A. *and* LATHAM G. P. (1990) *A Theory of Goal Setting and Task Motivation*. Englewood Cliffs, NJ, Prentice-Hall.

Meyer H. H., Kay E. *and* French J. R. P. Jr. (1965) 'Split roles in performance appraisal'. *Harvard Business Review*. Vol. 43. pp123–9.

Robins S. P. (2001) *Organizational Behavior*. 9th edn. Englewood Cliffs, NJ, Prentice-Hall.

Zander A. *and* Newcomb T. (1967) 'Group levels of aspiration in United Fund campaigns'. *Journal of Personality and Social Psychology*. Vol. 6. pp157–62.

13 HIERARCHY OF NEEDS THEORY

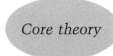

Core theory

Also known as

    Need theory

    Hierarchy theory

Key author(s)

    A. H. Maslow

Summary of theory

Maslow proposed that motivation is based on a number of human needs. These are arranged in a hierarchy that requires the 'lower', more basic needs to be satisfied before the increasingly less basic ones above. Maslow identified five key *categories of need*:

5 self-actualisation needs – eg the need for personal growth and development

4 esteem/ego needs – eg the need for status, self-respect

3 belonging and love needs – eg the need to be part of a family or social group

2 safety needs – eg the need for shelter and warmth, the need for order

1 physiological needs – eg to stave off hunger and thirst

Maslow's hierarchy is usually illustrated as a pyramid with physiological needs at the base, self-actualisation at the top.

    Physiological needs are the 'lowest' forms of need in the

hierarchy. Although independent of each other these needs may be satisfied in various ways or act as channels for other needs. Maslow points out that 'the person who thinks he or she is hungry may actually be looking more for comfort, or dependence, than for vitamins or proteins. Conversely, it is possible to satisfy the hunger need in part by other activities such as drinking water or smoking cigarettes' (Maslow, 1954). In everyday reality it is unlikely that many readers will ever experience this level of need. To do so, for example, would be to experience life-or-death hunger rather than simply a wish for something to eat.

Although it is likely, similarly, that most people, if not all, in the Western world have satisfied their *safety needs*, it is worth remembering that this level includes the need to seek order. In times of extreme insecurity (eg war, disease and natural catastrophes) Maslow believes that people regress from higher needs to the lower needs to seek safety. Maslow cites 'the common preference for a job with tenure and protection, the desire for a savings account, and for insurance of various kinds' (Maslow, 1954) to support this point.

Physiological and safety needs are considered the basic lower-order needs. They are also needs that tend to be met through external inputs – food, drink, and so on. In a work context, pay, job security and other external elements of the job will affect these lower needs – either directly (as in job security) or indirectly (as in pay, which allows people to meet their basic needs). It is only once these needs are satisfied that Maslow feels people are driven to satisfy the higher-order social needs of belonging, esteem and self actualisation.

Belonging and love needs include the giving and receiving of affection. Maslow states that when such needs are unsatisfied, 'a person will hunger for relations with people in general – for a place in the group or family – and will strive with great intensity to achieve this goal' (Maslow, 1954). Maslow makes the point that 'in our society the thwarting of these needs is the most commonly-found core in cases of maladjustment and more severe pathology' (*ibid.*).

Maslow reported that *esteem needs* were made up of two types of desire. Firstly, there is 'the desire for strength, achievement, adequacy, mastery and competence, confidence

in the face of the world, and independence and freedom'
(Maslow, 1954). Secondly, there is 'the desire for reputation
or prestige . . . status, fame and glory, dominance, recognition,
attention, importance, dignity, or appreciation' (ibid.). He
goes on to report that 'thwarting of these needs produces
feelings of inferiority, of weakness, and of helplessness.
These feelings in turn give rise to either basic discouragement
or else compensatory or neurotic trends' (ibid.).

Once esteem needs have been satisfied, Maslow notes that
'we may still often (if not always) expect that a new discontent and restlessness will soon develop, unless the individual
is doing what *he* or *she*, individually, is fitted for' (Maslow,
1954 – his italics). Maslow becomes quite philosophical at
this point, declaring that 'What humans *can* be, they *must*
be. They must be true to their own nature' (ibid. – his italics).
The form these *self-actualisation needs* take varies greatly
from person to person. 'In one individual they may take the
form of the desire to be an excellent parent, in another they
may be expressed athletically, and in still another they may be
expressed in painting pictures or in inventing things' (ibid.).
Although Maslow's early work did not address the consequences of self-actualisation needs' being met, he later (1962)
acknowledged that such needs could never be completely
attained or satisfied because self-actualisation needs are
endless.

Unlike lower-order needs, higher-order needs are usually
satisfied internally. They are the result of a person's *feeling*
that he or she belongs, has self-esteem, and so on. Maslow
states that higher-order needs are also less critical for sheer
survival and are usually less urgent, such that individuals
may be prepared to postpone gratification for long periods. In
a work setting, job satisfaction, personal development, and so
on are higher-order needs.

Hierarchy of needs theory is based on the premise that
individuals seek to satisfy unmet needs and that they will
most often seek to satisfy the next level of needs once the
needs below it have been satisfied. Maslow suggests that
people can become so focused on satisfying the current level
of need that they may treat it as a higher priority, for a time,
than a lower need. For example, if someone is working hard

to complete an assignment by a tight deadline, he or she may do so to the detriment of more basic physiological needs such as thirst or hunger. Also, needs that have been satisfied over long periods may diminish in importance. If people have never experienced real starvation, for example, they could treat food as relatively unimportant. However, lower-order needs are considered 'prepotent' – in other words, life-or-death hunger or thirst and a *real* need for shelter, for example, always take precedence over higher-order needs.

Maslow's theory is often portrayed as rigid, in such a way that movement from one level of the hierarchy to another is possible only once a lower need has been fully satisfied. Maslow did not actually say that. What he did say (Maslow, 1954) is:

> So far, our theoretical discussion may have given the impression that these five sets of needs are somehow in such terms as the following:
>
> If one need is satisfied, then another emerges.
>
> This statement might give the false impression that a need must be satisfied 100 percent before the next need emerges. In actual fact, most members of our society who are normal are partially satisfied in all their basic needs and partially unsatisfied in all their basic needs at the same time. A more realistic description of the hierarchy would be in terms of decreasing percentages of satisfaction as we go up the hierarchy of prepotency. For instance, if I may assign arbitrary figures for the sake of illustration, it is as if the average citizen is satisfied perhaps 85 percent in his physiological needs, 70 percent in his safety needs, 50 percent in his love needs, 40 percent in his self-esteem needs, and 10 percent in his self-actualisation needs.
>
> As for the concept of emergence of a new need after satisfaction of the prepotent need, this emergence is not a sudden . . . phenomenon, but rather a gradual emergence by slow degrees from nothingness. For instance, if prepotent need A is satisfied only 10 percent, then need B may not be visible at all. However, as this need A becomes satisfied 25 percent, need B may emerge 5 percent; as need A becomes satisfied 75 percent, need B may emerge 50 percent; and so on.

Maslow also pointed out that not everyone would conform to the hierarchy. Although most people seemed to have the basic needs he outlined, and in the order he indicated, Maslow identified some exceptions:

☐ Self-esteem seems to be more important than love to some people – in particular, to those who think the most likely people to be loved are strong and powerful. If they lack love, such people may behave in a way they think is strong and powerful but is often aggressive. They seek self-esteem for the sake of love rather than for self-esteem itself.

☐ Some innately creative people find the drive for self-actualisation arises despite the lack of satisfaction of more basic needs.

☐ Higher-level needs may be permanently lost in some people. This is likely where the person has never really moved away from basic lower-level need satisfaction (eg as a result of chronic unemployment) and will therefore never move to the higher levels of the hierarchy.

☐ Some people deprived of love in early childhood may experience permanent loss of love needs during the rest of their lives.

☐ Some people with high ideals or values may become martyrs and give up everything else for the sake of their beliefs.

Maslow cautions that there are many things that drive behaviour. He states that although his theory claims a person 'will *want* the more basic of two needs when deprived in both, there is no necessary implication here that he will act upon his desires' (Maslow, 1954 – his italics).

Examples (see **Character profiles**)

When Rachel was sorting out her house move, she found it hard to get motivated to do work needed for her professional qualification studies. She realised she was more focused on fixing herself up with a place to live (her basic safety needs) than she was on developing her skills for a long-term goal. She agreed with her tutor to take a six-month break from the course. This allowed her to concentrate on the purchase of her flat. She resumed her studies as agreed, and with her flat sorted out she regained her motivation to study.

Frank has reached the stage where he feels most of his needs have been met. He does not have to worry about money because he has a generous pension plan and paid his mortgage off several years ago. He has a close family and some good friends. However, Frank can see that he may feel a 'bit useless', as he puts it, when he retires. Much of his self-esteem is wrapped up in who he is at work. He always feels a stab of pride when he tells people what he does professionally, and realises this will vanish when he retires. Frank has decided that to counter this he will see if he can help out at a local college – perhaps by giving talks on their management courses. In this way his self-esteem might be maintained.

Key points

- Maslow's theory is based on needs classified in a hierarchy. The five basic needs identified are:
  1 physiological needs
  2 safety needs
  3 belonging and love needs
  4 esteem/ego needs
  5 self-actualisation needs.
- Needs move from the basic lower-order physiological and safety needs to higher-order needs.
- Lower-order needs are usually met via external satisfaction. Higher-order needs are usually met through internal satisfaction.
- Lower-order needs are considered prepotent (naturally dominant).
- Self-actualisation needs are never fully met.
- People are generally motivated to satisfy each level of the hierarchy only when the lower level/levels has/have been satisfied to a greater rather than lesser extent.
- Exceptions to the generalisation about moving up the hierarchy of needs in order include:

- Self-esteem seems more important than love to some people.
- Some creative people are driven to meet self-actualisation needs despite lack of satisfaction of more basic needs.
- Higher-level needs may be permanently lost in some people.
- People deprived of love in early childhood may experience permanent loss of love needs.
- Some people may become martyrs and give up everything for their beliefs.

Commentary

Maslow's theory is very popular, despite little validation of it in later research (see Hall and Nougaim, 1968, and Lawler and Suttle, 1972, for example). The theory has attracted criticism regarding its premise that people work on satisfying needs at a higher level only once all lower-level needs have been met. This, as noted above, is not an entirely valid criticism for Maslow did say that people are more likely to be partly satisfied at each level before moving on. However, Maslow suggests that there is still a hierarchy present – that people are unlikely to meet higher-order needs to any greater extent than they do lower-order ones.

In a letter to Hall and Nougaim as they carried out their research, Maslow indicated that he thought the emergence of various needs coincided with key stages in life. So (for the 'fortunate') safety and physiological needs are met during childhood, belonging and love needs during adolescence, esteem needs during early adulthood, and self-actualisation as people approach their fifties. If this is indeed the case, it would have an important bearing on research and the age-profiles of the groups being used.

A major problem with the Hierarchy of needs theory is how to measure needs – both in terms of how strongly they are felt and of how someone knows they have been met (Wahba & Bridwell, 1976). This is a particular issue for observers who are trying to assess whether someone else's needs have been met, especially at higher levels, because really only the individual involved can *feel* they have been met.

Other problematical aspects of this theory are how to categorise certain needs and even whether the order of the hierarchy itself is correct. Even Maslow suggests that some people see self-esteem needs as more important than love. The theory fails to address why some needs remain motivators even though they have apparently been satisfied. Alderfer criticised this lack of clarity and developed his theory partly as an attempt to overcome this, and other, shortcomings in Maslow's theory.

As for the theory's not explaining why some people continue to be motivated to meet needs that have apparently already been met, Alderfer referred to this as 'frustration-regression' – meaning 'that when a person is not satisfied by attaining less concrete, more uncertain ends, he "regresses" to needs which are somewhat more concrete and less uncertain as to their attainment' (Alderfer, 1969). See **Existence-relatedness-growth theory** (Chapter 10) for further information on this point and on the one made in the previous paragraph.

Another reason this theory is difficult to apply directly to work is that needs are not met through one source. For example, the sense of belonging may be satisfied outside of a work setting for some people, and those people are therefore unlikely to seek close friends, social ties or even close team-based relationships at work. Self-actualisation may be satisfied by activities outside work. This means that a person may be an excellent performer at work and one a manager thinks has potential to progress – but may simply not be interested in self-development plans, feeling that he or she is progressing well enough in his or her activities at home.

Recognition of some sort of hierarchy may help managers understand that issues at a lower level on the hierarchy may well diminish the motivational effects of anything higher up, and that what motivates a person on one day may change if his or her circumstances change. So if someone is worried about serious financial problems (affecting basic-level needs such as food and shelter), it is unlikely that he or she is going to be much motivated by self-development plans. Hierarchy of needs is also an interesting theory to apply to wider settings such as organisational growth. For example, while an organisation is struggling to meet basic needs (eg short-term cash flow) it is perhaps unlikely to be motivated to seek to meet higher needs (eg long-term learning strategies).

References

HALL D. T. *and* NOUGAIM K. E. (1968) 'An examination of Maslow's need hierarchy in an organizational setting'. *Organizational Behavior and Human Performance.* Vol. 3. pp12–35.

LAWLER E. E. *and* SUTTLE J. L. (1972) 'A causal correlational test of the need hierarchy concept'. *Organizational Behavior and Human Performance.* Vol. 7. pp265–87.

MASLOW A. H. (1943) 'A theory of human motivation'. *Psychological Review.* Vol. 50. pp370–96.

MASLOW A. H. (1954) *Motivation and Personality.* New York, Harper & Row.

MASLOW A. H. (1962) *Toward a Psychology of Being.* New Jersey, D. Van-Nostrand.

MASLOW A. H. (1987) *Motivation and Personality.* Revised by Frager R., Fadiman J., McReynolds C. and Cox R. 3rd edn. New York, Harper & Row.

WAHBA M. A. *and* BRIDWELL L. G. (1976) 'Maslow reconsidered: a review of research on the need hierarchy theory'. *Organizational Behavior and Human Performance.* Vol. 15. pp212–40.

14 HYGIENE THEORY

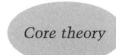

Core theory

Also known as
Two-factor theory
Motivator-hygiene theory
Satisfaction-motivation theory

Key author(s)
F. Herzberg

Summary of theory
Hygiene theory is based on the premise that the things people find satisfying in their jobs are not always the opposite of the things they find dissatisfying. This is because the things that lead to job satisfaction are distinct from those that lead to job dissatisfaction. The theory also contends that motivation is a function of job satisfaction. Herzberg (1987) suggests that motivation as a function of a fear of punishment or failure to get extrinsic rewards should actually be called 'movement' and is not motivation at all. Motivation, according to Herzberg, is 'a function of growth from getting intrinsic rewards out of interesting and challenging work' (*ibid.*).

Herzberg challenges the definitions of 'job satisfaction' and 'job dissatisfaction', saying that one is not the opposite of the other. He makes it clear that 'the opposite of job satisfaction is not job dissatisfaction but, rather, *no* job satisfaction; and similarly, the opposite of job dissatisfaction is not job satisfaction, but *no* job dissatisfaction' (Herzberg, 1987 – his italics).

Herzberg's research investigated situational factors that gave rise to certain attitudes at work – the attitudes that had arisen and the effects they had caused in the job. On the whole, those elements of the job that resulted in a positive attitude, or job satisfaction, were to do with the job itself. The elements that resulted in a negative attitude, or job dissatisfaction, were to do with the context within which the job was done.

Elements of the job that Herzberg found led to dissatisfaction he labelled *hygiene factors*. These relate to the elements of a job that are expected to be present, usually the ones that are externally provided – they are extrinsically rewarding. If the elements are adequate, people feel neutral about them; if they are absent, people are demotivated. Organisations get rapidly diminishing returns in motivation once they exceed 'adequate' – people do not continue to be more motivated each time these elements are improved. For example, although people are unlikely to refuse more pay or better working conditions, more of these elements would not necessarily motivate people to work harder.

Hygiene factors include (in order of strength of connection with dissatisfaction, such that 1 indicates the strongest connection):

1 working conditions – the physical characteristics of the environment
2 interpersonal relationships – the characteristics of work-related interactions between the individual and others in the organisation
3 supervision – the competence and fairness (or otherwise) of the first line manager
4 company and policy administration – the adequacy (or otherwise) of the company organisation and management, and the effects of policies, in particular those relating to the management of people
5 job security – the objective signs of security (rather than feelings of security), which include length of contract and company stability or instability
6 salary – any financial compensation.

Elements of the job that Herzberg found led to satisfaction he labelled *motivators*. These are elements of the job that make it satisfying. Lack of them could lead to dissatisfaction, but efforts to improve on them lead to increased motivation. Motivators are often elements of a job that people find rewarding in themselves – intrinsically rewarding.

Motivators include (in order of strength of connection with job satisfaction, such that 1 indicates the strongest connection):

1 achievement – including completing a challenging job and solving a challenging problem
2 recognition – including praise for a job well done and direct feedback on the results of one's work from customers and from the work itself
3 the work itself – including such elements of the job as creativity, challenge, variety, an opportunity to do the job from beginning to end
4 responsibility – including being accountable for one's own efforts or those of others, and being given responsibility for resources and self-scheduling
5 advancement – promotion.

Although salary appears here solely as a hygiene factor, it was also a motivator, but ranked only sixth in connection with job satisfaction. Overall, Herzberg reckoned it to be more closely connected to dissatisfaction than satisfaction because salary has a longer-term, more potent effect on job dissatisfaction than it does on job satisfaction. He felt that salary was a 'mover', and not a motivator, in that it rewarded the need to avoid economic deprivation and the need to avoid being treated unfairly. Salary as a positive feature of job satisfaction was mentioned mostly in relation to its links to recognition rather than because of the money itself.

The other factor investigated which did not appear to have a strong effect on job satisfaction or dissatisfaction was personal life. This was not whether someone's personal life affected work but whether work affected an individual's personal life, and the attitudes it caused when it did. For example, if a company required an employee to move location, the result might be a negative work-related attitude if the family was not keen to move. In fact, Herzberg reports, 'many of our respondents very pointedly informed us that they did *not* let the tensions of the job affect their families' (Herzberg *et al*, 1959 – his italics). Herzberg *et al* wondered whether this was 'a sign of the psychological sturdiness of our sample' and pondered over whether 'perhaps we should have asked their wives' (*ibid.*) – their research being based primarily on jobs held by men.

Hygiene theory contends that people are more satisfied, and thus more motivated, by elements of the job itself rather than by the environment within which they work. Herzberg suggests that such motivation has a positive effect on work performance, although he did not conduct independent studies into it.

Other key areas to which job satisfaction are linked include:

- [ ] turnover of staff – Those who are dissatisfied are, not surprisingly, more likely to quit than those who are satisfied. Herzberg also reports on 'psychological quitting', which is what happens when staff do not actually leave but 'withdraw' from the job – perhaps only putting in what is required to keep them employed.
- [ ] attitude toward the company – There was a close link between job satisfaction and a positive attitude toward the company.
- [ ] mental health (general well-being rather than mental illness) – People tended to link poor health and job dissatisfaction but did not as readily link good health and job satisfaction.
- [ ] interpersonal relationships – There appeared to be very little connection between job satisfaction or dissatisfaction and interpersonal relationships. Herzberg concludes that this is probably because 'the degree to which a person lets his feelings about his job spill over into the conduct of his interpersonal relationships is more a function of his psychological dynamics as an individual than of anything else' (Herzberg *et al*, 1959).

The theory concludes that if job satisfaction leads to greater *productivity*, then it makes sense that any improvements in motivators should lead to an improvement in performance. Herzberg suggests that the work itself, responsibility and advancement bring about the most long-term improvements in job satisfaction. Although recognition and achievement are more short-term in their effects on job satisfaction, they should not be ignored. Herzberg suggests that jobs could be improved by restructuring them to increase the opportunities available to the employee to achieve goals that are meaningfully related to the job. Jobs do not have to be more interesting *per se*, but they should be 'set up in such a way that, interest or no, the individual who carries them out can find that their operations lead to increased satisfaction' (Herzberg *et al*, 1959). This issue is explored further in **Job characteristics theory** (see Chapter 16).

Examples (see **Character profiles**)

One of Neil's first tasks in his new job was to implement an office move that had been planned by his predecessor. The move was within the same building but to a different floor. His team knew about the move and clearly had reservations about it, so Neil organised a meeting to discuss their concerns. He was surprised that they were so concerned about what he considered trivial things. For example, they did not like the decor on the new floor, and said (quite correctly, as it happened) that it was shabby. They also felt aggrieved that they were losing easy access to the fully-equipped kitchenette that was on their current floor. The new kitchenette had only a kettle.

Although Neil thought these issues were minor in the grand scheme of things, he could see they were having a major effect on productivity. He therefore put a case to his manager to get the new floor decorated and to kit out the kitchenette with a microwave and fridge. He involved the staff in choosing the new colour-scheme and selecting the new kitchen equipment. Overall, the budget for this was small, but the effect on productivity was profound. After the move, staff felt they were better off than before.

One of Frank's first jobs was in a factory. He remembers when the organisation created a personnel department. The new department encouraged managers to treat staff more as individuals than just as parts of the machinery, with the promise that productivity would increase. Early attempts to improve the environment mostly involved reforming working conditions and introducing a series of personnel policies.

The new initiatives certainly removed many of the issues the factory workers had formerly complained about on a regular basis, and started to make the workers feel more valued than they had done in the past. There was an initial positive impact on productivity – but it was not until the jobs themselves started to be redesigned that workers felt actually motivated to work harder. Productivity took an early dive while the new jobs were bedded in, but the gains after people had been trained and become used to the new way of working were substantial.

Key points

- □ Hygiene theory is based on the premise that things leading to job satisfaction are distinct from those leading to job dissatisfaction. Things people find satisfying in their jobs are therefore not always the opposite of things they find dissatisfying.
- □ Motivation is a function of job satisfaction. Motivation as a function of a fear of punishment or failure to get extrinsic rewards should actually be called 'movement'.
- □ Those elements of the job that lead to dissatisfaction are *hygiene factors*. They include (in order of strength of connection with dissatisfaction):
  - working conditions
  - interpersonal relationships
  - supervision
  - company and policy administration
  - job security
  - salary.
- □ Those elements of the job that lead to satisfaction are *motivators*. They include (in order of strength of connection with job satisfaction):
  - achievement
  - recognition

- the work itself
- responsibility
- advancement.

☐ Salary is also a motivator. Salary as a positive feature of job satisfaction is mentioned mostly in relation to its links to recognition rather than because of the money itself.

☐ Personal life appeared not to have a strong effect on job satisfaction or dissatisfaction.

☐ Overall, people are more satisfied, and thus more motivated, by elements of the job itself rather than by the environment within which they work.

☐ Other key areas to which job satisfaction is linked include:
- turnover of staff
- attitude toward the company
- mental health
- interpersonal relationships.

☐ If job satisfaction leads to greater productivity, it makes sense that any improvements in motivators should lead to an improvement in performance.

Commentary

Hygiene theory is a popular theory and the first to suggest that job satisfaction is not simply the opposite of job dissatisfaction. Critics of the theory point out that a lack of motivator must, by definition, be 'unsatisfactory' and therefore be dissatisfying. At the opposite end of the scale, the presence of a hygiene factor is satisfactory and therefore satisfying. Thierry and Koopman-Iwema refer to this as the *Herzberg controversy*.

This theory also challenged the basis of other motivation theories in that Herzberg distinguished between 'movement' (on which many other theories are based) and 'motivation'. Research shows that elements that improve motivation at work are those that appeal to personal growth and intrinsic rewards. There is also evidence that productivity increases when motivation is improved.

Hygiene theory does, however, have its critics, and Herzberg accepts that there are shortcomings in his approach. In particular, he accepts that to a certain degree interviewees had to be guided on what they were to talk about, and that this could have contaminated the data. He also accepts that interviewees may have found it 'painful ... to report of themselves that their work was poor or inefficient' (Herzberg *et al*, 1959) and might therefore have reported job satisfaction as linked to the job itself and job dissatisfaction as connected with extrinsic factors.

Robins (2001) lists five key criticisms of Hygiene theory:

☐ The methodology used by Herzberg does not take into account that often, when things are going well, people take the credit themselves, and when things are not, they blame others or their situation.

☐ Because the people undertaking the research had to interpret what people were saying about their jobs, there may well have been some unreliability in how responses were recorded. The same response could have been recorded differently by different people or by the same person on different occasions.

☐ There was no overall measure of satisfaction against which people could rate their jobs. This meant that individuals could dislike part of their job and yet still think the overall job acceptable. This point was expanded by Hackman and Oldham, who pointed out that the theory offered no suggestions on how to measure the presence or absence of motivating factors in existing jobs, which makes it difficult to evaluate the effects on intrinsic motivation of the success (or otherwise) of changes in job characteristics.

☐ Situational factors were ignored.

☐ The relationship between satisfaction and productivity was not independently proven (it was taken from people's own accounts of their inputs) and could therefore only be assumed.

Hackman and Oldham regard that a key flaw in Herzberg's theory is that it assumed everyone would be motivated by the same things – ie enriched jobs (jobs in which there has been an increase in 'motivators'). Later studies showed that some people are more likely to respond positively to enriched jobs than others. Hygiene theory provides no help in determining how such individual differences should be dealt with. Herzberg accepts 'that people who gain satisfaction from contextual factors would do well in jobs with a low potentiality for job-related satisfactions' (Herzberg *et al*, 1959).

Herzberg's interviewees were nearly all 'professional' people in middle management positions (mostly engineers and accountants) in a wide range of businesses, mostly manufacturing. This is a key factor in the limitations of the theory. They were chosen mainly because of their ability to communicate their feelings – and because it was this population who were most likely to be interested in the results. This means the theory is perhaps more specifically a 'middle management' theory of motivation than a general one.

Despite the criticisms, Hygiene theory is a key theory of motivation. It is useful for managers to consider hygiene factors when thinking about motivation. Staff attitude surveys often highlight dissatisfactions with hygiene factors. Getting hygiene factors sorted out is certainly important, but this theory suggests there is only so much that is beneficial, and that effort should go into improving the motivators if motivation is an issue.

References

HACKMAN J. R. *and* OLDHAM G. R. (1976) 'Motivation through the design of work: test of a theory'. *Behavior and Human Performance.* Vol. 16. pp250–79.

HERZBERG F. A., MAUSNER B. *and* SHERWITZ L. (1959) *The Motivation to Work.* New York, John Wiley.

HERZBERG F. A. (1987) 'One more time: how do you motivate employees?'. *Harvard Business Review.* Vol. 46. pp109–20. (Note: This article includes a reprint of an article that appeared in *Harvard Business Review* in Jan–Feb 1968.)

ROBINS S. P. (2001) *Organizational Behavior.* 9th edn. New Jersey, Prentice-Hall.

THIERRY H. *and* KOOPMAN-IWEMA A. M. (1984) 'Motivation and satisfaction'. In Drenth P. J. D., Thierry H., Willems P. J. and de Wolff C. J. (eds) *Handbook of Work and Organizational Psychology.* Chichester, John Wiley & Sons Ltd.

15 INTERNAL–EXTERNAL CONTROL THEORY

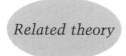

Related theory

Also known as

I-E theory

Key author(s)

J. B. Rotter.

Summary of theory

Internal–external control (I-E) theory builds on **Reinforcement theories** (see Chapter 17) and is an elaboration of **Attribution theory** (see Chapter 5). I-E theory suggests that reinforcement depends to some extent on an individual's perception of the cause of an outcome. The more someone feels an outcome is due to their own efforts, the more likely it is that the behaviour that produced the outcome will be reinforced. Outcomes seen as the result of external forces – such as luck – are unpredictable, and behaviour is therefore not so readily reinforced.

Rotter (1966) developed the *internal–external dimension* ('I-E dimension') to measure 'locus of control'. This is the extent to which people feel they are in control of the situations they are in, and therefore the extent to which they are confident of directing events. Rotter (*ibid.*) describes the extremes of the dimension:

☐ *External control* is when a person feels that the outcome of his or her actions is as 'the result of luck, chance, fate, as under the control of powerful others, or as unpredictable because of the great complexity of the forces surrounding him'.

☐ *Internal control* is when a person 'perceives that the event is contingent upon his own behaviour or his own relatively permanent characteristics'.

At the external end of the dimension ('E') people feel they have little or no control over events. At the internal end ('I') people feel they are able to influence and control their environment. Individuals may be located anywhere between the extremes.

As noted in the **Reinforcement theories** chapter (Chapter 17), reinforcement acts to strengthen expectancy that a particular behaviour or event will be followed by a particular outcome again in the future. The implication here is that the nearer the 'E' end of the scale someone is, the weaker the links he or she is making between actions and outcomes. For example, Efran (1963) studied students' tendency to repress failures rather than successes. The results suggested that those at the 'E' end of the scale are more ready to remember 'failures' because they make weak, or no links, between their actions and outcomes – they do not perceive failures as a reflection on their ability. Those at the 'I' end of the scale make strong links between their actions and the outcomes of events, and are therefore more ready to repress memories of 'failure' because they see them as a reflection on their ability.

Studies on links between I-E and response to external control or suggestion showed that people at the 'I' end of the scale tend to be more resistant to manipulation from others because they feel their control over their environment is being adversely affected. Yet if there is advantage from conforming, the 'I' person would do so but still feel it is his or her choice. Rotter concludes that 'The individual who perceives that he does have control over what happens to him may conform or may go along with suggestions when he chooses to and when he is given a conscious alternative. However, if such suggestion or attempts at manipulation are not to his benefit, or if he perceives them as subtle attempts to influence him without his awareness, he reacts resistively' (Rotter, 1966). (See also Crowne and Liverant, Strickland, Getter, Gore.)

Rotter suggests that the location of an individual on the I-E dimension is influenced by cultural factors. The more individualistic the culture, the higher the focus on achieving success as a result of one's own efforts, the more likely the population will lean towards the 'I' end of the scale. Cultures are not necessarily national and may be based on class, intelligence or other groupings.

Rotter concludes his 1966 paper with a summary:

> A series of studies provides strong support for the hypotheses that the individual who has a strong belief that he can control his own destiny is likely to (a) be more alert to those aspects of the environment which provide useful information for his future behaviour; (b) take steps to improve his environmental condition; (c) place greater value on skill or achievement reinforcements and be generally more concerned with his ability, particularly his failures; and (d) be resistive to subtle attempts to influence him.

Examples (see **Character profiles**)

Rachel is near the 'E' end of the I-E dimension. She saw the purchase of her flat as something she could not influence greatly – she reckoned she was in the hands of the estate agent, her solicitor and the vendor. However, there are some situations she feels more in control of. For example, at work she is beginning to feel she can do something about her situation, and has therefore been working towards achieving professional status by studying for her professional qualification.

Neil is near the 'I' end of the I-E dimension. A few years ago, in a previous job, his manager asked him to undertake a project. Neil felt angry at the way it was presented to him. Rather than offering a choice, his manager basically told him that if he did not undertake the project, Neil's chances of promotion would be badly affected. Because he felt he had no choice, Neil did not feel motivated by the project, even though it was one that he would normally have enjoyed doing. If only his manager had given him a choice! If only his manager had said that it would enhance Neil's chances of promotion if he did the project (rather than saying that it would scupper his chances if he did not), Neil believed he would have felt a lot more motivated.

Key points

- Internal–external control (I-E) theory builds on **Reinforcement theories** (see Chapter 17) in that reinforcement depends to some extent on an individual's perception of the cause of an outcome.

- The I-E dimension measures people's perceived 'locus of control' (see **Glossary**). At the 'I' end of the dimension, people feel they are in control and are responsible for, and thus can influence, their situation. At the 'E' end of the dimension, people feel they are influenced by their situation and thus have no control over their circumstances.

- This theory implies that the nearer the 'E' end of the scale someone is, the weaker the expectancy that certain actions will result in particular outcomes.

- People at the 'I' end of the scale tend to be more resistant to manipulation from others. However, if there is some advantage to be had from conforming, they may do so, feeling it is their choice to do so.

- The more individualistic a culture, the greater the chance that the general population will lean towards the 'I' end of the scale.

Commentary

Like **Attribution theory** (see Chapter 5), Internal–external control (I-E) theory is not a theory of motivation. However, because it builds on Attribution theory it is included for the same reason – ie it can help managers gain insight into the motivations that drive behaviour.

I-E theory has been criticised for its focus on the I-E dimension only as a personality variable. It appears to ignore other influences, such as differences between causes. For example, the theory tends to assume that all causes are equally stable. Thierry and Koopman-Iwema (1984) point out that it is the *degree of stability of causality* that more strongly influences future outcomes than the I-E dimension. So if an individual explains the outcome of his or her actions as resulting from his or her own capacity and/or efforts, it is because these causes are relatively stable rather than because the person is more naturally an 'I' type. Likewise, if an individual explains the outcome of his or her actions as resulting from the difficulty of the task and/or luck, it is because these causes are relatively unstable rather than any inherent 'E' personality type. Thierry and Koopman-Iwema therefore contend that previous experience (particularly performance) only affects the expectancies concerning outcomes of future behaviour when the causes of these previous experiences are attributed to stable characteristics.

The I-E scale is also general, so it is hard to predict specific behaviours, even if it is known where on the scale someone is. However, even if more specific locus of control scales were developed, the issues of other influences would still have to be taken into account. It would not be realistic to specify that 'I' or 'E' types will *always* behave in a certain way.

This theory has close links with the concept of *persistence*, which has only recently been attracting the attention of occupational psychologists. This concept is of particular interest in relation to perseverance after failure at a task. There are links between how long people are prepared to persist in doing something and their perception of the cause of the failure. If a person has high internal locus of control, and high standards, he or she is more likely to persist after failure – even if performance deteriorates as a result.

I-E theory implies that people at the 'E' end of the scale are far more difficult to motivate than those at the 'I' end because they do not feel their actions will change the situation. The implication is that such individuals must change their perceptions in order to change their motivations.

I-E theory is useful when considering motivation issues at an individual level. It should be used with caution, however, because there is no easy way to know at which end of the scale an individual is on any particular issue. We suggest that managers should not assume that a basic knowledge of the theory is enough to make decisions about other people's motivations without further analysis and exploration – and even then, they should proceed with caution!

References

CROWNE D. P. *and* LIVERANT S. (1963) 'Conformity under varying conditions of personal commitment'. *Journal of Abnormal and Social Psychology.* Vol. 66. pp547–55.

EFRAN J. S. (1963) *Some personality determinants of memory for success and failure.* Unpublished doctoral dissertation. Ohio State University.

GETTER H. (1962) *Variables affecting the value of the reinforcement in verbal conditioning.* Unpublished doctoral dissertation. Ohio State University.

GORE P. M. (1962) *Individual differences in the prediction of subject compliance to experimenter bias.* Unpublished doctoral dissertation. Ohio State University.

JAMES W. H. (1957) *Internal versus external control of reinforcement as a basic variable in learning theory.* Unpublished doctoral dissertation. Ohio State University.

PHARES E. J. (1957) 'Expectancy changes in skill and chance situations'. *Journal of Abnormal and Social Psychology.* Vol. 54. pp339–42.

ROTTER J. B. (1966) 'Generalized expectancies for internal versus external control of reinforcement'. *Psychological Monographs.* Vol. 80. pp1–28.

ROTTER J. B. (1967) 'Beliefs, attitudes and behavior: A social learning analysis'. In Jessor R. *and* Feshbach S. (eds) *Cognition, Personality and Clinical Psychology.* San Francisco, Jossey Bass.

STRICKLAND B. R. (1962) *The relationship of awareness to verbal conditioning and extinction.* Unpublished doctoral dissertation. Ohio State University.

THIERRY H. *and* KOOPMAN-IWEMA A. M. (1984) 'Motivation and satisfaction'. In Drenth P. J. D., Thierry H., Willems P. J. and de Wolff C. J. (eds) *Handbook of Work and Organizational Psychology.* Chichester, John Wiley & Sons Ltd.

16 JOB CHARACTERISTICS THEORY

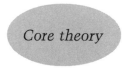

Core theory

Also known as

Job design theory

Key author(s)

J. R. Hackman and G. R. Oldham

Summary of theory

Hackman and Oldham undertook research to find out why it was that work redesign was considered a worthwhile strategy for organisations to follow. As they state in their 1976 paper, 'Though the benefits of work redesign . . . are widely touted in the management literature, in fact little is known about the reasons why "enriched" work sometimes leads to positive outcomes for workers and for their employing organisations.' Their theory is built on earlier research between job characteristics and individual responses to the work.

The *Job characteristics model* used in this theory consists of five 'core' job dimensions which prompt three psychological states which, in turn, lead to a range of beneficial personal and work outcomes.

The five *job dimensions* (also known as *job characteristics*) key to this theory are (all quotes from Hackman and Oldham, 1976):

☐ *skill variety* – 'the degree to which a job requires a variety of different activities in carrying out the work, which involve the use of a number of different skills and talents of the person'

- □ *task identity* – 'the degree to which the job requires completion of a "whole" and identifiable piece of work – that is, doing a job from beginning to end with a visible outcome'
- □ *task significance* – 'the degree to which the job has a substantial impact on the lives or work of other people, whether in the immediate organisation or in the external environment'
- □ *autonomy* – 'the degree to which the job provides substantial freedom, independence, and discretion for the individual in scheduling the work and in determining the procedures to be used in carrying it out'
- □ *feedback* – 'the degree to which carrying out the work activities required by the job results in the individual obtaining direct and clear information about the effectiveness of his or her performance'.

These dimensions prompt three *psychological states* (all quotes from Hackman and Oldham, 1976):

- □ *experienced meaningfulness of the work* – 'the degree to which the individual experiences the job as one which is generally meaningful, valuable, and worthwhile'
- □ *experienced responsibility for the outcomes of the work* – 'the degree to which the individual feels personally accountable and responsible for the results of the work he or she does'
- □ *knowledge of the results of the work activities* – 'the degree to which the individual knows, and understands on a continuous basis, how effectively he or she is performing the job'.

These states are core to this theory. If they are experienced positively (eg an individual learns that she has performed well on a task that she finds meaningful), this theory holds that the person is intrinsically motivated to perform well again in the future. If the person does not perform well, he or she will be motivated to regain the intrinsic rewards felt from a positive experience, and will therefore work hard to improve performance.

These three states all have to be present to incur high intrinsic motivation. It is unlikely that someone will feel intrinsically motivated to improve performance on a task if it is one he or she does not feel is important or if he or she has no feedback on the results of his or her endeavours.

The job dimensions relate directly to the psychological states. The first three dimensions of skill variety, task identity and task significance contribute to the meaningfulness of the work; the fourth dimension, autonomy, contributes to the responsibility for the outcomes of the work; and the fifth dimension, feedback, contributes to the knowledge of the results of the work activities.

Perception is key when defining these terms. For example, the degree to which individuals find their work meaningful depends on *their* perceived skills, *their* definition of a 'whole' job and *their* definition of task significance – not anyone else's. That said, people's perceptions are heavily influenced by social standards and norms. As Hackman and Oldham suggest, 'Employees who tighten nuts on aircraft brake assemblies, for example, are much more likely to perceive their work as meaningful than are workers who fill small boxes with paper clips...even though the skill levels involved may be comparable' (Hackman and Oldham, 1976).

Hackman and Oldham suggest that being able to measure job dimensions allows jobs to be rated on their motivating potential. The *motivating potential score* (MPS) is a measure of the degree to which the job dimensions are met. It is not possible to have a high MPS score if dimension four (autonomy) and dimension five (feedback) are rated poorly. However, it is possible to have a reasonably high MPS score on a job if only one of the first three dimensions (skill variety, task identity and task significance) score highly. The theory contends that intrinsic motivation should be highest when a job has a high MPS.

Hackman and Oldham criticised other motivation theories (eg Herzberg's **Hygiene theory** – see Chapter 14) for assuming that people react in the same way to their work. Careful not to do the same, they introduced a measure called individual *growth need strength* (GNS). This is a measure of the degree to which people have a need for personal growth and development. The theory contends that people with high GNS will 'respond more positively to a job high in motivating potential than people with low growth need strength' (Hackman and Oldham, 1976).

If GNS is high, it impacts on motivation in two key ways:

☐ an increased likelihood, or ability, of people to experience the psychological states when the job dimensions are positive

☐ an increased likelihood, or ability, of people to respond positively to the psychological states.

These impacts explain why some people, given the same job and same situation, react more positively than others.

Although there were some people in the study with very low GNS, Hackman and Oldham did not find evidence that job enrichment has a negative effect on people – for example, those who may feel unable to cope with more complex jobs. They concede that the gains from those low on GNS may be less than their high-GNS colleagues, but say, 'The present findings provide *no* reason to expect that the ultimate impact of working on enriched jobs will be more negative than positive for any group of employees, regardless of their level of growth need strength' (Hackman and Oldham, 1976 – their italics).

Hackman and Oldham list four key *personal and work outcomes* that are affected by relationships between core job dimensions, critical psychological states and growth need strength:

☐ internal work motivation
☐ high-quality work performance
☐ satisfaction with the work
☐ absenteeism and staff turnover.

These outcomes are more positive for jobs with high MPS than for jobs with low MPS. However, research demonstrates that the link between outcomes and high motivating potential is stronger for the first three outcomes than it is for absenteeism and staff turnover. This may have to do with the way in which the information was collected. For example, absenteeism was measured as a number of days. There was therefore no allowance for *occasions* to be measured. It could be that an employee with an excellent attendance record overall but who had one long absence could have skewed the figures.

Hackman and Oldham developed the *Job diagnostic survey* as a tool to measure the three key elements of this theory (job characteristics/dimensions, psychological states, and individual growth need strength) in actual work situations.

Hackman (1991) offered some guidelines for installing planned changes in jobs:

☐ Analyse ('diagnose') the work system prior to change.
☐ Keep the focus on the work itself.
☐ Prepare ahead of time for unexpected problems.
☐ Evaluate continuously.
☐ Confront the difficult problems early.
☐ Design change processes that fit with change objectives.

Examples (see **Character profiles**)

Mandy was recently talking about her job with a friend. She was trying to explain why she was motivated in this job when in a previous, very similar job she had not been. Both jobs were varied, and in both Mandy felt that she was working on worthwhile, whole projects, and that she was largely given control over them. In the end she concluded that the biggest difference was that in the previous job she had never known how well she was doing. The organisation never gave feedback, and a more senior manager always did the follow-up with the customer. Unless the results were bad, consultants tended to work on the basis of 'no news is good news'. In her current job, Mandy was getting detailed feedback on her work – not only from the partners and her colleagues but also from the customers.

Frank was recalling his early days working in a factory. He remembers when the organisation decided to change the jobs so that a team became responsible for a whole process, rather than for one small part of that process. Some of the benefits outlined by the management team to try to 'sell' the changes included the opportunities for workers to develop skills to help them advance. Some of Frank's colleagues were not interested in such development – they just wanted to do a job, get paid, and go home. Yet although some workers benefited personally out of the change more than others, overall the change resulted in a more satisfied, motivated workforce.

Key points

- ☐ Job characteristics theory contends that a person's intrinsic motivation is affected by his or her psychological state, the characteristics of his or her job, and how he or she responds to complex and challenging tasks.
- ☐ The Job characteristics model consists of five 'core' job dimensions which prompt three psychological states which, in turn, lead to a range of beneficial personal and work outcomes.
- ☐ The five job dimensions (also known as job characteristics) are:
  1 skill variety
  2 task identity
  3 task significance
  4 autonomy
  5 feedback.
- ☐ The three psychological states that have to be present to incur high intrinsic motivation are:
  - experienced meaningfulness of the work (linked to dimensions 1, 2 and 3)
  - experienced responsibility for the outcomes of the work (linked to dimension 4)
  - knowledge of the results of the work activities (linked to dimension 5).
- ☐ Personal and work outcomes are:
  - internal work motivation
  - high-quality work performance
  - satisfaction with the work
  - absenteeism and staff turnover.

- ☐ The individual, influenced by social standards and norms, defines the terms used in the psychological states.
- ☐ If the psychological states are experienced positively, a person will be intrinsically motivated to try to perform well in the future in order to repeat positive gains achieved previously.
- ☐ The motivating potential score (MPS) is a measure of the degree to which job dimensions are met. It is possible to have a reasonably high MPS score on a job with only one of the dimensions 1, 2 and 3 scoring highly. High MPS is not possible if dimensions 4 or 5 are rated poorly.
- ☐ Intrinsic motivation should be highest when the job has a high MPS.
- ☐ Individual growth need strength (GNS) is a measure of the degree to which a person has a need for personal growth and development. People with high GNS are likely to respond more positively to a job with high MPS than people with low GNS.
- ☐ Personal and work outcomes are more positive for jobs with high MPS than for jobs with low MPS. Research shows that the link between outcomes and high MPS is stronger for the first three outcomes than it is for absenteeism and staff turnover.
- ☐ Job diagnostic survey is a tool developed to measure job characteristics/dimensions, psychological states, and growth need strength.

Commentary

Hackman and Oldham developed the ideas put forward in their 1976 paper and published a book in 1980. This addressed some of the shortcomings in their earlier paper. For example, the design of jobs for work groups was not covered initially but was thereafter included in their book. Overall, research generally supports Job characteristics theory. It seems to be the case that jobs that are designed around the core dimensions do motivate people more than those that are not.

The research was conducted in an organisation setting and involved 658 employees working in 62 different jobs in seven organisations. The jobs were wide-ranging (including blue-collar, white-collar and professional work), and industrial and service-sector organisations were included. Some critics of this theory question its validity because of the way in which the research was conducted (eg Roberts and Glick, 1980). People on being questioned might have made links between the questions and adjusted their answers to fit. For example, if asked about task significance and their satisfaction in the job, they might have made connections that they would not have made if either factor had been researched separately. Later research (see Algera, 1983), however, has supported Hackman and Oldham's theory in that the relationships between job dimensions and attitudes of job-holders are similar regardless of the sources used.

Hackman and Oldham were careful to ensure that they did not imply that everyone would react the same way to enriched jobs. To this end they introduced the growth need strength (GNS) dimension. Some researchers suggested that people low on GNS might react negatively to enriched jobs because they found them too much to cope with psychologically or because they did not value the outcomes (eg Hulin and Blood). However, Hackman and Oldham reported discovering 'no evidence to support such contentions . . . the signs of the relationships between the job characteristics and the outcome measures are positive even for people in the bottom quartile of the growth need measure' (Hackman and Oldham, 1976).

Although the theory contends that people with low GNS would still benefit, but not as much, from enriched jobs, Roberts and Glick point out in their critique of the theory that 'no attempt was made to identify desirable task attributes for low-GNS individuals' (Roberts and Glick, 1980).

Suggested links between job dimensions and psychological states have caused some debate. Hackman, in a later article, explained that 'the job characteristics operate *through* the psychological states in influencing the outcome variables . . . rather than influencing the outcomes directly' (Hackman, 1991 – his italics).

Job characteristics theory is one of the few motivation theories specific to an organisational setting. Hackman and Oldham have created clear guidelines on how it can be implemented, and many of the suggestions are in line with good management practice. Because job dimensions rely on the perceptions of the job-holder, organisations cannot be expected to please everyone if jobs are enriched in the same way. However, it is a theory that has plenty of practical application.

References

ALGERA J. A. (1983) ' "Objective" and perceived task characteristics as a determinant of reactions by task performers'. *Journal of Occupational Psychology*. Vol. 56, No. 2. pp95–107.

HACKMAN J. R. (1991) 'Work design'. In Steers R. and Porter L. (eds) *Motivation and Work Behavior*. New York, McGraw-Hill.

HACKMAN J. R. *and* OLDHAM G. R. (1976) 'Motivation through the design of work: test of a theory'. *Organizational Behavior and Human Performance*. Vol. 16. pp250–79.

HACKMAN J. R. *and* OLDHAM G. R. (1980) *Work Redesign*. Massachusetts, Addison-Wesley Publishing Company.

HULIN C. L. *and* BLOOD M. R. (1968) 'Job enlargement, individual differences, and worker responses'. *Psychological Bulletin*. Vol. 69. pp41–55.

ROBERTS K. *and* GLICK W. (1980) 'The job characteristics approach to task design: a critical review'. *Journal of Applied Psychology*. Vol. 66, No. 2. pp193–217.

17 REINFORCEMENT THEORIES

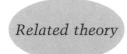

Related theory

Also known as

Instrumental learning

Key author(s)

There are many examples of reinforcement theories, and for practical reasons we have drawn the key points together under this heading. Many of the key points made here are based on a review of Reinforcement theories in Tosi *et al*.

Summary of theory

Reinforcement theory is a learning theory based on the premise that behaviour is influenced by the consequences of previous actions. The theory assumes that a person has been motivated to take a particular action in the first place: it is then concerned only with how the person responds to the consequences of his or her actions.

There are four main types of consequences each of which can have different effects. Tosi *et al* (1994) present a list:

☐ *positive reinforcement*, where desirable consequences are linked to a behaviour (eg praise after a good job done) – The effect of this is to increase the probability that the behaviour will be repeated.

☐ *negative reinforcement/avoidance learning*, where undesirable consequences are removed (eg learning that answering the telephone quickly stops the supervisor shouting at the team every time the telephone rings) – Again, the effect of this is to increase the probability that the behaviour will be repeated.

□ *punishment*, where undesirable consequences can be applied (eg disciplinary interview) or desirable consequences can be taken away (eg removal of privileges) – The effect of this is to reduce the probability that the behaviour will be repeated. In some cases, however, it may *increase* the probability that the behaviour will be repeated if the person being punished feels rewarded by the punishment. This latter point can be illustrated by the situation in which some children repeat behaviour that has been punished in the past because it gets them attention.

□ *extinction*, where a previously established reinforcer which is maintaining a behaviour stops being used – The effect of this is to reduce the probability that the behaviour will be repeated. For example, if individuals' ideas are forever being criticised by their manager, they may withhold their ideas. Putting a stop to the criticism may make it less likely that people will go on withholding their ideas.

The strength of reinforcement is affected by different patterns of reinforcement. These are called *reinforcement schedules* and include:

□ *continuous* – reinforcement every time the behaviour occurs (eg error messages on a computer system)

□ *fixed-interval* – reinforcement after a fixed period of time (eg six-monthly appraisals)

□ *variable-interval* – reinforcement occurs at irregular periods (eg mystery shopper audits – see **Glossary**).

□ *fixed-ratio* – reinforcement after a fixed number of activities (eg payment for every 100 items sold)

□ *variable-ratio* – reinforcement after a variable number of activities within a range (eg regular weekly monitoring, but random spot-checks on quality).

In every schedule, the closer the reinforcement to the behaviour, the stronger it is.

Another factor affecting the strength of reinforcement

is the frequency – the more frequent the reinforcement, the stronger it becomes. Continuous reinforcement therefore results in the strongest reinforcement. Fixed-interval reinforcement tends to have most effect immediately before the reinforcement. For example, if performance is reviewed every three months, it tends to be improved just before the appraisal. Unknown time intervals – ie those that are variable – can result in sustained performance because the reinforcement could occur at any time. However, performance may drop immediately after a variable-ratio reinforcement because the chances that there will be another reinforcement soon after the last may not be high. In addition, performance is less likely to be sustained the longer the time interval between each reinforcement.

Frequency also affects how quickly a behaviour is 'unlearned'. Continuous reinforcement may result in the fastest learning, but it will also result in the most rapid falling-away of the behaviour once the reinforcement stops. Intermittent and partial reinforcement may result in slower learning, but behaviours tend to continue for longer once the reinforcement stops. This may be partly because individuals continue to anticipate future reinforcement, even if the time interval is much longer than usual.

The strength of reinforcement also depends on how the person who gets the reward perceives it. The more directly the reinforcement is seen to be related to the individual's behaviour, the stronger it will be. For example, if a person considers the praise he or she receives to be indiscriminate, there are no particular behaviours that can be specifically linked with that praise and so there is no link between the reinforcement and the person's behaviour. However, if the praise is directed towards a particular behaviour, it will be perceived to reinforce that behaviour, and repetition of that behaviour is more likely.

The validity of the reinforcement is affected by perceptions of the reinforcer's position in giving feedback. For example, if feedback is given by someone an individual considers to be in no position to give feedback, reinforcement is less likely to occur.

Reinforcement is developed further in **Social learning**

theory (see Chapter 18). This theory takes into account the influence of the situation on reinforcement, and notes that behaviours can be learned not only through direct reinforcement but also through observation of others. See **Social learning theory**, Chapter 18, for further information.

Examples (see **Character profiles**)

When Mandy took her first job in consulting, she attended the organisation's induction programme. The training centred on the use of the client management software the organisation used. There were a series of 'failsafes' built into the system designed to prevent users from making serious mistakes. Some of the error messages were accompanied by an audible signal to alert the user to the error. Mandy and her colleagues found these 'alarms' embarrassing. The feeling of embarrassment meant that the trainees were motivated to get it right first time and not make any errors!

Neil's organisation introduced a quality-checking programme to encourage staff to complete customer orders correctly. The programme was set up on the basis of random checks on work completed during a week. In the early days the reinforcement did not work very effectively because the quality-checkers checked a specified amount of that week's work. Once the teams knew the checks had been completed for that week, they felt that the pressure was off. Neil changed the system so that the quality-checkers checked a specified number of pieces from the *previous* week's work. That way, staff could never be sure which pieces would be checked, and the reinforcement was more successful.

Key points

□ Reinforcement theories are learning theories based on the premise that behaviour is influenced by the consequences of a person's previous actions and by how he or she responds to those consequences.

□ The four main types of consequences are:
  – positive reinforcement
  – negative reinforcement/avoidance learning
  – punishment

- extinction.
□ The strength of reinforcement is affected by reinforcement schedules.
□ There are five main reinforcement schedules:
  - continuous
  - fixed-interval
  - variable-interval
  - fixed-ratio
  - variable-ratio.
□ In every schedule, the closer the reinforcement to the behaviour, the stronger it is.
□ The more frequent the reinforcement, the stronger it becomes. This affects the speed at which the behaviour is picked up, and also how quickly it is dropped once the reinforcement ceases.
□ The strength of reinforcement also depends on how the person who gets the reward or punishment perceives it. The more directly the reinforcement is seen to be related to the person's behaviour, the stronger it will be.
□ The more valid the reinforcer's position to give feedback is perceived to be, the more likely reinforcement is to occur.
□ Reinforcement theory is developed further in **Social learning theory** (Chapter 18) which accounts for situational influences on reinforcement.

Commentary

Reinforcement theories are primarily learning theories – ie they help explain how people learn from the results of previous activity. They underpin a number of motivation theories, and it is for that reason that we have included a summary of Reinforcement theories in the book.

Reinforcement theories have been widely supported in later research much of which has been based on animals, students and people in mental hospitals. It is only in the last 15 years or so that research into how Reinforcement theories apply in a work situation has been carried out. One of the key differences between laboratory-based experiments and the 'real' world of work is that the time interval between action and reinforcement is usually much longer in work settings (eg in the case of pay). Another difference is how people's response to reinforcement schedules can change in a work setting. An experiment by Latham and Dossett (see Latham and Huber, 1992) showed that continuous reinforcement was more effective as a motivator when skills are being learned, and variable-ratio reinforcement was a more effective motivator to maintain performance once people are experienced.

A key criticism of Reinforcement theories, when applied to human learning and motivation, is that they are too simplistic. Because reinforcement relies on personal experience, the theory ignores the learning and motivation that occurs because of observed experience. It therefore cannot explain deviant behaviour – that is, behaviour that is contrary to what has been learned in the past. Perhaps this is a peculiarly human trait, and so one that will not occur during experiments using animals. See **Social learning theory** (Chapter 18) for further information.

Reinforcement theories cover the extrinsic reinforcement of behaviour and do not cover intrinsic reinforcement. Intrinsic reinforcement is, by definition, granted by individuals to themselves. Such intrinsic rewards might be pride in a job well done or annoyance that a goal has not been achieved. Reinforcement of an intrinsically motivating task via extrinsic rewards can have a negative effect on intrinsic motivation. See **Cognitive evaluation theory** (Chapter 6) for further information.

Organisations should think carefully about the implications of Reinforcement theories on motivation. Reinforcement relies on the rewards, or punishments, an individual perceives that he or she is getting as the outcome of an action. If managers wish to motivate staff to behave in certain ways, rewards or punishments must reinforce the desired behaviours. There are many subtle ways in which organisations may undermine the motivation of their staff to behave in the desired way. For example, many new management approaches (some may call them 'fads') fail early on because the new behaviours are not reinforced.

References

LATHAM and HUBER in HOPKINS B. L. *and* MAWHINNEY T. C. (eds) (1992) *Pay for Performance: History, controversies, and evidence*. New York, Haworth Press.

ROTTER J. B. (1966) 'Generalized expectancies for internal versus external control of reinforcement'. *Psychological Monographs*. Vol. 80. pp1–28.

SKINNER B. F. (1938) *The Behavior of Organisms*. New York, Appleton-Century.

TOSI H. L., RIZZO J. R. *and* CARROLL S. J. (1994) *Managing Organizational Behavior*. 3rd edn. Massachusetts, Blackwell Publishers.

18 SOCIAL LEARNING THEORY

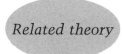

Related theory

Also known as

SLT
Social Learning Theory of Personality
Vicarious learning theory

Key author(s)

J. B. Rotter
A. B Bandura

Summary of theory

Social learning theory (SLT) is an extension of **Reinforcement theories** (see Chapter 17). Whereas Reinforcement theories work on the basis that behaviour is reinforced each time an action results in an expected outcome, SLT adds that people also learn that reinforcement, to a large degree, changes depending on the situation that a person is in. Rotter states that for the theory the word *social* was used 'because it stresses the fact that the major or basic modes of behaving are learned in social situations and are inextricably fused with needs requiring for their satisfaction the mediation of other persons' (Rotter, 1954).

The key aspect of SLT is its focus on the social influences on how people value goals or needs. Rotter *et al* (1972) outline four points concerning *the nature of needs*.

☐ Early needs, and perhaps some later ones, largely arise

from the association of new experiences with some sort of reinforcement. Most later goals or needs are acquired as a means of satisfying earlier, learned goals.

☐ Parents, siblings and other influential family members or friends are key in reinforcing early behaviours and thus shaping early goals.

☐ Behaviour may have been based on internal reinforcement (ie through a person's own experience) or external reinforcement (ie through outcomes observed in others). External reinforcement (imitation) can be as strong as internal reinforcement (McBrearty, Marston and Kanfer, 1961). In fact, many of our early learning experiences are through imitation.

☐ Many behaviours can lead to the same goal, and a group of behaviours all culminating in the same effect therefore develops a greater degree of intergroup similarity than does a group of randomly selected behaviours. In this way a behaviour may be of more value in relation to its occurrence with other behaviours than it would be on its own.

So SLT contends that the motivation to behave in a certain way is driven by the goals that are largely learned through reinforcement by, and within, our social groups. By implication, then, managers may presume that certain behaviours can be predicted based on the behaviours of others in the group. At a general level this may be true – but beware the manager who applies this to managing individuals: there is a lot more to behaviour than simply learning from reinforcement. This is why, even among close members of the same family, people behave in different ways.

SLT consists of four basic concepts that help to explain some of the reasons for differences between individuals in the same group.

☐ *behaviour potential*: the likelihood that any given behaviour will occur – It is a relative concept in that there are invariably a range of behaviours that could occur, so behaviour potential can be strong or weak (or anywhere in between). For example, it could be said that if a person is looking for a job there is strong likelihood that he or she will send in applications in response to job adverts.

- □ *expectancy*: the likelihood that any given behaviour will be reinforced as expected by the individual – Expectancy can range from no likelihood of reinforcement to certain likelihood of reinforcement. For example, a job-seeker who looks in a newspaper or trade magazine for job adverts has high expectancy of finding them. If the job-seeker looks in a comic, he or she has no expectancy of finding a job advert!

- □ *reinforcement value*: the degree of preference for any given reinforcement, assuming the individual has a free choice – For example, if the job-seeker could pick any job, the one he or she actually picks would have the highest reinforcement value. Reinforcement value is as perceived by the individual.

- □ *psychological situation*: the situational context in which the behaviour is demonstrated – People learn that some situations are more likely to be conducive to the desired outcome than others. Because no two situations are exactly the same, people's generalised reflections on situations in the past influence how they will behave in similar situations in the present.

Rotter (1954) states that behaviour can be predicted:

> The potential for behaviour x to occur in situation 1 in relation to reinforcement a is a function of the expectancy of the occurrence of reinforcement a following behaviour x in situation 1 and the value of reinforcement a.

For example, let's say behaviour x is to smile; situation 1 is meeting a new colleague and reinforcement a is previous experience that smiling helps to break the ice. Using Rotter's formula we can declare that the potential for smiling to occur when meeting a new colleague (in relation to the previous experience of the positive effects of smiling) is high because the expectancy of the occurrence of breaking the ice following a smile when meeting new colleagues is high, and breaking the ice is valued.

Motivation to behave in certain ways is therefore not just

the result of reinforcement but also of expectancy, the value of the predicted outcome, and the situations in which people find themselves.

Expectancy and reinforcement value are very closely linked. If a person fails to achieve a goal, 'the reinforcement itself may become associated with the unpleasantness of failure and diminish in value' (Rotter *et al*, 1972). This close link can cause dissatisfaction when expectancy is low and the value of the goal is high. For example, the value of promotion at work may be high but an individual may feel that he or she will not be able to achieve it. The motivation to strive towards promotion will therefore diminish. It is a situation that almost becomes a self-fulfilling prophecy because as the motivation to work towards a perceivedly unattainable goal decreases, the goal becomes ever less likely to be achieved.

A discrepancy between high goal value and low expectancy can also result in attempts to achieve the goal through illegitimate means, against either the law of the land or the rules of the organisation (see Merton, 1957). Someone who seeks the goal of a bonus through high output of work but who has low expectancy that he or she will actually be able to achieve it, may resort to 'creative' ways of manipulating the system in his or her favour. The use of illegitimate means to obtain desired goals is particularly prevalent in situations where the individual feels that the environment has conspired to put him or her in that position, rather than any lack of effort. For example, if a staff member comes to believe that she will never progress in an organisation however hard she tries because her manager does not like her, she may conclude that the situation is the result of factors outside her control and may therefore feel justified in using 'illegitimate' ways of gaining her desired promotion (perhaps by bypassing her manager when applying for other jobs).

Examples (see **Character profiles**)

When Mandy took her first job in consulting she had a lot to learn about client management, having never really had to do it in any previous job. Mandy learned a considerable amount from the induction programme, which centred on the use of client management software. The experienced consultants were also very helpful, and one in particular (Robert) became Mandy's unofficial mentor. Looking back on this relationship in later years, Mandy realised that much of what she learned from Robert was through observing how he dealt with clients and imitating it, rather than from anything written down or delivered on a learning event. Her behaviours became so similar to those of Robert's that colleagues used to joke that she was his 'clone'.

Key points

☐ Social learning theory (SLT) is an extension of **Reinforcement theories** (see Chapter 17). It focuses on the social influences on people's goals and the value they put on them.

☐ There are four key points about the nature of needs:
   - Needs are learned or acquired.
   - Early goals appear as the result of satisfactions and frustrations that are mostly controlled by other influential people.
   - Regularly occurring behaviour is available through reinforcement during previous experience.
   - Needs exist within functionally-related systems.

☐ Because behaviour is influenced and shaped by others, there tends to be some degree of conformity of behaviour within the influential group. However, this generalisation would be an inappropriate premise to apply to individuals as an assumption.

☐ The four concepts that explain individual differences within a group are:
   - behaviour potential
   - expectancy
   - reinforcement value
   - psychological situation.

☐ SLT contends that motivation to behave in certain ways is the result of expectancy, the value of the predicted

outcome, and the situations in which people find themselves.

☐ If expectancy is low, motivation can be adversely affected
even if the value of the goal is high. This becomes, to
some extent, a self-fulfilling prophecy. Some people may
resort to illegitimate means to obtain such goals.

Commentary

Social learning theory (SLT) is a learning theory and not
strictly a theory of motivation. We have included it as a
related theory because of its obvious links to core theories
and other underpinning theories such as **Reinforcement theories** (see Chapter 17). SLT may help managers understand
why it is that some people seem motivated to behave in
different ways despite similar backgrounds, identical training,
and so on.

There are close links between this theory and **Internal–
external control theory** (I-E theory – see Chapter 15). In
fact, Rotter developed I-E theory to enhance SLT. He contended that expectancy is not only based on experience
and observation but also on an individual's ability to
generalise the expectancy across a range of similar situations.
So individuals with a perception of internal control are
more likely to link behaviours and outcomes than people
with a perception of external control. Rotter admitted that
the I-E concept was originally supposed to be a peripheral
feature of SLT and not a whole theory in its own right (Rotter,
1975)!

SLT is more complex than Reinforcement theory because
it considers behaviour resulting not only from the reinforcement *experienced* by the individual but from the
reinforcement *observed* by the individual. It is an attractive
theory to apply to any organisational setting in which managers wish to influence the motivation to behave in a certain
way because it suggests that a 'Do as I do' style of learning
is a valid approach to take – managers do not have to wait
for people to *experience* reinforcement.

Of course, this explains why the extension of the 'Do as I
do' cliché – ' . . . not as I say' – also applies. This theory goes

some way to showing how it is that people are motivated to behave in ways that conform to the 'accepted' norms of their group, even if those norms are contrary to the behaviours espoused in policy. For example, individuals who join a department that has long-established employees in traditional roles often take up the 'ways of working' demonstrated by these staff, despite what they are told during induction or learning events.

SLT offers a complex approach to understanding learning and motivation. It is hard to decipher exactly what has reinforced behaviour – other than a combination of early reinforcements from influential others and observation of those around them. It relies on the importance that an individual confers on the influential others – not unlike referent groups in **Equity theory** (see Chapter 9). In other words, it is hard for a manager to understand what has reinforced certain behaviour. As a theory it is perhaps more useful in helping managers understand that behaviour is influenced by many disparate inputs rather than in deciphering and interpreting what those influences are.

References

BANDURA A. (1977) *Social Learning Theory*. New Jersey, Prentice-Hall.

McBREARTY J. F., MARSTON A. R. *and* KANFER F. H. (1961) 'Conditioning a verbal operant in a group setting: direct versus vicarious reinforcement'. *American Psychologist*. Vol. 16. p425 (abstract).

MERTON R. K. (1957) *Social Theory and Social Structure*. Illinois, Free Press.

ROTTER J. B. (1954) *Social Learning and Clinical Psychology*. New Jersey, Prentice-Hall.

ROTTER J. B., CHANCE J. E. *and* PHARES E. J. (1972) 'An introduction to social learning theory'. In Rotter J. B., Chance J. E. and Phares E. J. (eds) *Applications of a Social Learning Theory of Personality*. New York, Holt, Rinehart & Winston.

ROTTER J. B. (1975) 'Some problems and misconceptions related to the construct of internal versus external control of reinforcement'. *Journal of Consulting and Clinical Psychology*. Vol. 43. pp56–67.

19   THEORY X AND Y

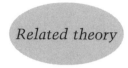

Also known as

Key author(s)
   D. M. McGregor

Summary of theory

   Theory X and Y was based on McGregor's view that the relationship between managers and employees could be vastly improved if the assumptions that had developed about how people behaved at work were changed from a Theory X view to a Theory Y view.

   Theory X was the view prevailing at the time of McGregor's writing. It was based largely on the Scientific Management school of thought, and proposed that increased productivity could result from breaking jobs down into small units of work and giving workers a small range of clearly defined tasks to do. The theory was based on specific assumptions about contemporary workers:

☐ They were inherently lazy and avoided effort wherever possible.

☐ Their goals were contrary to those of the organisation.

☐ They resisted any change.

☐ They were poor decision-makers.

Because of these assumptions, organisations had to set up systems to motivate and manage workers. Such systems included:

- [ ] a minimal number of situations in which workers had to make decisions
- [ ] extrinsic rewards, mostly financial
- [ ] very close supervision
- [ ] tight discipline and strict correction of performance to encourage conformance
- [ ] detailed training and guidance on how to do the jobs.

Theory Y was McGregor's response to what he saw as being Theory X's shortcomings. It was also based on specific assumptions about workers:

- [ ] They all have potential to develop within their current roles and, in many cases, beyond.
- [ ] They are able to take responsibility for their work.
- [ ] Their goals can be the same as those of the organisation.

Following these assumptions, organisations would have to set up systems different from the traditional ones in order to manage and motivate their workers. Such systems would include:

- [ ] responsibility delegated to workers where possible
- [ ] jobs enlarged to encompass whole, meaningful processes
- [ ] people empowered to make relevant decisions within their job remit
- [ ] training and guidance directed towards aligning personal goals with those of the organisation.

McGregor felt that as long as Theory X was the predominant theory of management there could be no trust between management and employees, and very little opportunity for relationships between the two parties to improve. The more dependent an organisation makes its employees on the management systems and controls, the less likely those employees are to be intrinsically motivated to perform well at their jobs. McGregor believed that this could not result in a productive relationship in the long term.

Examples (see **Character profiles**)

Frank's first job was on a production line producing car components. He had strict orders to follow on how he was to do his job and how much he was to produce in any given week. Frank quickly learned that the most significant decision he was expected to make was when to tell the supervisor that a decision was needed! In some ways he enjoyed the job for the first year or so. It was comforting never to have to make a decision and to be told exactly what to do all the time. He was motivated to work while the pressure was on but enjoyed the few times when the supervisor was away and life lightened up a little.

Frank was good at his job and was promoted to a supervisory role. There was very little training for this role: supervisors were expected to learn 'on the job'. He found it stressful to have to be on top of things all the time. Yet if he did not control things, production suffered. He began to feel that his was not a healthy relationship with his workers, many of whom he was sure were capable of taking on much more responsibility – it was just that the company did not trust them an inch.

Key points

☐ Many organisations following the Scientific Management approach to motivation at work viewed their workforce in a way that was described as Theory X by McGregor.

☐ Theory X assumes that workers are lazy, are poor decision-makers, hate any change, and want different goals from those of the organisation.

☐ Theory X organisations had management systems that outlined each job in great detail, trained workers in that detail, limited the situations in which workers had to make any decisions, and closely monitored the workers, punishing those who went out of line and rewarding those who kept in line mostly through extrinsic, financial means.

☐ Theory Y organisations assumed workers could take responsibility for their work, and develop in their jobs. Goals could be seen as mutually compatible.

☐ Theory Y organisations would have management systems that encouraged responsibility and empowered employees within jobs broad enough to take in a whole process rather than just a few tasks. A unitarist approach to employee relations was taken in that it could be assumed that the goals of the organisation would be those of the individual.

Commentary

Although this is not a theory of motivation, Theory X and Y can influence how motivating factors are regarded within an organisation. If a Theory X approach is taken, extrinsic rewards – such as pay – are closely linked with performance in order to motivate people to perform well in their jobs. If a Theory Y approach is taken, the organisation is more likely to consider how to create a working environment in which employees may discern intrinsic rewards in their jobs – through job enrichment, for example.

McGregor's ideas were very similar to those put forward by the Human Relations movement (not to be confused with Human Resources Management, which came later). This movement emerged in Chicago, USA, in the 1940s, from research that suggested that organisations and their employees would benefit from a move away from a pluralistic win/lose manager/worker relationship towards a unitarist win/win relationship. Features such as those outlined in McGregor's Theory Y organisation were said to have a beneficial effect on organisational performance.

Others writing at the same time as McGregor took a similar line (see Argyris, Likert, Stogdill). All seemed to agree that a rigid, bureaucratic organisational structure stifles human ability to work flexibly to be productive. The more rigid the controls, the more the relationship between manager and worker is akin to a parent-and-child relationship – involving all the dependencies that come with it.

The unitarist view of people management put forward by McGregor and others has not always been popular. Some theorists question the concept of the 'human side of enterprise' (to use McGregor's phraseology). There are studies that show a participative management style is not always the best if productivity is considered key (see Podsakoff and Schriesheim, 1985, and Sims, 1980). Generally, however, the more controlling and directive the management style, the more extrinsic the motivation of the workers. This requires management systems and processes that maintain the tight levels of control to be rigidly and constantly applied in order that it is effective. Such measures are usually resource-intensive.

The simplistic nature of Theory Y was not lost on McGregor who, towards the end of his life, started work on *Theory Z*. Theory Z recognised that the objectives of the organisation could be different from those of its employees – and that this was not necessarily a bad thing. Individuals could be motivated to meet their own needs, which might be at odds with those of the organisation. The trick was to manage it so that the fundamental needs of both were met. Theory Z was expanded in a later book by Ouchi (1981), who used the theory to outline the Japanese style of management in which long-term employment and a focus on teamwork were key.

The ideas put forward by McGregor and others may now seem rather too simplistic, yet managers may still recognise the core of many of those ideas in other motivation theories. It is unlikely that any organisation would deliberately set out now to be a 'Theory X' or 'Theory Y' organisation, but McGregor's work may help managers to understand how motivation can be affected if management styles reflect one or other theory.

References

ARGYRIS C. (1957) *Personality and Organization: The conflict between the system and the individual.* New York, Harper & Row.

ARGYRIS C. (1964) *Integrating the Individual and the Organization.* New York, John Wiley.

LIKERT R. (1961) *New Patterns of Management.* New York, McGraw-Hill.

McGREGOR D. M. (1960) *The Human Side of Enterprise.* New York, McGraw-Hill.

OUCHI W. G. (1981) *Theory Z: How American business can meet the Japanese challenge.* Massachusetts, Addison-Wesley.

PODSAKOFF P. A. *and* SCHRIESHEIM C. A. (1985) 'Leader reward and punishment behavior: a methodological and substantive review'. In Straw B. and Cummings L. L. (eds) *Research in Organizational Behavior.* San Fransisco, Jossey-Bass.

SIMS H. P. Jr (1980) 'Further thoughts on punishment in organizations'. *Academy of Management Review.* Vol. 5. pp133–8.

STOGDILL R. M. (1959) *Individual Behavior and Group Achievement.* New York, Oxford University Press.

PART II

PRACTICAL APPLICATIONS

20 AN INTRODUCTION TO PRACTICAL APPLICATIONS

This part of the book enlarges on some of the motivational issues facing organisations, and indicates how motivational theories could apply. We examine motivational issues at organisational, team-and-group and individual level. Each chapter is set out in a standard format so that readers can easily find the information they are seeking. This format corresponds to:

Title
There are three parts to the title. Firstly, there is the level at which motivation issues are being discussed. Secondly, there is a one-line summary which clarifies the level. Lastly, there is the specific issue to be discussed in the section.

Introduction
A brief overview of what is covered in the chapter.

Application of theory
This covers how motivation theory can apply to issues facing organisations at the level of the chapter. Theory names have been **emboldened** for ease of reference.

Each chapter is broken up into key applications where appropriate.

We have illustrated points using examples from real situations. To ensure that the organisations involved remain anonymous, however, we have not referred to them by name. At times, we have brought together key points from two or more situations to create one example.

| | *We use the term 'manager' to describe anyone who manages the activities of others.* |
| **Key points** | A list of the main points made in the chapter. |

We recognise that each situation faced by someone with a motivation issue will have nuances that make it different from every other situation, even if there are many similarities. However, our aim for the practical application chapters is to highlight how motivation theories could apply in a range of day-to-day work situations in sufficient depth for most readers to be able to relate theory to their own circumstances.

21   JOB DESIGN

Introduction

In this section we discuss the design of the job – not the rewards attached to it, or the way in which jobs are managed. Although these two elements clearly have an impact on job design, issues relating to motivation in those areas are discussed elsewhere. 'Job design' here refers to the description of the tasks that make up a job and, in some cases, of how the job should be done, as compiled in a formal job description, role profile or similar document.

Many organisations design jobs with a 'blank sheet of paper' approach – in other words, they ask themselves how work would ideally be organised into jobs that maximised the enterprise's effectiveness as an organisation. This is usually easier for new organisations or new business units. Most organisations, however, find themselves designing jobs as the result of organisational change – a situation implying that while the people may stay the same, it will be the jobs that are changing. Motivation issues are therefore key.

Application of theory

There are two key applications in job design:

☐ designing new jobs (whether for a new unit or redesigning within an existing unit)

☐ designing jobs around individuals.

Designing new jobs

To design new jobs implies that either there are no jobs or job-holders at present (eg when starting a new organisation or creating a new business unit, team or department in an existing organisation) or there is a need to redesign existing jobs (eg as the result of an organisational restructure or merger).

The key theory relating to job design is **Job characteristics theory** (see Chapter 16). This theory suggests that jobs should be designed in such a way as to maximise intrinsic motivation, and should therefore contain skill variety, task identity (involving a 'complete' task), task significance, autonomy and feedback. It also helps if job-holders do jobs they consider meaningful and in which they feel accountable for the results.

Creating jobs that contain the characteristics listed above requires organising job tasks to encompass a complete activity (a process from beginning to end) and giving job-holders the resources to undertake those tasks. 'Complete' does not necessarily mean from conception to conclusion of the whole process, but it does mean that there must be a clear start and finish. For example, opening accounts in a bank is a whole process whereas checking the application forms is not. Skill variety is likely to be a natural outcome of this design.

Significance must be reinforced throughout the organisation. It is no good expecting people to think of their jobs as significant if they are treated as the 'lowest' members of the organisation, if their jobs are never mentioned in briefings, if their learning is considered low-priority, and so on.

Theory X and Y (see Chapter 19) supports these characteristics in that it suggests the type of environment in which most people would be intrinsically motivated to work is one in which workers are trusted and given responsibility. Environments in which employees are considered lazy and untrustworthy are likely to be those in which there is close supervision and guidance and a focus on extrinsic rewards to motivate. Not an intrinsically motivating environment, we would suggest.

Job characteristics theory (Chapter 16) suggests that feedback is a key characteristic of an intrinsically motivating job. This is supported in **Control theory** (see Chapter 7), which is based on the need for systems to have clear standards and feedback good enough to ensure that corrective action can be taken when necessary. This is also supported by **Reinforcement theories** (see Chapter 17) which suggest that the more frequent the feedback, the more the behaviour is reinforced. Reinforcement is not necessarily positive, although no doubt most organisations would prefer that it is.

A note of caution should be sounded here. **Cognitive evaluation theory** (see Chapter 6) suggests that the more controlling the job-holder regards the feedback, the less likely he or she will feel intrinsically motivated. Jobs designed to appeal to people not interested in the content of the job, just the rewards it brings, may actually require detailed controlling feedback to sustain motivation.

Needless to say, not everyone views feedback in the same way – the identical feedback can be perceived as controlling by one person and as informational by the next. However, as a general rule, frequent feedback is probably going to be considered most informational in the early stages of learning a task or job. As the person becomes more competent, feedback can become less frequent (although we are not suggesting that eventually managers give no feedback at all!). When designing a job, feedback should be considered in terms of induction into the job as well as necessary, ongoing feedback.

Clear standards have been mentioned as key. Individual performance objectives are covered in another chapter, but if new job descriptions are to include standards, **Goal-setting theory** (see Chapter 12) suggests they should be specific and challenging in order to be motivating. Standards will have to be clearly specified somewhere, even if they are not included in job descriptions.

We suspect managers in most organisations want to design jobs that maintain levels of interest, whatever the motivation. **Activation theory** (see Chapter 4) suggests that people are motivated to maintain a personal, optimum level of activation or stimulation. If an organisation designs jobs that are highly repetitive and routine, it is effectively designing for *reducing* levels of activation. This is because the initial novelty of the new job, creating an initial rise in activation, will soon wear off, taking stimulation of activity levels down with it. The results of this can be counter-productive to the organisation, though not necessarily to the individual. Where critical tasks have to be done in a routine way, it may be best to programme these into the first part of a daily schedule when (for most people) activation levels tend to be higher.

Equity theory (see Chapter 9) suggests that people should understand why differences exist between jobs. Feelings of inequity are likely to cause people to be motivated to do something to redress the situation, particularly if they feel they are the ones losing out. If new jobs are part of a larger organisational structure, explaining how they fit in should be part of the communication strategy. Better still, get people (or their representatives) who are already part of the organisation involved in designing the jobs. This should minimise the potential for unfairness to be built in, for generally – this theory contends – people work to establish fair systems. Jobs designed through involving others need not be very different from those a single individual may have designed. However, because it is the *perception* of fairness that is key, involving others is likely to get more buy-in than not.

Although not strictly about job design, **Hygiene theory** (see Chapter 14) outlines a number of factors without which people are likely to feel demotivated. These include working conditions, salary, supervision and company policies. Organisations that design jobs to motivate, but in situations that are not motivating, are not maximising the potential of the organisation. This theory lists motivating factors such as achievement, recognition, responsibility and advancement. If these are built into the design of a job, this theory suggests, people are more likely to be motivated to do the job.

As a general rule, **Job characteristics theory** (see Chapter 16) suggests that although most people respond positively to well-designed jobs, the greatest benefit is gained for the organisation from those who feel a need for growth and development (called *growth need strength*). Both **Existence-relatedness-growth theory** (see Chapter 10) and **Hierarchy of needs theory** (see Chapter 13) suggest that people's motivations vary depending on how basic their needs are. The more short-term and physical the need (eg for food, clothing, shelter, and so on), the more basic it is, and therefore the more a person will seek to meet this need over and above other longer-term, more social needs (eg for relationships and personal growth).

The above point does not mean that low-paid jobs should not be designed with higher motivations in mind. An intrinsically motivating job can accommodate both intrinsically and extrinsically motivated people. An extrinsically motivating job design is unlikely to work for both.

Designing jobs around individuals

There may be times when an organisation wishes to design a job around a specific individual – perhaps when a business unit is small enough to allocate its tasks around the skills and preferences of its people. There may also be times when an individual is 'between' jobs (eg after finishing a project and before starting another) when an organisation wishes to design a job for that one person. There may also be special circumstances in which an organisation is willing to design a job to suit an individual (eg returning to work after a long-term sickness absence, winding down before retirement, or threatening to leave and so remove highly valued skills). Many of the points made above in the section on designing new jobs apply here too.

Job characteristics theory (see Chapter 16) suggests that there are a range of characteristics which could be designed into a job to make it intrinsically motivating. These could be easy to ignore if the job being designed is for a short-term need. Managers should consider the impact on motivation of giving someone a task that does not involve these characteristics. What does it say about the value of the individual to the organisation? If long-term motivation is important, we would advise that managers treat such short-term assignments with the same care as is needed in job design overall.

The job characteristics mentioned in the above theory also apply to creating permanent jobs for individuals. If this is in a team environment, the jobs can reflect individuals' preferences. However, the danger of giving all the interesting tasks to a few people, leaving the less interesting tasks for others, should be avoided. **Equity theory** (see Chapter 9) suggests that people will not be motivated to work in an environment they consider unfair. At least, their motivation will be to redress the inequity. So when creating jobs in this situation, organisations should not fail to consider the perceptions of fairness of all the members of the team.

Activation theory (see Chapter 4) suggests that people have an optimum level of activation or stimulation. If the job being designed is to cover a period in which there are other stimulating activities filling a person's life, a job with low levels of stimulation may actually be what is required.

Existence-relatedness-growth theory (see Chapter 10) and **Hierarchy of needs theory** (see Chapter 13) both suggest that people will focus on the more immediate, short-term basic needs as a priority if they feel these are under threat. There may be times when an individual is dealing with a crisis in his or her life that an organisation will design, or redesign, a job for that individual. This is likely to be considered short-term, and many might not consider it to be job redesign at all. However, managers may need to reduce 'extra' activities such as career development over this period.

> A manager was returning to work after 18 months of sickness absence relating to stress. It was agreed that he should return to work part-time for an agreed number of weeks, before going full-time. The organisation agreed that in the initial period, the job he would do, while important, would be fairly routine. This was intended to ensure that he was not given too much too quickly. There were many aspects of returning to work (meeting new colleagues, re-establishing relations with old colleagues, and getting up to date with the many changes that had occurred while he was away) that would be stimulating in themselves, so a routine job would guarantee that his level of activation would not exceed his stress levels.

Key points

Motivation theories suggest that if an organisation considers its jobs rewarding in themselves, and it is prepared to treat its employees as trusted members of the team aiming for the same goals, jobs should be designed in such a way as to maximise intrinsic motivation. The key points below draw out the main themes of the theories as they apply to job design.

- ☐ Jobs should be interesting, significant, autonomous, and a 'whole job'.
- ☐ Somewhere job standards should be made clear and challenging (perhaps in the employee's listed objectives rather than in the employee's job description).
- ☐ People should be able to get regular feedback on their performance. Feedback should be designed to be informational rather than controlling in order to ensure that intrinsic motivation is not adversely affected.
- ☐ The things most people accept as 'given' should already be in place (policies, salary, good working conditions, etc).
- ☐ Those affected (or their representatives) should ideally be involved in job design from the start.
- ☐ People are most likely to respond to well-designed jobs if they are looking to grow and develop. However, even those that are not are unlikely to respond negatively.
- ☐ People who are seeking to meet the most basic of human needs (food, shelter, etc) are likely to be extrinsically motivated more by the rewards a job brings than by the content of the job itself. However, by designing jobs that cater only for such needs, organisations are in danger of alienating those who have 'higher' needs and not allowing for personal development and growth.

22 COMMUNICATION

Introduction

In relation to the strategies, policies and tools an organisation has to make sure its employees know about, communication is delivered in many different ways: team briefings, newsletters, in-house websites, annual results broadcasts, 'away days', and so on. Yet another important aspect of communication is how a manager explains and handles day-to-day issues. But there are also strategic decisions about what information should be communicated, to whom, and when.

Staff attitude surveys consistently report that employees feel they do not have enough information. We suspect it is not *more* information they want, however, but more *relevant* information – ie about what the organisation is planning, and how it affects an individual's immediate environment and job. Motivation can be positively influenced through effective communication strategies, or negatively through ineffective ones.

Application of theory

There are two key applications within organisational communications:

☐ how an organisation communicates
☐ what an organisation communicates.

How an organisation communicates

An organisation communicates with its employees by means of a wide range of methods, as outlined in the introduction above. although motivation may not be the key purpose of some of these methods of communication, we assume organisations do not intend their communications to *demotivate*.

The method an organisation chooses to employ when

communicating gives a message in itself – the method of delivery should fit the message. Organisations could consider this in relation to **Job characteristics theory** (see Chapter 16). One of the key elements of this theory is that people find jobs that are meaningful more motivating than those that seem meaningless. If an organisation communicates to one group of employees using high-tech glossy presentations and to another via poorly-photocopied sheets of paper, what message does that give? Employees in the second group are likely to think their jobs are less meaningful than those of employees in the first group. On its own this may not be demotivating, but if it is part of an overall attitude in relation to a particular group of jobs, it can be.

Equity theory (see Chapter 9) also suggests that these 'hidden' messages can produce demotivated employees (or employees motivated instead to address an inequity!). For example, if a message is communicated differently to different groups, it is the *perceived* inequity that will demotivate – whether or not management consider the reason for the differences just.

Reinforcement theories (see Chapter 17) are also interesting to apply to how organisations choose to communicate. If there is a key behaviour that an organisation wants to encourage, this message should be supported in the medium the organisation chooses to use for delivery. For example, if the organisation wants to motivate people to work towards high quality, all the ways in which it communicates this message should support this. Organisations should not expect high quality to be taken seriously if it appears to staff that the message is delivered in a shabby way.

A government agency in a monopoly relationship with their suppliers (in that the particular service was offered only via the agency) had built up an ethos of 'take it or leave it'. In order to motivate the suppliers and the staff in the agency to improve the relationship, a customer-focus programme was introduced. The message of the programme was reinforced through the involvement of the suppliers in the design of future policy and the requirement that any projects affecting the suppliers had henceforth to include representation of their views.

When delivering a message, the messenger may wish to consider **Activation theory** (see Chapter 4). This theory suggests that people's motivation to listen to a message – even one that is important to them – is adversely affected if it is delivered in a way that does not stimulate. Most managers can probably recall times when a long speech given in a monotone voice was difficult to concentrate on, even when the topic was interesting.

What an organisation communicates

In relation to the *information* an organisation communicates to its employees, it is no good expecting to motivate staff to work towards a particular goal through presentation alone. If the information is not clear, or not enough, the message will not get through. We suggest that motivation is often the key purpose behind much of the information an organisation communicates, and that motivation theories therefore have a direct relevance.

One of the key areas for communication is feedback on performance. This can be at all levels – from relaying organisation and team results to individual results. **Cognitive evaluation theory** (see Chapter 6) suggests that feedback which is perceived as controlling can reduce intrinsic motivation. Organisations and managers would do well, therefore, to ensure that the feedback is informational. Feedback might be regarded as controlling if information is used to set future targets.

An organisation was giving feedback to its employees about the financial performance in the previous year. Overall, the figures were looking good, despite a difficult year in their particular sector. The chief executive used the figures to congratulate all the staff for their hard work and then immediately went on to announce that this showed they could produce the goods, even in difficult times, and that he was therefore setting an even more challenging target for next year. This had the effect of demotivating staff.

Cognitive evaluation theory (Chapter 6) suggests that the feedback in the example was demotivating because it was perceived as being controlling – in other words, it was being used to control future behaviour. Management's use of the information to control future behaviour was sufficient to create demotivation. If individuals had been free to use the previous year's results to set their own targets, the communication might have been perceived as informational and motivating. The management team could then 'roll up' individual targets into an annual target. Motivation would have been maintained and any shortfalls in desired targets could still be addressed in one-to-one meetings.

If people are to be motivated by information about performance, they should ideally understand the distinction between what is in their control and what is not. Both **Attribution theory** (see Chapter 5) and **Internal–external control theory** (see Chapter 15) suggest that people attribute the cause of behaviour either to their own actions or to actions outside their control. Messages communicated by the organisation should encourage links to causes. For example, organisations that communicate results as being caused by the state of the economy, or a piece of good (or bad) luck, are effectively saying the efforts of staff do not really contribute much – positively or negatively. Likewise, if results that were actually affected by luck are communicated as being the result of the good (or poor) performance of individuals, people's motivation can be affected.

Organisations would do well to make it clear in their communications the elements people can control (and can therefore be motivated to do something about) and what elements are outside their control (and therefore a waste of time and effort trying to control). This clearly applies at all levels of feedback.

Reinforcement theories (see Chapter 17) make the point that messages that are reinforced are more motivating than those that are not. If there is a key message that an organisation or manager wishes to get people motivated to work towards, it would be naïve to think that a single mention – even if the importance is stressed – is enough. The message should be reinforced appropriately and often.

It is worth considering what messages are being reinforced via monitoring systems.

An organisation wanted people to be equally motivated towards achieving quality goals as quantity goals. Despite many messages to support this, in reality people focused more on quantity than quality. Each week the performance statistics were produced giving feedback on the previous week's outputs. Because every piece of work was processed through the computer system, quantity measures were always on 100 per cent of the work. Because quality checks were done at random (and often cancelled through pressure of work), quality measures were often on a small percentage of the work. The message that quantity was more important than quality was thus being reinforced every week.

Information that helps people to understand how a policy works is important in a communication strategy. **Equity theory** (see Chapter 9) states that perceptions of inequity motivate people to try to redress the situation. If an organisation feels this sort of motivation is unproductive, clear explanations of policies must be communicated. For example, a pay policy that is confusing and unaccompanied by clear guidelines about how it works is likely to cause many people to feel it is unfair.

Another issue that is worth managers' considering when communicating a generic message (ie one to a group rather than to an individual) is what elements are likely to motivate different groups. **Existence-relatedness-growth theory** (see Chapter 10) and **Hierarchy of needs theory** (see Chapter 13) both suggest that people with immediate short-term needs are likely to be motivated by things that will meet these short-term needs. People who feel these needs have been met are likely to be motivated by things that will meet their longer-term needs. This might be considered for example when advertising for new staff. At the junior level, an organisation may choose to emphasise extrinsic benefits. At the senior level, although benefits might be mentioned in the advert, the emphasis may be on opportunities for development.

When communicating business plans and targets, organisations should keep in mind the key tenets of **Goal-setting theory** (see Chapter 12), which are that motivating goals should be clearly stated, should be challenging, and should matter to the individual. Commitment to goals is also increased when the person, or people, for whom they are the targets are involved in setting them. There is more information about this in the **Objective-setting** chapter (Chapter 30).

Key points

If an organisation wishes to make motivation a key outcome of its communication strategy, messages should be designed in such a way as to maximise motivation, or at least minimise demotivation. The key points below draw out the main themes of the theories as they apply to communication strategy.

☐ Communication should be clear and easy to understand.

☐ Messages should be reinforced through the medium chosen to relay them.

☐ Messages should be reinforced in other relevant communication systems and processes.

☐ Communication of results should relay honest messages about the causes of those results.

☐ The way in which messages are delivered should be varied enough to hold people's attention.

☐ Informational messages (eg feedback) should be separated from anything that may make them seem controlling if intrinsic motivation is to be unaffected.

☐ Generic communication should be tailored to the likely motivation needs of the audience.

23 REWARD

Introduction

Although 'reward' as viewed here is largely pay, we also include other financial rewards such as bonuses and fringe benefits, and non-financial reward systems such as recognition schemes and employee-of-the-month schemes. A 'reward system', as referred to in this section, is therefore a catch-all term primarily encompassing pay strategies but applying also to other types of reward.

A major consideration of any reward system is what it is intended to achieve. The time-frames past and future influence whether reward is to reflect past input or whether it is to encourage future input (motivation). Those designing or delivering reward systems should be asking 'Is this reward intended to reflect past performance or is it intended to encourage future performance?'

To some extent, every reward involves both these elements, but it is the emphasis that is key. Many problems with reward systems seem to arise from the confusion between the intended outcome and the perceived reality of it. In this section we examine how motivation theory applies when linking reward to motivation.

Application of theory

There are two key applications in reward.

☐ design of reward systems
☐ delivery of reward systems.

Design of reward systems

As noted above, before designing a reward system it would be useful to analyse what it is supposed to achieve. Motivation theories will inform that decision.

One of the key theories that apply to the design of reward systems is **Hygiene theory** (see Chapter 14). This theory suggests that pay is considered by many to be dissatisfying if it is not adequate, but more of it is not necessarily motivating. What people do find motivating, however, is the work itself, being recognised for good work, having responsibility, and so on. So if a reward system is to be motivating, it may be wiser for the organisation to consider the motivating elements rather than simply focusing on pay. It does not have to be expensive, as an example may show.

A financial organisation had reduced the grades in its mortgage section to three: A (mortgage clerk), B (senior mortgage clerk), and C (supervisor). This system caused discontent at A grade because there was no distinction between a new starter and an experienced mortgage clerk.

A programme was introduced for A-graded staff which divided their development into four key stages – a foundation stage and three further modules. Alongside this development programme a reward system was introduced. After completing the compulsory foundation module plus one other, a person might be 'promoted' to A2. After completion of the second and third modules, promotion to A3 and A4 might be awarded. At each stage there was also a small pay rise.

When investigating the results of the system it was found that the mortgage clerks were more motivated in their jobs, and that although the pay rise was welcome, it was the advancement and recognition that was felt to be the most motivating element.

Hygiene theory (Chapter 14) assumes that most people have their basic needs satisfied already. **Hierarchy of needs theory** (see Chapter 13) and **Existence-relatedness-growth theory** (see Chapter 10) suggest there may be times when people are motivated purely by money. These times are likely to be when basic short-term needs require to be met as a priority over longer-term developmental needs. Reward systems directly linking a job-holder's effort to the money he or she receives each pay period are likely to motivate in these circumstances.

Hierarchy of needs theory (Chapter 13) and **Existence-relatedness-growth theory** (Chapter 14) also suggest that people at the higher end of the needs spectrum are less likely to be motivated by money and more likely to be motivated by things that will enhance their development and growth. Organisations could consider this when designing reward systems for senior-level staff. Money is not unimportant, but trying to motivate by simply providing more of it is unlikely to be wholly successful.

Those designing reward systems should be wary of making too many assumptions about where people are, or should be, on the needs hierarchy. As illustrated in the mortgage clerk example above, junior-level staff were motivated by elements of the reward system over and above the money.

Cognitive evaluation theory (see Chapter 6) presents a warning message about rewards. This theory suggests that the closer rewards are linked to performance, the less intrinsically motivated a person is likely to be to do that job. This is most likely when rewards are considered controlling rather than informational. To some extent, all rewards involve elements of both, but it is the emphasis as perceived by the recipient of the reward that has the effect.

Cognitive evaluation theory (Chapter 6) can also affect reward systems for voluntary work – either within the voluntary sector or in relation to extra efforts within a paid job. If a reward is given to someone for spending his or her own time on something, and that reward is seen as controlling, it has to be a reward that is available every time the activity is undertaken.

In an interview about what motivates him to compete, Richie Cunningham, an elite triathlete, said that when he first started out his motivation was largely the challenge of seeing how good he could get, and that competing gave him a buzz. Since he started to earn his living out of competing, however, he has commented that now what motivates him is the money, and that he views competitions as going to work.

Source: *220 Triathlon* magazine, Issue 137, December 2001

This example links **Cognitive evaluation theory** (Chapter 6), **Hierarchy of needs theory** (Chapter 13) and **Existence-relatedness-growth theory** (Chapter 10). Richie's intrinsic motivation changed once extrinsic rewards were directly linked to his performance. His motivation became extrinsic – and the rewards have to be maintained in order for him to continue to be motivated. Richie is also motivated by the extrinsic rewards because his short-term needs have to be met. If he was financially secure through other means, his motivation to compete might be more like it was when he started out.

Cognitive evaluation theory (Chapter 6) also suggests that the closer an organisation links pay to *specific* activities, the more likely intrinsic motivation will decrease. Performance-related pay, which links pay rises to an overall appraisal score, is therefore likely to affect intrinsic motivation less than piece rate pay, by which pay is linked directly with the number of units produced or dealt with.

Organisations should also think about the longer-term effects of introducing contingent financial rewards on motivation. For example, a bonus paid to everyone as a 'thank you' for good performance is likely to have a less negative effect on intrinsic motivation than a bonus that is linked to an individual's appraisal score.

Some readers may think it does not matter whether someone is intrinsically or extrinsically motivated – as long as they are motivated. To some extent that is true. However, the more extrinsically motivated someone is, the more the organisation has to ensure that the things which motivate him or her are ever-present. **Cognitive evaluation theory** (Chapter 6) suggests, in most cases, that this requires clear direction on how to do the job, close supervision, clear procedures for linking pay to performance, and decision-making at a senior level. It is resource-intensive and sustainable only while the control systems are in place.

Cognitive evaluation theory (Chapter 6) and **Hygiene theory** (see Chapter 14) suggest that pay is perceived as the way in which organisations get people committed to their jobs. Without pay, most of us would not go to work. Once employees are committed, however, other than by ensuring that pay remains competitive, organisations should perhaps seek further ways of motivating staff.

This point is key when considering performance-related pay (PRP) schemes. Research suggests that these schemes rarely increase motivation, despite the fact that increased motivation is the express intention of many of them. In a good number of cases, such schemes actually represent rewards for past performance, and are not perceived by staff as incentives to perform well in the future. **Reinforcement theories** (see Chapter 17) suggest that another reason for the failure of PRP schemes to motivate is that the reinforcement is too distant – that reinforcement as such just does not happen because pay rises are usually agreed annually and not until *after* the job performance has been assessed.

This last point can influence how a PRP scheme is designed, and presents a dilemma. The more directly pay is related to performance, the more it is likely to be motivating – but at a cost. It is likely to be considered extrinsically motivating (with all the attendant costs); it may not be directly linked to the organisation's profits (so labour costs may increase out of step with profits); it is likely to motivate only when short-term financial needs are paramount; and it encourages individualistic behaviour which is contrary to many organisations' intentions regarding teamwork.

If pay is not the best way of motivating through rewards, what is? **Hygiene theory** (Chapter 14)and **Job characteristics theory** (see Chapter 16) suggest that it is those things that are built into the job itself that can motivate. In terms of rewards, then, a system which uses these elements is likely to be more motivating than one which focuses on money alone. For example, advancement and feedback are seen as key motivators and are things that could be included in creative reward systems.

A key factor many people expect of reward systems is that they should be fair. **Equity theory** (see Chapter 9) suggests that although people have their own perceptions of fairness, they nonetheless tend to refer to socially accepted norms. There are implications here for organisation-wide reward packages. Although people generally learn what is considered 'appropriate reciprocation', it cannot be assumed that the same package will suit everyone in an organisation, and the opportunity to tailor benefits to meet individual needs may be invaluable, given that rewards are intended to motivate.

Equity theory (Chapter 9) also suggests that the involvement in the design process of those whom the system includes (or their representatives) increases the chances of a system that is acceptable. Managers should also note, however, that research suggests that the more disparity there is in pay, the more likely it is to cause conflict, even when the disparity is equitable (or seemingly so). This implies that a system which produces wide gaps in pay between people on the same grade may be a cause of conflict and, therefore, a source of demotivation.

Delivery of reward systems

Once a reward system has been designed, it has to be delivered. This involves the management of pay systems at organisational level as well as at individual management level. Individual performance management is not covered in this chapter, and readers should refer to the **Individual-level chapters** (Chapters 30 to 33) for further information on this aspect of reward delivery.

Expectancy theory (see Chapter 11) suggests that people have to be able to make clear links between their actions and expected outcomes in order for them to be motivated. If a reward system is designed to be motivating, it should deliver on expectations. For example, if there is a recognition scheme designed to motivate people to deliver top-class customer service, there should be a good likelihood that they are eligible for a reward. If the scheme rewards only one person at a time and eligibility is across large numbers of people, the odds for each individual of receiving a reward are minimal, and the scheme is therefore unlikely to motivate.

That is not to say such schemes should not exist. **Reinforcement theories** (see Chapter 17) suggest that each time a reward is given it reinforces the importance of the desired behaviour. Organisations should perhaps consider how reward systems can motivate across a wide number of initiatives, rather than relying on one or two.

Rewards should also be applied fairly if they are to be motivating. **Equity theory** (see Chapter 9) supports this. It is no good having a fair reward system that is implemented unfairly. This theory suggests that reward systems perceived to be unfair may motivate people to try to do something about it. Of the many actions that people can take to try to reduce dissonance, most would be considered counter-productive to an organisation, and therefore best avoided.

Equity theory (Chapter 9) implies that managers and organisations have the opportunity to deal with conflict that stems from feelings of inequity. For example, explaining to one employee why another is receiving greater rewards than he or she is may be all it takes to resolve an issue – perhaps he or she was simply unaware of the reasons. Increasing rewards may not be expensive – perhaps all that is needful is more verbal recognition or the establishing of recognition schemes such as special mentions in the organisation's newsletter. Rewards must be sufficient or they may be rejected. For example, if someone feels that he or she is being paid several hundred pounds less than their referent group, a very small pay rise may be considered more insulting than no pay rise at all.

Key points

Most reward systems are designed with motivation in mind. Motivation theories suggest that organisations should handle the motivation intentions of any reward strategy with care. The key points below draw out the main issues.

☐ When designing a reward system, organisations should consider whether its focus is to reward past behaviour or motivate future behaviour.

☐ Money is generally seen as a motivator only by those who have short-term financial needs. For many people at work, money gets them in the door and commits them to their job, but the theories suggest that it does not actually motivate.

☐ Rewards that motivate tend to be those that link to job characteristics such as advancement and feedback on progress.

☐ Reward systems that focus on motivating via extrinsic means require resource-intensive control systems to support them.

☐ An individual's intrinsic motivation can change to extrinsic if rewards are perceived as controlling rather than informational.

☐ Reward systems should be seen to be fair to all those who are part of the system if they are to avoid demotivating.

☐ Rewards designed to motivate must be perceived as realistically achievable by all those in the scheme.

24 LEARNING FOR CURRENT JOBS

Introduction

Although strategy design and implementation should revolve around how individuals are dealt with, this chapter focuses on the strategic level, not on the individual. For information on the management of an individual's learning, readers should refer to the **Individual-level chapters** (Chapters 30 to 33).

Learning encompasses any activity in which someone discovers and adopts new behaviours or skills. We use the term 'learning event' to cover organised activities and events that concentrate on learning specific techniques. We use the term 'development' to describe the ongoing learning through which an individual develops the use of a technique, behaviours and skills to increase his or her expertise. Motivation issues relating to learning for future jobs are covered in the chapter on **Career development** (Chapter 25). Motivation issues relating to learning for a current job are covered in this chapter.

In describing learning events, we consider all sorts of activity – off and on the job. We also include support once a person gets back to work as part of an effective learning strategy.

Application of theory

Hygiene theory (see Chapter 14) suggests that having a learning policy is not a motivator in itself, but not having one (or having one that is poorly implemented) could be a demotivator. It would seem that when learning is perceived as a low priority within an organisation, there may be dissatisfaction.

There are two key applications in learning for current jobs.

☐ design
☐ delivery.

Design

The motivation theories that apply to the design of learning events at organisation level focus on how to motivate people to attend the events and develop their skills, and on how to design features into the events that will maintain a learner's motivation.

All learning events have goals. **Goal-setting theory** (see Chapter 12) suggests that the best goals are those that are clear and challenging. **Achievement theory** (see Chapter 3) suggests, for those who are high achievers, that challenging goals are more motivating than ones which are too stretching, or are not stretching enough. Both theories should therefore influence how learning events are designed. If a goal is considered too challenging by the learners, it can demotivate. Such a goal, broken down into interim, stretching but achievable goals, becomes more motivating.

The term 'achievable' is defined by the individual. In the early days of learning, therefore, organisations should design in reinforcements that goals are achievable. **Reinforcement theories** (see Chapter 17) suggest that this may be done by reference to previous learning (eg by pointing out that the skills are similar to ones previously learned successfully). **Social learning theory** (see Chapter 18) also suggests that it can be done by reference to others (eg by pointing out that skills are similar to ones learned by successful colleagues in the past).

Control theory (see Chapter 7) suggests clear goals are not enough – people need to know how they are doing against those goals in order to feel motivated to take corrective action. Feedback is therefore important. When designing learning events, thought should be given to how this feedback will be received by the learner. Feedback does not always have to be verbal. For example, error messages on computer systems are a form of feedback, as are comments from fellow-learners. Self-analysis can provide feedback as long as the learners can be objective about their performance and they are familiar enough with the expected standards to know when they have been met or exceeded.

Although feedback is important, **Control theory** (Chapter 7) implies that learners must understand how to rectify a discrepancy. Event design should take this into account. People who clearly understand what standards they are striving to achieve and clearly understand they are not meeting them but do not know what to do to change the situation are likely to be demotivated. **Goal-setting theory** (see Chapter 12) reiterates this point, stating that clear goals should be backed up with clear instructions.

Goals and standards are effectively setting up 'discrepancies' in those who do not currently meet them. **Drive theory** (see Chapter 8) suggests that such discrepancies motivate people to close the gap. Learning has to be perceived to meet a need in order for it to be motivating. This need has to be perceived by the individual. Introducing learning events to support a clearly stated, new organisation standard should therefore motivate people to learn the necessary new skills more than events that do not seem to link to any organisational need. This can be illustrated by an example.

A large organisation with telephone-based service centres set a new standard of three minutes duration for the average telephone call – less time than the previous average. This was to support new customer service standards. No time-frame was set within which training should be delivered, and it was decided to make it a part of individual performance objectives only once a person had attended a learning event. The organisation did not state why the new customer service standards were important, or on what basis they had been drafted.

The longer the delays in delivering the learning event, the less motivated people became to achieve the standard, or attend the event. The organisation had outlined the new customer service standards clearly, and continuous monitoring gave clear feedback to individuals that enabled them to realise when they had gone adrift from the new standard. However, the lack of time-frame within which the training had to be completed suggested the training was not a priority, and staff were not at all sure why a three-minute average call-time was important anyway. Consequently, staff were not motivated to reduce the average time of their telephone calls. The need was not demonstrated by the organisation.

This example illustrates how a need has to be made evident in order for people to be motivated. In this case the organisation had either to create an extrinsic need (eg staff had to learn the new skill because from a certain date their performance would be measured against it) or to appeal to an intrinsic need (eg staff who wanted to provide better customer service had to realise that this was one way in which it could be achieved), or effect a combination of both.

Even if there is an obvious organisational need, it has to be translated as relevant to the individual's job. **Expectancy theory** (see Chapter 11) suggests that in order to be motivated, people have to see a link between what they are learning and a worthwhile outcome for them in their situation. This may influence whether learning events are delivered 'on the job', how exercises are designed, and how the event is marketed in the first place. The more learning can be designed to reflect the job itself, the more relevance learners will see – and the more motivated they are likely to be to learn.

It could be argued that individuals will always be motivated to attend learning events, or else they would not turn up! However, we suspect that most organisations would prefer motivation to be based on what the learner could learn rather than on avoiding conflict with his or her manager!

Activation theory (see Chapter 4) can also influence how learning events are designed. This theory suggests that people have an optimum level of stimulation – above or below this level people will try to reduce or increase stimulation. A motivating learning event is therefore one which creates an optimum level of arousal. Although this may be a simple concept to grasp, the challenge is that everyone has a potentially different optimum level of stimulation. So while event designers can work on the generalisation that most people are most likely to be most stimulated first thing in the morning, whatever their optimum levels, they should consider how the learning events they design can cope with differences. This can be done partly by catering for the likely learners on an event (eg matching the variety and pace to that experienced in the trainee's jobs) and partly by building in flexibility to cater for varying levels of stimulation (eg designing activities in which trainees can dictate the pace of events).

Delivery

We want here to focus on the population of staff within an organisation who have responsibility for event delivery (line managers, members of the human resources department, etc), including also job support after the event has been delivered.

Organisations can demonstrate the value of learning events by ensuring that managers explain the relevance of the event before individuals are nominated for it. This is also the ideal time to discuss the value of the outcome of the event. **Reinforcement theories** (see Chapter 17) suggest that the more a behaviour is reinforced (through reward systems, recognition schemes, criteria for advancement, and so on), the more likely it is going to be seen as desirable, and therefore the more people are likely to be motivated to acquire it. **Social learning theory** (see Chapter 18) suggests that this can be achieved through reinforcement via the communicated experience of others, and does not have to be experienced first-hand by an individual.

When discussing design we raised the importance of feedback. **Cognitive evaluation theory** (see Chapter 6) suggests that the way in which feedback is perceived can affect the intrinsic motivation of the individual. If feedback is considered informational, it can enhance intrinsic motivation. If it is considered controlling, it can reduce it. For example, consider a modular learning event where progression from one level to the next level depends on passing an assessment. If there are limited opportunities to pass an assessment (eg learners can fail only twice before being taken off the event), it is likely that the feedback (ie the results) will be considered controlling. If there are unlimited opportunities to pass the assessment, individuals may be more motivated by the learning itself, and see the assessment as informational feedback on progress.

An implication that can be drawn from this example is that the more extrinsically motivated someone is to learn, the more likely he or she is to 'do just enough to get through'. The prime objective may be to *pass*, rather than to *learn*.

How many trainers have asked learners what they want to get out of an event, only to find that some of them do not actually know why they are there in the first place? As noted in the section on design, **Expectancy theory** (see Chapter 11) suggests that people have to perceive a link between learning and a worthwhile outcome for them to be motivated. This applies in learning event delivery as well. The trainer or coach should make these links throughout the event. The manager also has a key role in ensuring that such links are stressed before and after the learning event.

Drive theory (see Chapter 8) outlines another key implication for the manager's role in supporting learning. This theory indicates that habits are difficult for people to change, and that in times of anxiety people tend to revert to familiar, reinforced habits. The implication here is that managers must ensure that people are supported in using their new habits once they have completed the learning event. In particular, this means allowing an individual time to practise his or her new skills. Many managers admit that all too often their staff finish a learning event and are then not given sufficient time to transfer their learning to their jobs. Consequently, any motivation to put a new skill into practice is hindered, and old habits do not become as old as perhaps they should!

Equity theory (see Chapter 9) has implications for how and when learning events are delivered. If staff are to feel that they have an equal chance of performing at their best, they should see that learning events which support this are available to them. Availability is not just about creating an event – it is about thinking through when and how it is delivered.

Trainers must be flexible in the delivery of learning events. **Activation theory** (see Chapter 4) outlines a number of disruptive behaviours that may occur if people are feeling over- or under-stimulated. Trainers need to have several solutions to such situations in reserve – for example, taking a short 'comfort break' if people seem to be finding the event overwhelming, or adding on extra activities if people seem to be underwhelmed!

A call centre was being set up as a 24-hour 365-days-a-year site. People were recruited to work specific hours, and although some worked shifts, the majority worked the same pattern of hours every week.

In the early days of the centre, learning events were established to enhance people's telephone and customer service skills. However, these events were available only during the daytime. People who worked during the night felt that this was unfairly holding them back from performing at their best. They found this demotivating and a source of conflict.

The organisation took action to address their concern. The original event was redesigned so that some elements involved self-directed distance-learning-type material (with time and resources for study provided). The 'classroom' elements were delivered by trainers appointed to work some nights and by night-time managers trained to deliver some elements. This action successfully resolved the situation.

Key points

Motivation theory suggests that organisations should consider the points below when designing and delivering learning events.

- □ A learning policy may be perceived as an indication of the importance of learning in an organisation. Having one is unlikely to be motivating in itself, but not having one (or having one that is poorly implemented) could be a demotivator.

- □ A learning need is created by a drive to meet a business or personal need. Organisations should ensure that such a need is clearly demonstrated. Learners should perceive the relevance of the learning and that the learning event will help them achieve a desired outcome.

- □ A need will be strongest when the desired behaviour or skill is reinforced through other management systems and processes (eg reward systems, recognition schemes). Managers also have a key role in ensuring that the need is reinforced through day-to-day management, including support for the learner to use the new skills once trained.

☐ Learning events should have clear and challenging standards and goals. Trainers should help learners understand how they are going to achieve challenging goals, particularly at the outset when the skill being learned is new.

☐ The ability to meet a challenge can be reinforced by reference to previous successful learning or by reference to comparable others who have successfully learned from the learning event.

☐ There must be feedback systems in place to ensure that people know how they are performing against standards and goals.

☐ Feedback should ideally be seen as informational to sustain intrinsic motivation. Feedback perceived as controlling may cause motivation to focus on extrinsic rewards rather than on the intrinsic rewards of the learning itself.

☐ Learning events should be available to all those who could benefit from them.

☐ Learning events should maintain levels of stimulation and not over- or under-stimulate learners.

25 CAREER DEVELOPMENT

Introduction

A caring organisation sets up internal programmes to help employees to progress in their career. 'Career' could either be a specific, clear path (eg in the medical profession) or a general path (eg holding different jobs within a single company). Most career development programmes (CDPs) are likely to be closely tied in with the organisation's succession plan, even if that plan is not a detailed one.

'CDP' is the term we use to apply to a whole range of learning activities that support an intention to develop the skills and behaviours necessary for progression. This includes formal learning events, externally-provided courses/qualifications, and solo study. We also describe, in general terms, the support an individual may require from the organisation.

There may be times when an organisation uses CDPs as a motivational tool alone – ie with no specific intention that the staff should remain with the organisation for the full duration of their careers. We suspect that this is rare, however, and that most organisations would expect to benefit from the outputs of CDPs in some way.

Application of theory

There are two key applications in career development.

☐ succession planning
☐ design and delivery.

Succession planning

A succession plan is drafted by an organisation with the intention of developing staff to provide a pool of job-holders as potential recruits for other roles within the organisation. Such plans may be very comprehensive (eg outlining specific roles and detailing structured CDPs which lead to those roles) or quite loose (eg outlining a general need for management skills without identifying any specific role).

Motivation issues are likely to focus on how to enthuse people to take part in CDPs and on how to avoid demotivating those not taking part.

In order for succession plans to motivate people to want to develop, there has to be an expectation that the outcomes are worthwhile. **Expectancy theory** (see Chapter 11) suggests that people will be motivated to work to achieve a worthwhile goal when they can see a link between their actions and a worthwhile outcome for themselves. When drafting a succession plan – even a general one – organisations should therefore consider how CDPs are going to link in with other human resource (HR) strategies. For example, people are unlikely to be motivated to take part in a CDP that has no apparent links to the recruitment strategy for other roles (unless, of course, they see it as developing useful skills for their progression to another organisation!). An example illustrates this, below.

A large organisation had a succession plan which involved a CDP for senior clerical staff to encourage them to develop the skills necessary to take on a supervisory role. It had been noted that recruiting such staff externally was proving expensive and that experienced staff were leaving the organisation because they could see no way of 'getting on'.

The CDP was a comprehensive well-structured programme made up of off-the-job learning events. In the early days, the motivation to attend the programme was high and it was often over-subscribed. However, after it had been running for a couple of years, the motivation to attend (or to remain on) the programme fell away, and the succession plan looked to be in trouble.

The HR department investigated the background of those recruited to supervisory level over the previous two years and found that those who had been on the CDP were no more likely to get a supervisory job than anyone else in the organisation.

As a result of the investigation the HR department restructured the CDP to include a lot more planned on-the-job learning. The programme was also changed to include the project and support work individuals

> were undertaking. These extra tasks were developing supervisory skills but had previously not been included in the CDP.

One of the key words used in **Expectancy theory** (Chapter 11) to describe the goals being pursued is 'worthwhile'. Staff may perceive the connection between action and outcome, but if they do not perceive the outcome as something worth pursuing, then motivation to join – or stay on – the programme will not be high.

Another issue to consider when drafting a succession plan is how to prevent it from becoming a source of demotivation for those that do not take part. **Equity theory** (see Chapter 9) suggests that any selection system perceived as unfair has the potential to demotivate. The organisation should ensure not only that the selection criteria for the CDP are clearly stated, and can be justified, but also that they are communicated to, and understood by, everyone in the organisation.

Design and delivery

This section deals with issues that apply to the whole CDP. Issues relating to the design of learning events are covered in more detail in the **Learning for current jobs** chapter (Chapter 24).

Motivation issues are likely to focus on how to motivate people to continue on the programme and achieve the goals of the CDP.

As noted above, **Expectancy theory** (see Chapter 11) implies that there has to be a perceived link between an action and a worthwhile outcome in order for people to be motivated. This is not easy when designing a CDP because there is likely to be a fair interval of time between starting the programme and seeing results. **Reinforcement theories** (see Chapter 17) suggest that reinforcers distanced in time from the actions are weak in their effect. All these theories indicate that regular reinforcements should be built in to the programme to maintain motivation. Such reinforcements might be in the form of short-term goals that are set within the CDP. Success on the programme could then be perceptible without having to wait until the end. One organisation dealt with this as out-lined below.

A CDP for a senior clerical role was designed for a government agency. The programme was likely to take from about eighteen months to two years to complete. Success on the programme guaranteed a senior role (ie there was no further selection process). A learning contract was drafted that contained a number of key stages both parties agreed to. Each stage had to be completed to ensure success on the CDP.

This modular approach ensured that staff on the CDP had short-term goals to aim for as well as an overall long-term goal to achieve.

The organisation made sure there were incentives for staff to join, and remain on, the CDP. **Goal-setting theory** (see Chapter 12) suggests a number of incentives (feedback, time-limits, participation, competition, praise, and money) that motivate people to set and achieve goals. Those designing CDPs should consider how such incentives might be incorporated into their programmes.

Just because an incentive has been established does not mean it will remain an incentive. **Control theory** (see Chapter 7) contains reminders that incentives can change as a result of an alteration in the individual's circumstances. This point can be illustrated using **Existence-relatedness-growth theory** (see Chapter 10) and **Hierarchy of needs theory** (see Chapter 13). These theories suggest that people tend to be most motivated to attend to longer-term higher-order needs when their lower-order needs have been met. For example, people who are motivated to meet the short-term needs of paying bills, establishing security, and so on, are less likely to be motivated to attend, or remain on, CDPs than those who are confident that such short-term needs are being met. This is not to suggest that CDPs should be offered only to those in the higher salary brackets! But it does suggest that CDPs that offer incentives likely to appeal only to self-actualisation and growth needs are less likely to motivate staff with short-term needs than those CDPs that also offer incentives which appeal to safety and existence needs.

Reinforcement theories (Chapter 17) and **Social learning theory** (see Chapter 18) imply that people learn from experience and observation. People are therefore motivated to repeat behaviours they have deemed (either through their own experience or through that of others around them) 'successful'. This is a particular challenge when designing CDPs because an organisation may wish to encourage behaviours for a future role that are not appropriate for the role being undertaken currently. Consider the following example.

> A CDP was developed in an organisation to develop supervisory skills for clerical staff who aspired to be team leaders. One key difference in behaviour between the two roles (of clerk and team leader) was the level of attention to detail. As a clerk, an employee was required by the organisation to be attentive to detail. As a team leader, a person was expected by the organisation to take a broader view. This clearly posed a challenge for those on the programme, and those supporting them.
>
> The organisation dealt with it by developing the ability to see things from a broader perspective through off-the-job project work. This meant that those on the CDP could easily separate the times when it was appropriate to take the broader view and the times when they needed to focus on the detail.

The clerical staff on the CDP in the above example were motivated to develop the behaviour required for the future role without being demotivated by the conflict this could have created with behaviour in their current role.

Key points

Motivation theories can help in the design of succession plans and career development programmes by making generalisations about how people may be motivated to join, and remain on, the programmes. The key points below are raised as important issues to consider.

☐ Organisations should take care over how CDPs link into other human resource (HR) strategies in order to ensure that staff can see a link between their actions and the outcome.

- Staff on CDPs should see the outcome as something worth pursuing to encourage the motivation to join, or stay on, the programme.
- Organisations should ensure that selection criteria for the CDP are clearly stated, can be justified, and are communicated to, and understood by, everyone in the organisation.
- There should be regular reinforcements built in to the programme to maintain motivation. These could be in the form of short-term goals set within the CDP.
- Those who design CDPs should consider how incentives might be incorporated into the programme to maintain motivation.
- Incentives can change as a result of altered circumstances of the individual. CDPs should ideally offer incentives that appeal to a range of needs if they are to appeal to all types of staff.
- Organisations should consider how they are to motivate people to develop behaviour for future roles that may clash with behaviours expected in current roles.

26 ORGANISATIONAL CHANGE

Introduction

This chapter is about changes in organisational structure, including attempts to change culture (eg following a merger). Issues covered in other organisation-level chapters that impact on organisational change (eg communication) have not been repeated here.

During a period of change most people move through various emotional stages. These are illustrated by Sugarman's (1986) 'transition curve'.

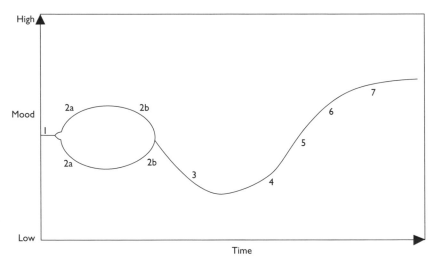

The vertical axis represents mood. The horizontal axis represents time. We are using the curve to illustrate the example of staff reaction to an organisational change affecting their jobs. The points are described and amplified below:

Point	Description	Amplification
1	Immobilisation – people feel overwhelmed by the implications of the change.	All features of the new situation are almost too much to think about.
2a	Elation if the change was desired. Despair if it was not.	Excitement about the new job, or exasperation at being forced into a new role or situation.
2b	Thoughts on how to minimise the effects of the change.	Playing down the desired new job or building up the undesired one.
3	Self-doubt as a growing sense of the implications sets in.	Doubts start to creep in about whether the new job is right for them.
4	Accepting the reality – converting any perceived crisis to opportunity.	Whether the new job is desired or not, the positive aspects of it are considered.
5	Considering and testing out new options.	Each person starts the job and begins to think about whether it suits him or her or not.
6	Attempts to learn from the new situation.	The person is settling into the idea of the new job. He or she is likely to be motivated by it at this stage.
7	Integration – people have incorporated the change.	The new job lives up to expectations, and each person feels his or her life has improved because of it.

Neither axis has a scale because it is relative. Some people's responses will not change a great deal; others' will change a lot. In some situations the transition curve will last a few hours; for other people it may take weeks or months. Some people may not move beyond point 3 without help or further changes to their circumstances.

During organisational change it may be helpful for managers to understand this curve. The intention is not to avoid the negative feelings – it is to accept that they will occur and to take account of the results. In motivational terms the organisation should seek to minimise the time people spend at points 2 and 3, and support people endeavouring to find the motivation to move forward.

Application of theory

There are two key applications in organisational change.

☐ preparing for change
☐ managing the change.

Preparing for change

Depending on the scale of the change and how voluntary it is, motivation theories could shape what alterations actually take place. For example, if an organisation is restructuring to meet new demands, motivation theories may help to inform the design of the new structure. If, however, the change is the result of a hostile takeover, there may be limited opportunities to shape the change.

During any period of change, people usually feel threatened. The security of a known and familiar situation, even if it was disliked, is changing to something unknown. **Hierarchy of needs theory** (see Chapter 13) suggests that when lower-order needs are threatened, they become the focus of motivation. Safety is a lower-order need, and includes safety in the situation people perceive themselves in. This helps explain why in times of change there is often a conflict when those managing the change expect staff to be motivated by the future whereas in fact staff are mostly motivated to find out how secure their position is now. This may also be because those who are preparing for the change have moved along the transition curve a lot further than those who have just found out about the change. The implication for preparing for change is therefore to ensure that a period of low productivity is built in, and should not come as a surprise.

This focus on lower-order needs can also be seen in **Hygiene theory** (see Chapter 14). Basic needs, such as working conditions, can be demotivators if they are considered not good enough. This suggests that if change impacts on hygiene factors, even an office move, it can have a demotivating effect. **Equity theory** (see Chapter 9) suggests that people will compare their situation to that of others (or that of themselves in the past) in order to establish whether they think a situation is fair. Linking Hygiene and Equity theories, managers could see how such 'basic' changes, such as a move to an office that is perceived to be of a lesser standard, can be demotivating. Those who are designing the change should take into account the possible demotivating effects of any alteration in hygiene factors and consider how they will be dealt with when the change takes place.

Equity theory (Chapter 9) is important to take into account when planning change. In almost every change situation the organisation is effectively supplying staff with a possible new referent group. This might mean that staff compare their new situation with the one just past, or compare themselves with another business unit. Again, if this is considered at the planning stage, any perceived inequities could be anticipated. Communication and involvement are key here – firstly because there may be perceptions of inequity arising from misinformation, and secondly because there may be perceptions that nothing is going to be done about any inequity. Consider how one organisation dealt with this potentially demotivating situation.

An organisation was in the process of merging with another organisation from the same sector. It was quickly realised that although some of the job titles were very similar, the roles the job-holders fulfilled were quite different. In order to avoid a potentially demotivating situation, those planning the merger set up a series of meetings between representatives in each organisation of people who were doing similar jobs (ie based on job content, *not* job title).

Apart from many other benefits, this enabled people in both organisations to realise that job titles were far less important than job content. Feedback within team meetings meant this information was quickly communicated back to each department in the merging organisations and a potentially demotivating situation of perceived inequity was averted.

If change is likely to affect the structure of the jobs in the organisation, there should be careful consideration of how the new jobs will be designed. **Job characteristics theory** (see

Chapter 16) suggests that jobs with characteristics such as responsibility for a 'whole' job and variety are more intrinsically motivating than those without. Organisational change should be planned to ensure that jobs have at least as many of these characteristics as before. More information about job design can be found in the **Job design** chapter (Chapter 21).

For people to want to work towards a new goal, that new goal has to be perceived as worthwhile. **Goal-setting theory** (see Chapter 12) suggests that the most motivating goals are those that are challenging, clearly specified and considered valid by those working towards them. When planning any change, organisations should ensure that *why* the new goal is worthwhile is clearly specified and communicated. It is sometimes easy for managers who have planned a change to forget that they have a lot more information about the change than others, and to stint on good-quality information when the change is announced.

Managing the change

In this section we explore issues that may help managers identify and deal with motivational problems which arise from change.

One reason many people find change hard to deal with is that they feel it is outside their control. **Internal–external control theory** (see Chapter 15) suggests that those with an internal locus of control (see **Glossary**) are likely to focus on what they can control (eg their reactions to the change). These people are more likely to remain motivated throughout a change than those with an external locus of control, who feel they are subjected to everything that happens and they are powerless within the situation. Although this is a rather simplistic interpretation, and in reality people are not all one or the other, this theory may help managers in turn to help people deal with change. Throughout the change process it would be useful for managers to reinforce those aspects of the change that *are* in the control of the staff, and be honest about those aspects that are not. This will help people to retain motivation for things in their control, and prevent them from beating their heads against the brick walls of things not in their control.

An organisation announced a structural change, and communicated the new business plan to deal with this change via a series of briefings delivered by the regional director in each office. How each office dealt with the implementation of the plan was left up to the local senior management teams.

Three months after the briefings, a review of progress was conducted. It was found that those regional directors who had focused their implementation plans on how they were going to deliver the goals set out in the business plan were doing much better than those who had challenged the business plan and held off developing their implementation plans until the issues of concern were resolved.

The active directors had focused on issues that were in their control (implementation plans) rather than those that were not (the set goals). The hesitant directors were spending (some might say, wasting) time resisting things that were outside their control.

Once implementation of the change begins, systems and processes designed to support the change should be closely managed. **Equity theory** (see Chapter 9) suggests that people may feel demotivated if they believe they are being over-compensated. This situation can occur during times of change where key people may be left without a job in the short term. Dealing with these situations to the benefit of all parties may help to avoid demotivation. For example, systems for fully-paid sabbaticals may create a situation in which a valued employee can still feel valued while he or she is 'between' jobs.

One of the ways in which people can deal with change is to leave the situation. However, **Equity theory** (Chapter 9) suggests a particular course of action has to be perceived as realistic to make it an option worth considering. For example, if an organisation is in a location where there are few jobs of a similar nature around, 'leaving the situation' may not seem a realistic option for an employee. Moving to another area might well be considered out of the question for a parent of school-aged children if schooling is regarded as too important to disrupt, for example. If someone feels 'trapped' by change, he or she is unlikely to be highly motivated.

Expectancy theory (see Chapter 11) indicates that a person's behaviour may be based on the expectancy that that behaviour will result in a particular outcome. In the early days of change, a certain degree of trust may be essential accordingly. If an organisation is introducing a new set of standards, for example, people will have to trust that any required new behaviour will be rewarded. **Reinforcement theories** (see Chapter 17) state that each time a person makes the link between his or her own behaviour and the desired outcome, the behaviour is reinforced. Day to day during a period of change, therefore, the organisation should ensure that new behaviours are being reinforced through recognition, praise, reward systems, and so on.

Behaviour that does not meet the new standards may take some time to disappear. This is partly because people need to experience, or witness, the reinforcement for themselves, and partly because old habits die hard. **Drive theory** (see Chapter 8) suggests that strongly reinforced behaviours (as ones that were appropriate in the pre-change regime are likely to be) are those that people are motivated to fall back on in times of anxiety. Anxiety is exactly what some people will be feeling at the very time when new behaviours are required.

Key points

Change is almost the only sure aspect of the business world today. If organisations are to maintain (or even create) motivation during these times, the planners and implementers of change should consider the key points below.

☐ Goals should be clear, challenging and valid in order to be motivating. Validity can be easy to forget – explaining *why* a goal is valid is as important as the goal being clear and challenging.

☐ People are likely to focus on basic short-term needs (eg job security) when they are threatened. A period of low productivity while this is being dealt with should be expected during any major change.

☐ New situations will be compared with old ones, or with new referent groups. If a situation is perceived as being inequitable, there may be adverse consequences in terms of motivation – even if the inequity is the result of over-compensation.

☐ Choices must be perceived as realistic for them to be considered real choices. Organisations should be aware of the demotivating impact of 'trapping' people in situations they feel they cannot change.

☐ New behaviours required by a change must be reinforced throughout the organisation. There is likely to be a hiatus while old habits are being replaced by new, so a supportive environment should be encouraged.

☐ Those implementing change should ensure that they focus activity on those things that are within the control of the staff. It is likely to be demotivating to encourage effort to change the unchangeable.

☐ Any diminution of working conditions (or other hygiene factors) may cause demotivation, even if the issue seems to managers to be minor in the total scale of things.

☐ New jobs should be designed to maintain, or enhance, characteristics that lead to intrinsic motivation such as variety and job-holder responsibility.

Reference

Sugarman L. (1986) *Life-span Development: Concept, theories and interventions*. London, Methuen.

27 MANAGING PERMANENT GROUPS AND TEAMS

Introduction

This chapter is about how motivation theories might apply when managing permanent groups and/or teams. The word 'team' is henceforth used throughout to cover both teams and groups. Our definition of 'permanent' in this context is that the team is part of the way in which the organisation has structured its core business. In other words, there is no 'expiry date' to the team's activities. We acknowledge that such teams may be new – for example, as the result of an organisational structure change – but they all have a perceived longevity (until the next structure change!).

Some of the issues examined in this chapter could apply to temporary teams. However, because we have focused on permanent teams, managers of temporary teams should pick out only those issues that affect their particular circumstances, and otherwise refer to the **Managing temporary groups and teams** chapter (Chapter 28) for information more relevant to their situation.

There is one type of 'permanent' team we have not considered in this section – one that is part of the organisational structure but is made up of people on temporary contracts. Although this team may have an ongoing role, the individuals have an 'end date' to their part. Because of this temporary nature, we have considered the issues relating to this type of team in the **Managing temporary groups and teams** chapter (Chapter 28).

Application of theory

There are two key applications in the management of permanent teams.

☐ selection

☐ managing performance.

Selection

Although most of the issues of motivation in team management are day-to-day performance matters, people have to be motivated to apply to join the team in the first place. Selection processes include any formal way of recruiting staff, and can range from interview through to detailed application processes and assessment centres. It is in the interests of all parties in the selection process to ensure that candidates are motivated to do their best. Motivation theories can help managers to achieve this.

Expectancy theory (see Chapter 11) suggests that people are motivated when they can make clear links between their actions and the outcomes. This implies that if candidates cannot see the relevance of the elements of the selection process, they could become demotivated. Briefing information should clearly explain the links between the exercises and the skills or competencies required for the job they are applying for. An example illustrates how one organisation tackled this.

A major bank made it a policy that before attending an assessment centre all candidates would be sent a briefing pack. This pack contained definitions of all of the competencies to be examined during the centre. Every definition included a list of indicators representing examples of the behaviour regarded as demonstrating each competence. There was also a detailed overview of the job in which clear links were made between the competencies and the requirements of the job.

The assessment centre exercises were chosen to reflect the banking sector. Out went the 'shoe-shop' setting that had been used previously, and in came the 'bank branch' type of environment. Although technical knowledge of banking was not always being sought (eg at more junior levels), this change of setting ensured 'face validity' of the exercises.

One reason that people look for another job is that they have
unresolved issues in the one they are trying to leave. For
example, **Equity theory** (see Chapter 9) suggests that individuals may choose to leave a situation they think is unfair.
If belonging to a restructured organisation or a new team can
provide a situation in which a person perceives equity, then
the issue is resolved and the person no longer wants to leave.
However, if the issue is not resolved and the person brings the
issue with him or her into the new organisational structure or
team, that new team could be taking on someone who quickly
becomes demotivated. This may particularly apply in relation
to internal candidates. Managers could explore the reasons
for leaving during an interview – although we accept that this
will not always elicit an entirely honest response. Managers
can, however, be honest about the job and what it has to
offer. That way at least the candidate can think through
whether any inequitable situation will be addressed through
taking up the new job.

Some candidates will have thought through examples to
use during interviews to highlight their strong points. **Attribution theory** (see Chapter 5) suggests that people may
attribute the causes of their successes and failures to different
influences. People with a high need for achievement are likely
to attribute the outcomes of challenging tasks (successful or
not) to their own skills, abilities and efforts. People with a
high fear of failure may well ascribe the outcomes to luck,
chance or the environment they are in. There are links
between this and **Internal–external control theory** (see
Chapter 15), which suggests that people with internal locus
of control (see **Glossary**) believe they influence their environment, and that people with external locus of control believe
their environment controls them.

The reason managers may be interested in what people
attribute their successes and failures to during selection is
that it may be crucial in relation to jobs which involve any
sort of personal responsibility. People who feel at the mercy
of their environment may be demotivated in a job in which
they are held accountable for all outcomes. We are not suggesting that such people should automatically be dropped
from the selection process. We are suggesting that this may

be an issue worth exploring further, and one that might influence the contents of the induction programme.

Managing performance

Most of the motivational issues faced by managers of permanent teams arise when managing day-to-day performance matters. One of the key challenges that confront team managers is how to interpret and deliver organisation-wide policy and procedure at team level. To varying degrees, team managers often have scope to shape how their team operates.

Team managers may have some scope to design how the work is processed within the team. **Equity theory** (see Chapter 9) suggests that people are not going to be motivated by a system they see as being unfair. This applies to any system, any process. Systems and processes can be as apparently 'minor' as who makes the teas and coffees – some people can harbour a real sense of injustice about the unfairness of such situations. This theory suggests that the best way to avoid such perceived inequity is to come to an agreement with the team about how things will work. For example, if there is a necessary but unenjoyable job that has to be done, agreeing a system with the team is more likely to result in a perceivedly equitable situation than imposing something. An example shows how one organisation dealt with this.

A call centre had to provide cover during office hours over Christmas and New Year. A high percentage of the staff wanted to take the days off between Christmas and New Year. But if everyone who wanted the time off was allowed to take it, adequate telephone cover could not be provided. Staff felt the system traditionally used of 'first come, first served' was unfair. The department head agreed therefore that as long as there was enough cover on the telephones, and as long as the work output was maintained, each team could decide how to allocate the holidays.

Each team ended up introducing a slightly different system, but generally people were happy with the result. Although people did not want to work over the Christmas period, they all agreed they preferred being in control of how holidays were allocated.

Although team managers may have limited scope in the design of jobs, the way work is allocated may be in their control. **Job characteristics theory** (see Chapter 16) outlines a number of features that motivating jobs possess. Team managers could use this to help distribute tasks among their team. For example, it is likely to be more motivating if the team manager allocates to each team member a variety of jobs and responsibility for a key area rather than dividing tasks so that each team member does only one part of the process. Task significance can also be influenced by the team manager. For example, if there is a task that is never mentioned in team briefings – or always mentioned in disparaging terms – it should not be surprising if the people who do that task do not view it as motivating!

Job characteristics theory (Chapter 16) throws up interesting challenges for autonomous work teams, especially in relation to the issue of autonomy. However, it does suggest that the same methodology can apply. In other words, rather than making one person responsible for a whole task, managers should ensure the team is. Team managers should still take account of the motivational aspects of the tasks people in such teams undertake each day.

Part of being a manager is reinforcing 'desired' behaviours. **Reinforcement theories** (see Chapter 17) contend that people are generally motivated to respond to particular situations in particular ways learned from past experience. **Social learning theory** (see Chapter 18) takes this further by suggesting that people also learn from observing others. Team managers therefore have a dual responsibility. Not only are they 'on show', in that their behaviour will influence what others perceive as acceptable, but they also have a responsibility to reinforce the desired behaviours of others through praise, recognition, and so on. Team managers are also responsible for discouraging undesirable behaviour.

Another challenge facing the team manager is the setting of team-based goals. **Goal-setting theory** (see Chapter 12) suggests that goals are motivating when they are challenging and clearly stated (and when the outcome is considered worthwhile). 'Challenging' does not mean 'impossible' – and this is where the good manager can maintain motivation even during stressful times. Consider the following two examples.

An organisation underwent a computer upgrade. During the implementation and staff training phase a vast backlog of work built up. The organisation wanted to clear the backlog as fast as possible. Rather than stick to the normal service standards, which would have been impossible during this time, the manager set interim objectives week-by-week to ensure that the backlog was cleared by a given date. The week-by-week targets were challenging but not impossible. The teams were motivated by them because they could see each week that went by that the backlog was getting smaller and could also see that there was an end date.

An insurance company was flooded with claims from one area following a bad storm that caused a lot of damage to property. The claims department felt overwhelmed with the claims – which caused their weekly intake of work to treble. The manager tried to keep the claims staff motivated by having a weekly meeting to let them know how things were progressing. She finished each meeting by asking everyone to put in as much effort as they could during the following week to try to clear the backlog. The backlog did decrease each week, but very slowly. Claims staff felt demotivated by the piles of work everywhere, and feared they would never get to the end of the operation.

In the first example motivation was maintained because the goals were not only challenging, they were specific. The manager had introduced a time-based incentive and gave feedback on progress. The manager in the second example gave feedback but failed to set specific targets – preferring to stick to the 'Do your best' type of challenge. This clearly did not work as well as the first manager's approach. **Goal-setting theory** (Chapter 12) supports this outcome, stating that a specific goal is more motivating than a general one, and that time-limits and feedback are effective incentives.

Key points

The management of permanent groups and teams requires team managers to consider how organisational strategy and policy can be implemented effectively at a local level. Motivation theories provide a framework in which some of the motivation issues this raises can be considered. The key points below were made in this section.

☐ Briefing information for selection processes should clearly explain the links between the exercises and the skills or competencies required for the job being applied for.

☐ During selection, managers should be honest about the job and what it has to offer in order to ensure that candidates can think through whether any inequitable situation can be addressed by taking up the new job.

☐ When recruiting and selecting for jobs that involve personal responsibility, it is worth exploring what people attribute their successes and failures to.

☐ The best way to avoid feelings of inequity within a team is to come to an agreement with the team about how things will work.

☐ Managers who have control over the way in which work is allocated in their team should try to ensure that jobs have variety, task significance, task identity, autonomy and feedback.

☐ The team manager's behaviour will influence what others perceive as acceptable. Team managers also have a responsibility to reinforce the desired behaviour of others and to discourage undesirable behaviour.

☐ Team-based goals are motivating when they are challenging, when they are clearly stated, and when the outcome is considered worthwhile.

☐ Incentives to achieve goals include knowledge of score, time-limits, competition, and praise or reproof.

28 MANAGING TEMPORARY GROUPS AND TEAMS

Introduction

This chapter is about how motivation theories might apply when managing temporary groups and/or teams. The word 'team' is henceforth used throughout to cover both teams and groups. Our definition of 'temporary team' in this context is that the team is part of the short- to medium-term vision of the organisation. In other words, there is an 'expiry date' to the team's activities. The team has a particular task to achieve and will no longer exist as such after this task has been completed. The team might be made up of people who have other jobs elsewhere in the organisation and are working part-time on the temporary team. The team might instead be made up of people recruited full-time on to the team – either seconded from permanent jobs within the organisation or recruited on a fixed-term contract to last the length of the project. The life-span of the team might be up to a couple of years. Any longer than that, and issues affecting motivation are likely to be more those that affect a 'permanent' team, and are therefore not dealt with in this chapter.

There is one type of 'permanent' team that we have considered in this section – one that is part of the organisational structure but is made up of people on temporary contracts. Although this team may have an ongoing role, the individuals have an 'end date' to their part. The issues faced by people who have an end date to their employment are similar to those faced by other 'temporary' teams, and are therefore considered in this chapter.

Application of theory

There are two key applications in the management of temporary teams.

☐ selection

☐ managing performance.

Selection

Although most of the issues of motivation in team management are day-to-day performance matters, people have to be motivated to apply to join the team in the first place. For the purposes of this chapter we are assuming that they have a choice. Selection processes include any formal way of recruiting staff, and can range from interview through to detailed application processes and assessment centres.

One of the key features of a temporary team is its limited 'shelf life'. **Expectancy theory** (see Chapter 11) suggests that people are motivated when they expect their actions to result in desired outcomes. During the selection process, managers should be encouraging staff to join the team. There should therefore be a clearly stated outcome desired by the employee. This requires some assumptions to be made by the management team, but extrinsic rewards such as a monetary bonus and intrinsic rewards such as personal development are likely to be worthwhile incentives to stress in the selection process.

To some extent managers may be able to predict what type of rewards may be worthwhile by thinking of the job in hand. **Job characteristics theory** (see Chapter 16) suggests that jobs with variety, responsibility, autonomy, and so forth, are more likely to be intrinsically motivating. Jobs without these features are more extrinsically motivating. **Existence-relatedness-growth theory** (see Chapter 10) and **Hierarchy of needs theory** (see Chapter 13) also suggest that people are more likely to be motivated by things that are instrumental in meeting their needs – short-term lower-order needs are probably going to be met mostly through financial rewards; longer-term higher-order needs are probably going to be met mostly through developmental rewards. If managers wish to motivate people to apply for temporary jobs, they may wish to stress the financial rewards for straightforward process-type jobs and the developmental rewards for more complex jobs.

Clearly, the above point is a generalisation and will not be true in every case. Even the most aptly stressed rewards may not be enough in some cases. For example, organisations should be cautious about how temporary teams have dealt with staff in the past. **Social learning theory** (see Chapter 18) suggests that staff learn from the experience of others how to behave in certain situations. Consider the following example.

A large organisation went through several major restructuring pro-grammes within a short space of time. Each change resulted in a number of project teams being set up to deal with issues specific to the most recent change.

Unfortunately, the project managers were not encouraged to deal with staffing issues beyond the end of their project, and the managers of permanent teams were not encouraged to consider project team members when selecting for permanent teams. This meant that many highly-skilled managers left the organisation at the end of their project because they did not have a permanent job within the new structure.

Joining projects soon became synonymous with being sacked. People learned that there was a strong likelihood of ending up out of a job if they joined a project, so they were not motivated to apply. Another consequence of this lack of co-ordination between temporary and permanent team managers was that the organisation was losing valuable skills.

Temporary teams may well be looking for people who can 'hit the ground running' – for example, project teams. During the selection process, managers should be clear about the skills they are looking for and ensure that these are explored during the selection process. **Achievement theory** (see Chapter 3) suggests that people with a high need for achievement (nAch) may overestimate their abilities, not necessarily in a deceitful way, but because they believe effort is key. People with high nAch are not necessarily going to apply for jobs that are clearly out of their league, but they may be motivated to apply for jobs that would stretch their capacities. If the manager of the team is prepared for the support this situation would require, such enthusiasm may be an asset to the team. However, if skills are needed immediately, enthusiasm may not be enough.

Managing performance

Most of the motivational issues faced by managers of temporary teams arise when managing day-to-day performance matters. Some of the challenges are the same as those that confront permanent teams. The issues we address here, however, are specific to the short-term nature of temporary teams.

Jobs are often less clearly defined on temporary teams, especially project-based teams. It can be tempting to divide jobs around single tasks, especially if time is of the essence. In this way training can be kept to a minimum and people can become accomplished at a single task, thus coming to be quicker at it than if they had to cope with many different tasks. **Job characteristics theory** (see Chapter 16) suggests that such jobs are not intrinsically motivating. Any benefits of speed may be lost as people become demotivated.

Another issue when considering jobs within the team is how tasks are split among the team members. The flexibility that some project teams may afford in terms of job design may also be the cause of resentment if jobs are not considered fairly distributed. **Equity theory** (see Chapter 9) suggests that it is the *perceived* equity of the balance of inputs and outputs that is of concern to individuals. Team managers should not only make sure they have a clear understanding of why jobs are distributed in a particular way, but make sure it is also clear to the team.

Whereas with permanent teams the team itself may not have clear objectives but the individuals within it do, it is our experience that this is reversed with temporary teams. The team itself frequently has specific objectives to achieve (eg written into a project specification), and often the individuals within the team get sketchy objectives at best. **Goal-setting theory** (see Chapter 12) suggests that if goals/objectives are clearly specified and challenging, they are also likely to be motivating. Team managers should therefore ensure that team goals are clearly translated and linked to individual goals.

Activation theory (see Chapter 4) may help plan the work of a temporary team, especially project teams. This theory suggests that people strive to maintain an optimum level of stimulation/activation. Although optimum levels are personal to each individual, managers might safely assume that routine jobs are likely to create low levels of activation. Many projects have stimulating beginnings and endings – it is often the bit in the middle that can be routine (data analysis, report-writing, and so on). Ensuring that routine work is interspersed with more stimulating work or creating challenges within the routine work may help team managers avoid demotivation as a result of low activation levels.

Clearly, one of the major features of the temporary team is that the people in it do not have a job once the team has met its objectives and/or their contracts come to an end. **Hierarchy of needs theory** (see Chapter 13) suggests that a lack of security is a lower-order need and therefore one that is likely to take priority over higher-order needs. The motivation to deal with security issues is most likely to occur with individuals towards the end of their tenure. A couple of examples show how two organisations dealt with this issue.

Due to a recruitment freeze, a government organisation staffed its filing team with staff on temporary contracts (usually three months at a time). If the temporary staff were good, and wanted to stay, their contracts were renewed. However, because only one week's notice was required from either party, the organisation often only advised the individual of any extension (or lack of it) the Monday before he or she was due to finish. Productivity from individuals always dropped just before their contract end date as they started to worry about whether they were going to be asked to stay. The manager reviewed the practice and agreed that although the one-week notice period would remain, the organisation would endeavour to advise temporary staff at least one month before the end date whether their contract was going to be renewed or not. In this way both the staff members and the organisation benefited.

An insurance company was running a number of projects reviewing working practices. The projects were mostly staffed with people from within the organisation. Learning from previous projects (when it was hard to keep people motivated at the end of the project because they were worried about their future), it was agreed that eight weeks before a project was due to finish project staff could take up to five hours per week (to be taken in any fashion they wished) to look for alternative work. This time was costed in to the project. Staff were allowed to use office facilities (PCs, telephones, photocopiers, etc) to help them in their search. In this way, staff remained motivated on the project to the end, and the organisation gained significant benefits in sustained motivation up to completion of the project, and also retained a high number of staff who found work within the organisation.

Key points

Managing temporary groups and teams presents the manager with some interesting motivational challenges. The key points below highlight some issues that should be considered when dealing with motivation on short-term teams.

☐ During the selection process, managers should use the 'selling-points' of the job to encourage people to join. Extrinsic rewards such as a monetary bonus and intrinsic rewards such as personal development are likely to be worthwhile incentives.

☐ Managers endeavouring to motivate people to apply for temporary jobs may wish to stress the financial rewards for straightforward process-type jobs and the developmental rewards for more complex jobs.

☐ Jobs with variety, responsibility, autonomy, and so forth are likely to be intrinsically motivating. Jobs without these features are likely to be extrinsically motivating.

☐ People with a high need for achievement (nAch) may over-estimate their abilities because they believe that effort is key. However, if skills are needed immediately, effort may not be enough.

☐ In temporary teams it can be tempting to divide jobs around single tasks, especially if time is of the essence. Such work is not likely to be intrinsically motivating.

Any benefits of speed may be lost if people become demotivated.

☐ Managers of temporary teams should make sure not only that they have a clear understanding of why jobs are distributed in a particular way, but that it is also clear to the team.

☐ If goals/objectives are clearly specified and challenging, they are also likely to be motivating. Team managers should ensure that team goals are clearly translated and linked to individual goals.

☐ Ensuring that routine work is interspersed with more stimulating work or creating challenges within routine work may help team managers avoid demotivation as a result of low activation levels.

☐ People on temporary teams are likely to be motivated to seek security, especially towards the end of their tenure. To prevent this from becoming a problematic issue, ways to deal with it may be built into the project plan at the outset.

29 MANAGING VIRTUAL GROUPS AND TEAMS

Introduction

This chapter is about how motivation theories might apply when managing virtual groups and teams. The term 'team' is henceforth used throughout to cover both teams and groups. Our definition of a virtual team is a group of people who report to one manager but who are dispersed across various geographical locations. Communication between the team members is likely to be via electronic or telephonic means. The team members may be based at home or at different offices belonging to the same organisation. Some virtual teams may work from 'tele-offices' set up to house people from a variety of organisations, offering office facilities such as photocopying, faxing, power and communication points for PCs, and so on. This way of working is generally referred to as 'teleworking'.

Team members may get together for face-to-face meetings but their bases are remote. We are not including sales teams based in a central office but who are mostly out on the road (although the issues could be very similar). We use the description 'remote' not to mean 'far from anywhere' (although some working locations could be so described) but to indicate that each workplace is sited quite separately from any of the workplaces of other team members.

Application of theory

There are two key applications in the management of virtual teams.

☐ selection
☐ managing performance.

Selection

Motivating people to apply for jobs in virtual teams is important because it is such a new concept. Getting the right people is key because many applicants may perceive benefits such as working from home to be attractive but may not have thought through the consequences.

Everyone has an optimum level of activation/stimulation, according to **Activation theory** (see Chapter 4). Those who move away from that level will be motivated to restore it to the optimum. This applies to both over- and under-stimulation. Some people find that having a job in an office creates a useful divide between home life and work life, not least because it offers a way for managing activation levels. It may be hard for some people to be stimulated by work if there is a lot of stimulation (eg children) at home. During selection, therefore, it is worth an organisation's checking on how issues such as childcare are to be dealt with in order to ensure that the individual can cope with any potential conflict between work and home life.

Of course, people may also find that work offers them the stimulation that they would not get at home. **Achievement theory** (see Chapter 3) and **Attribution theory** (see Chapter 5) suggest that those with a high need for achievement (nAch) consider much of their success is due to their own efforts. People with high nAch and without much to do at home may therefore burn themselves out by taking on more and more work. We are not suggesting that organisations turn down high-nAch people with not much going on at home! We are suggesting, however, that this issue is flagged up – that each applicant is challenged about his or her expectations of the job, and that the team manager is made aware of any issues of potential overwork.

There are a good number of needs that people are motivated to meet through work, not just money. Relatedness and growth needs, as outlined in **Existence-relatedness-growth theory** (see Chapter 10), may be fulfilled by many at work. When selecting people to work remotely, especially if they will be working alone, it should be part of the selection process to identify whether this will be an issue for them. Consider the following example.

In the early days of teleworking, working from home was considered ideal for those who found it hard to be mobile through disability. However, many in this position did not appear to be taking up the opportunities. It was then realised that such people often want to get out of their homes, and that going out to work was a good way for them to meet relationship needs.

Managing performance

When it comes to managing performance, managers of virtual teams must consider how to ensure that motivation can be established and maintained in the absence of many of the external incentives relied upon when people are all together in the same place. For example, working conditions, feedback and praise are more difficult to control when the team member is not in the immediate vicinity.

Assuming that most members of a virtual team will be working on their own, the manager must consider why each person is likely to have been so motivated in the first place. **Expectancy theory** (see Chapter 11) suggests that there has to be a worthwhile goal to achieve for people to be motivated. An organisation may assume the pay packet is enough to motivate most people. **Hygiene theory** (see Chapter 14) challenges this by suggesting that money will only go so far to ensure motivation. This theory outlines a number of hygiene factors (including money) considered essential to prevent demotivation but not likely to continue to increase motivation just because there is more of it.

These hygiene factors pose quite a challenge for the virtual team manager. For example, how is he or she to control the working conditions when someone is working from home? One organisation found this particular issue quite a problem.

In the early days of teleworking one insurance company undertook a feasibility study to investigate the possibility of setting some employees up to work from home. One of the challenges the study raised was how to establish suitable working conditions. Some of the issues outlined in the study included:

☐   Who was responsible for the insurance of equipment that was not

> exclusively owned by the organisation but would be used during the course of the working day (eg kitchen equipment)?
> ☐ How much influence did the organisation have over the siting of a suitable office space within someone's home?
> ☐ How should health and safety issues be tackled in premises not owned by the organisation?
>
> The feasibility study concluded that more work was needed to establish the answers to these questions before a pilot could be set up.

Now that teleworking is more popular, many organisations have dealt with these issues satisfactorily. However, working conditions, together with the other hygiene factors, should be thought about and tackled creatively if they are to be avoided as demotivators.

Hygiene theory (Chapter 14) also lists a number of motivating factors. These present less of a challenge for the manager of virtual teams but should still be considered. For example, managers should consider how they are going to ensure that recognition and advancement for remote workers are made possible and visible. A sense of achievement and of accomplishment in the work itself should be built in to the job – and is perhaps more critical for remote workers, who have fewer opportunities to seek reassurance from supervisors or colleagues than do those who have such support easily to hand.

Although not tested within virtual teams, as far as we know, it is reasonable to conclude that the job dimensions outlined by **Job characteristics theory** (see Chapter 16) should be key to all jobs. Some remote or virtual jobs, however, do not contain these dimensions because they are perceived to be easier to manage that way. Job characteristics theory outlines what a job requires in order to maximise the likelihood that the job-holder will be *intrinsically* motivated to undertake the job. The implication is that the fewer motivating features a job has, the more likely the individual will be motivated *extrinsically*. The implications of this for the virtual team manager are outlined by **Cognitive evaluation theory** (see Chapter 6). Systems for monitoring performance, and linking it closely with reward, need to be managed carefully and closely. This is not to say that such systems are wrong, but to highlight that the management systems and processes should match the way in which a job is intended to motivate.

One of the fears many managers have regarding managing virtual teams is that they cannot see what their teams are doing. In reality, many managers do not actually see what their teams are doing even if they are in the same building, but it is the perception that is key. For jobs with input-related goals (eg those specifying *how* a job should be done) this is clearly an issue. However, for jobs with output-related goals, remote working should be less of an issue and be easier to manage for both team member and manager. It does depend, though, on the quality of the goals. **Goal-setting theory** (see Chapter 12) suggests that the most motivating goals are those that are challenging and specific. There is no reason why goals set for virtual teams should not be as challenging and specific as for any other team.

One perceived benefit of remote working is that it enables people to avoid commuting problems associated with travelling to a central location. However, remoteness from the central workplace has different drawbacks. **Existence-relatedness-growth theory** (see Chapter 10) describes an individual's need for relationships. **Hierarchy of needs theory** (see Chapter 13) also describes this need. Because relationship needs are often partly met through work, the implications of remote working should be considered carefully. Some organisations deal with it by holding regular meetings (eg monthly) at a central location so that people can get together and talk. Another example illustrates how one organisation offered an opportunity to meet this need.

A call centre type of operation ran a pilot scheme using staff recruited from very remote, rural locations. In order that the members did not feel too isolated, the organisation installed a video link on each PC. Staff were encouraged to contact each other via the video link not only to discuss work-related issues but also for social contact during their breaks.

Staff working on the pilot reported that this was a great success and helped them to feel closer to colleagues, even though many were physically a long distance apart.

In the section on selection above we noted that those with high nAch may need to be managed carefully to ensure that they do not burn themselves out. This could happen if they take on more and more work to keep themselves feeling adequately challenged. Managers are not expected to manage someone's life outside the workplace – but they should be expected to ensure that an individual is not taking on too much.

Key points

Not being physically close to the team, and perhaps not having much control over the team members' working environment, presents quite a challenge for the manager of a virtual team. The key points below should help such managers consider how they can deal with motivational issues at the team level.

☐ During selection it is worth an organisation's checking on how personal issues are to be dealt with in order to ensure that an individual can cope with any potential conflict between work and home life.

☐ Applicants could be challenged about their expectations of the job to ensure that work/life balance issues have been considered.

☐ Team managers should be made aware of any issues of potential overwork that might result if people find it hard to separate their jobs from their personal lives.

☐ Organisations should not assume that people who have mobility problems will automatically want to work remotely. For such people needs (eg relationships) are often met through going out to work.

☐ There has to be a worthwhile goal to achieve for people to be motivated. Whereas money may be key for some, there are many other incentives for people to work for.

☐ Money may get people to join an organisation, and keep them at work, but it is less likely to motivate people than such factors as how the job is designed.

☐ Factors such as working conditions may pose more of a challenge for organisations when workers are not based in a place owned, or managed, by the organisation. Such factors need to be dealt with creatively if they are not to demotivate.

□ Some motivating factors, such as a sense of achievement and accomplishment in the work itself, may be designed into the job. Others, such as recognition and advancement, may present more of a challenge but are worthwhile dealing with in order to motivate.

□ The fewer motivating features a job has, the more likely that the worker will be motivated *extrinsically*. Management systems and processes should ideally match the expected drives of employees.

□ Output-related goals are easier to manage for remote workers than input-related goals. The most motivating goals are challenging and specific.

□ Work/life balance, although not the responsibility of the team manager, should be an issue that is discussed with team members from time to time to ensure that they are not burning themselves out by taking on too much.

30 OBJECTIVE-SETTING

Introduction

Objective-setting is important in establishing a focus for individuals' work efforts. We have separated objective-setting from performance management to emphasise the difference between motivational issues related to *what* people are striving towards (objective-setting) and motivational issues relating to *how* people keep working towards their objectives (performance management). Performance management issues are examined in other **Individual-level chapters** (Chapters 31 to 33).

Whereas some motivational theories help to inform how objectives are set, others shape the way objectives are structured. In setting objectives, annual or short-term, there is a need for a careful balance between defining what the organisation requires to be achieved and what the individual is motivated towards achieving. Without this balance, the best intentions on both parts may lead to a failure to achieve objectives.

Application of theory

There are similarities between objectives set annually and those set to meet short-term needs. SMART (*S*pecific, *M*easurable, *A*chievable, *R*ealistic, *T*imely) objectives are supported by motivation theories – in particular **Goal-setting theory** (see Chapter 12) and **Achievement theory** (see Chapter 3). However, although these theories help to generalise points about motivation, managers need to consider individual differences when actually establishing what is achievable by each person. For example, **Achievement theory** (Chapter 3) suggests that individuals with a high need for achievement (high nAch) relish challenging goals but these challenges should be within an individual's ability to achieve them. In the context of this theory, and in the context of SMART objectives, an achievable objective must be one the individual is skilled in and able to achieve, and be sufficiently resourced by the organisation – ie it must be both achievable and realistic.

Goal-setting theory (Chapter 12) indicates that individuals tend to produce higher levels of performance when they have specific goals. The theory also argues for the importance of feedback on progress toward, and achievement of, an objective. To provide such feedback it is essential to specify a measure of success. **Control theory** (see Chapter 7) endorses this argument with reference to the need for setting standards for work activities. The level of the standard used in feedback can also influence the level of a goal. The lower the standard that attracts positive feedback, the less likely a higher standard will be achieved.

Goal-setting theory (Chapter 12) refers to the use of incentives. For example, setting a target time by which to complete an objective can provide extra motivation for individuals. Other incentives include competition (and this could be against previous performance of the individual as well as against others), participation in goal-setting (although this, in itself, is not enough to ensure motivation), and praise (or reproof).

The act of setting an objective creates a discrepancy because it is highlighting a difference between the individual's starting position and what he or she is aiming to achieve as the objective. Given that **Drive theory** (see Chapter 8) suggests that individuals are motivated to reduce discrepancies or feelings of dissatisfaction, the act of setting an objective should be a good start for motivating an individual to get on with his or her job. However, **Goal-setting theory** (Chapter 12) suggests that the individual also needs clear instructions too.

There are two key aspects of objective-setting.

□ annual objectives
□ short-term objectives.

Annual objectives

Annual objectives usually provide the main overall focus for an individual's job or role activities. Typically, these objectives are linked to organisational objectives and fit within local business plans. **Expectancy theory** (see Chapter 11) indicates that for an objective to be motivating, individuals need to see how their work performance links to outcomes they can regard as meaningful and worthwhile. It helps therefore to make quite explicit the links between individual and organisational and/or departmental objectives. In this way individuals will be able to see how their efforts contribute to the overall efforts and achievements of the department or organisation.

Managers may wonder whether annual objectives have to be set at all. Research from both **Expectancy theory** (Chapter 11) and **Goal-setting theory** (see Chapter 12) shows that individuals are more productive when they have objectives than when they do not. Objectives in this instance could include prescriptive, predefined schedules or tasks.

Objectives that describe *how* a person should do his or her job restrict the individual's ability to adjust the work to fit his or her preferred approach. This may be the desire of the organisation, but it can be counter-productive. For example, **Activation theory** (see Chapter 4) suggests that individual activation levels fluctuate during a day or over longer periods. The setting of objectives based on inputs thus restricts an individual's ability to manage this. Output-based objectives (ie those that specify *what* is to be achieved) allow individuals to choose how they schedule aspects of their work to accommodate times of greater and lesser personal activation.

According to **Achievement theory** (see Chapter 3), individuals with a high need for achievement (nAch) seek challenging goals, and individuals with a high fear of failure (fF) may seek impossibly challenging goals. In the case of the former, the individual finds such goals stimulating. In the case of the latter, setting such objectives is likely to represent a defence mechanism by which targeting ridiculously challenging objectives enables the individual to excuse subsequent failure to achieve them. Individuals with high fF may alternatively set themselves very easy targets, and it may be difficult with new staff to establish whether aiming at an easy target is due to a lack of confidence or skill or due to fear of failure.

An example highlights the dangers of accepting objectives without considering motivational issues.

Following a disappointing first year in a company, Peter met with his manager to set objectives for the next year. Peter had delivered very little of one key objective (objective 'A'), and what he had delivered had not been to an acceptable standard. As a result, his overall appraisal rating was not high – which Peter found disappointing.

At the appraisal meeting Peter was asked about the objectives he felt he could deliver in the next year. Peter declared that he would only agree to the lowest acceptable targets in order to ensure that he would get a good appraisal at the end of the year. Despite the manager's willingness to drop objective 'A', Peter was insistent he wanted it to stay.

Peter's manager carefully explained why this might result in a pay award significantly below what Peter was capable of achieving. Despite a stated need for an increase in pay, Peter would not agree to more stretching but achievable targets or to dropping objective 'A'.

In this example Peter's manager made every effort to ensure that objectives were agreed and not imposed, as most motivation theories suggest. However, there were some things the manager did not fully appreciate or understand about motivation.

Because people with high nAch tend to view achievement in terms of their effort (rather than their ability), they may want to retain tasks and objectives others consider incompatible with their skills. This is perhaps what happened in Peter's case. **Equity theory** (see Chapter 9) states that people are likely to consider their objectives in relation to those set for others. In the above example, Peter believed that objective 'A' was considered by colleagues to be highly valued within the organisation. He also believed that the objective would be set for all staff in this role, and might have been concerned that colleagues would think he was being let off a key responsibility and they would have to pick up the extra workload.

Expectancy theory (Chapter 11) suggests that individuals take on challenges if they appear to be instrumental in providing something perceived as worthwhile – eg a significant pay increase or experience required for promotion. When setting objectives, managers should therefore ensure that the link between good performance and the achievement of desired objectives is made. **Control theory** (see Chapter 7) suggests that there are different levels of goal – lower-order goals contributing to higher-order goals (instrumentality in Expectancy theory). This is an important point because it implies that not all goals are of equal importance to the individual. In the above example, although Peter wanted a significant pay increase, the manager was unable to use that to motivate Peter to revise his objectives. This could be because Peter considered his perceived reputation as more important than the pay rise.

Managers need to be careful about how they make the links between reward and performance. **Cognitive evaluation theory** (see Chapter 6) states that if an individual feels the rewards are positioned in a controlling way, they could undermine intrinsic motivation. All rewards are, to some extent, controlling – it is how they are perceived that is key. In the above example, the manager's arguments regarding pay would have needed very careful positioning to prevent Peter from feeling his manager was only interested in getting Peter to meet his manager's needs.

Managers should establish and be prepared to deal with motivational issues before discussing objectives. **Existence-relatedness-growth theory** (see Chapter 10) and **Hierarchy of needs theory** (see Chapter 13) may provide some clues for the manager in this respect. For example, someone may be known to have taken a pay cut to accept a job, or may have discussed financial matters with the manager. In these cases, the manager might suspect that lower-order needs (needs due to the lack of money) could be a key driver. **Equity theory** (Chapter 9) can also help managers prepare. This theory suggests that people do not like being in a situation they consider unfair – issues that might also be dealt with during objective-setting.

In preparing for objective-setting meetings, however, the manager must be careful not to let primary assumptions take the place of actuality. For example, a manager who assumes that finance is an issue would need first to establish if the financial situation was indeed critical. It might turn out that being accepted by colleagues or retaining self-esteem was more important.

The preceding points relate primarily to ensuring that objectives are matched with the preferences and needs of the individuals striving to achieve them. Managers should take care not to let their own motivational preferences or viewpoints shape their team members' objectives. For example, managers with a high need for affiliation (nAff), as described in **Achievement theory** (Chapter 3), may be tempted to set objectives that are not challenging, believing that stretching objectives might cause them to be disliked by their team members. As we noted above, less stretching objectives may be less motivating than worthwhile stretching ones.

Managers with a **Theory X** (see Chapter 19) view are likely to set very clear and precise objectives, prescribing in detail how to achieve each objective and the rewards to be had for success. Most people are likely to find this type of objective-setting demotivating, not least because it takes no account of the needs of the person who is actually doing the job. Managers might review the motivation theories to establish their own motivational preferences and to understand the implications of their preferences for others.

Short-term objectives

Short-term objectives are deemed to be objectives set in order to meet *ad hoc* organisational needs. They may also represent additional challenges to capitalise on extra time available during periods of unexpectedly low business activity.

The general principles for setting short-term objectives and many of the points made about annual objective-setting also apply here. Some further, additional, points are made below.

Achievement theory (see Chapter 3) warns managers that

individuals with a high need for affiliation (nAff) may be tempted to agree to all requests to take on short-term objectives, so as to nurture or protect a positive relationship with their manager. Moreover, this theory suggests that individuals with a high need for achievement (nAch) are likely to believe they can always fit in another challenge and achieve by increasing their efforts. Managers must be disciplined when assessing an individual's ability to take on extra objectives, and ensure that they will be achieved – and not just feel relieved that someone said they would do it!

Activation theory (see Chapter 4) argues that under-activated individuals tend to increase their activation to a more acceptable level. In some cases this may be done with outside work activity, but it could also happen within normal working. If activation levels fall a long way below their optimum, an individual may seek significant alternative stimulation. Outside normal working this could take many forms – further study, voluntary work, part-time work, immersion in a hobby, and so on. Within work the individual may seek project work, provide colleagues with assistance, get involved in organising social activities, etc. Whether activation is sought within or outside work there are risks to the organisation, especially if these new activities become more stimulating than the individual's job. Consider the following example.

Mike was a highly productive engineer who had rapidly mastered his job and had been promoted to a new role. The role was not very demanding and was again quickly mastered. The organisation thought they had done enough to retain him.

Feeling a bit bored at work Mike got involved with a community education project and started teaching some of his skills to local people in the evenings. This interest grew, and he became more and more involved with the project as an unpaid trainer.

By now, Mike was doing just enough in his day job to remain effective and therefore to retain his income. Mike's manager made no effort to find out why he had changed, and was thunderstruck when Mike resigned to take up a less-well-paid full-time job with the community education project.

Short-term objectives are one way of raising the activation level for an individual and ensuring that new activities are adding value to the individual and the organisation. If his manager had set Mike short-term objectives (eg helping to train apprentices), the organisation might have kept hold of Mike's much-needed skills which the organisation had spent several years developing.

Existence-relatedness-growth theory (see Chapter 10) and **Hierarchy of needs theory** (see Chapter 13) can help managers realise when an individual's needs have shifted to a new level. Following a successful year an individual may receive a pay increase that takes him or her to a more comfortable lifestyle. As the next year progresses, the individual may start to seek satisfaction from more intrinsic activities such as personal development. In Mike's case the organisation could have considered discussing a development objective that fitted in with his interests in learning – eg supporting part-time study towards a qualification. This would have addressed both activation and hierarchy needs.

Managers should also be aware that short-term objectives may be required when longer-term ones are superseded (eg in times of crisis when the focus has to be on specific activities). Managers can put in a lot of time and effort ensuring that long-term annual objectives are set properly only to forget to use the same approach when shorter-term objectives require to be set.

Key points

Objective-setting is a key part of performance management. The points listed below summarise the key issues discussed in this chapter.

☐ Objectives should be stretching but achievable. Individuals should believe that the objective can be achieved by their own efforts.

☐ Objectives must be stated clearly and understood by the job-holder. Individuals need to know what standards they are working towards.

☐ Objectives must be seen to be fair.

- Individuals are more motivated when they have a sense of responsibility for the delivery of an objective.
- Individuals need to feel that they are working towards something that is desirable and worthwhile.
- Individuals with a high fear of failure may seek very easy or impossibly difficult objectives.
- Although objectives should be discussed and agreed, managers should not let their own preferences dictate the objectives of their team members.
- Where objectives are linked to reward, there should be no ambiguity about the link between the two.
- Feedback should be given in order to let the individual know how he or she is progressing.
- Feedback perceived as controlling can undermine intrinsic motivation.
- Individuals may take on less desirable objectives if they consider achieving those objectives to be instrumental in achieving something else that is more desirable.
- Individuals' preferences and needs are likely to change over time.
- Equal care should be taken with short-term objectives as is taken with longer-term ones.

31 MAINTAINING EFFECTIVE PERFORMANCE

Introduction

Most issues in maintaining effective performance are day-to-day and informal, but performance management also includes the more formal annual and interim reviews of performance against objectives. During day-to-day management, managers can have a significant impact on the motivation and possible demotivation of their staff.

Application of theory

Achievement theory (see Chapter 3) suggests that people with a high need for achievement (nAch) are likely to be self-motivated to achieve objectives they find worthwhile, challenging and achievable. This does not mean, however, that once objectives have been agreed, people can be left to get on unsupported. Continued motivation needs to be maintained with clear feedback on progress. The manager is one source or conduit for this, but feedback can also be built into work systems (eg error messages), correspond to a visible result of an activity (eg the reduction of a pile of filing), or be provided by others (eg customers and colleagues). **Control theory** (see Chapter 7) and **Job characteristics theory** (see Chapter 16) also emphasise the importance of individuals' obtaining knowledge about the results of their efforts.

A note of caution regarding feedback is sounded by **Cognitive evaluation theory** (see Chapter 6). This theory states that if feedback is perceived to be informational, intrinsic motivation will be enhanced. However, if feedback is perceived as intended to control a person's behaviour, it is likely to undermine intrinsic motivation.

Needless to say, not everyone views feedback in the same way. The same type of feedback might thus be considered controlling by one person and informational by the next. As a general rule, frequent feedback is probably going to be considered most informational in the early stages of learning a task or job. This should be specific and directly related to tasks so that the individual can learn. As the person becomes more competent, feedback can become less frequent and even less specific. However, this is not to suggest that managers can eventually give no feedback at all!

If a task is unlikely to be intrinsically motivating, feedback may be considered controlling but need not be seen as a negative thing. After all, if a task is not intrinsically motivating, extrinsic motivators have to be reinforced. **Expectancy theory** (see Chapter 11) suggests that one way of doing this is by giving feedback on progress towards both the objective and the reward – in other words, making the link between performance and reward.

By highlighting the above points, we are not proposing that intrinsically motivated people only require an occasional 'Well done!' **Reinforcement theories** (see Chapter 17) suggest that people who undertake new challenges may need a lot of encouragement and helpful feedback until they have learned what to do and developed their confidence in doing it correctly. After this, frequent feedback may be inappropriate, may be perceived as contrived and controlling, and may result in demotivation.

Reinforcement theories (Chapter 17) also suggest that reinforcement is less effective when it is so routine it becomes predictable. It is better that reinforcement is varied, in terms of both positive and negative reinforcement and the intervals between. Most managers would probably prefer to reinforce behaviour through positive reinforcement – by recognising and applauding positive behaviour – rather than by punishing negative behaviour.

Drive theory (see Chapter 8) relies heavily on reinforcement. People learn how to behave (or how not to) by reinforcement – ie by learning from the success (or otherwise) of previous behaviour. It is therefore important in performance management that the correct signals for reinforcement are given. This is particularly true when behaviour change is required (eg a change in customer service standards) or when new behaviours are needed (eg in a new job).

Managers should be aware of the potential impact of their behaviour on the motivation of others to adopt behaviours desired by the organisation. **Social learning theory** (see Chapter 18) suggests that individuals learn by imitation as well as from personal experience. For example, managers may encourage poor behaviour if they are seen to use the poor behaviour themselves and to be rewarded by colleagues after doing so. Similarly, when poor behaviour demonstrated by senior managers is accepted, applauded or not challenged, it should not be surprising that junior managers are more motivated to adopt the poor behaviour than to espouse the organisation's desired alternative.

Achievement theory (Chapter 3), supported by **Attribution theory** (see Chapter 5), describes achievement-oriented activities as being those in which a person feels responsible for the outcomes of the activities. If feedback confirms this view, all well and good. However, if feedback undermines this by attributing the cause of performance to mere luck or chance (eg by saying 'Bad luck!' when things go wrong, or 'That *was* lucky!' when they go right), the person giving the feedback could be eliminating some of the challenge and perceived responsibility – and therefore some of the motivation. Further undermining of motivation will also result if responsibility for outcomes, ideas or decisions is frequently being attributed to others or being usurped by the manager.

The feeling of control over the cause of one's actions is also covered in **Internal–external control theory** (see Chapter 15). This theory suggests that day-to-day performance management can support or undermine a person's view of his or her control of the environment. For example, if an employee is given a task to complete, the manager should consider how his or her actions and comments affect that employee's motivation to complete the task. Consider the example below.

> Marianne was a very collaborative manager and always sought the views of her team members before making decisions that affected them. Marianne had delegated an important task to Wendy, a team member, and always checked on progress during team meetings.
>
> During one such meeting Marianne became concerned about progress on the task and invited the other team members to suggest how Wendy might get back on track.
>
> Despite best intentions, Wendy left the meeting feeling very demotivated and asked that the task be delegated to someone else.
>
> Wendy thought she had been delegated the necessary responsibility to carry out the task and also felt able to complete the task. During the meeting, however, her manager had removed the sense of responsibility and implied a lack of confidence in Wendy's ability to deliver.

Achievement theory (Chapter 3) also suggests that feedback can be important to individuals with a high fear of failure. If clear objectives have been agreed, for which even such a person feels responsible, appropriate feedback should be used to reinforce a belief both that it will be achieved and that the person is responsible for achieving it.

Managing performance includes monitoring activation levels and recognising signs of over- or under-activation. **Activation theory** (see Chapter 4) suggests that when an individual's activation levels exceed or drop below his or her optimum level, the individual could show signs of a lack of motivation. The most obvious sign is when performance has already been affected, usually downward: this is dealt with in the **Managing under-performers chapter** (Chapter 32). In terms of day-to-day performance management, signs of distraction, boredom or restlessness should be analysed to see if activation is an issue. Short-term objectives might help address this. See the chapter on **Objective-setting** (Chapter 30) for further information.

Monitoring should also be concerned with assessing an individual's ability to cope. **Attribution theory** (Chapter 5) and **Achievement theory** (Chapter 3) suggest that people with high nAch consider most things to be achievable if they put in enough effort. Managers should question whether such people are pushing themselves too hard and/or taking on too many challenges. Managers should also be prepared to guide people if effort is being wasted. **Existence-relatedness-growth theory** (see Chapter 10) suggests that if higher-order needs are not being met, people may be motivated to work towards meeting lower-order needs even if they have already been met. Consider thc example below.

> Sally, a team leader in a large organisation, was finding her job very frustrating. She wanted to develop her skills so that she could be promoted, but felt that the organisation was not giving her the right opportunities. The result of this frustration was that she spent many hours on tasks she knew she was good at. She completed these tasks to a level of detail far in excess of what was required and despite her manager telling her such effort was not required.

Monitoring performance and giving feedback may require a manager to remind an employee of the longer-term objectives. **Drive theory** (Chapter 8) suggests that motivation is driven by a desire to reduce dissatisfaction. Management of perform-ance therefore suggests that managers can help by reminding the person why he or she is dissatisfied! This is not as silly as it may first seem. A person who has agreed to take on a project to help develop some of his or her key skills may become demotivated if performance management focuses only on the objectives of the project. However, although the objectives of the project clearly have to be discussed, the manager can assist the individual's motivation by empha-sising the long-term, personal developmental objectives of the project.

The apparent evenhandedness of a manager can also be key in maintaining the motivation of others. **Equity theory** (see Chapter 9) contends that people dislike inequity and will work to eliminate it. Performance management should ensure that such situations do not arise. Managers should think about how they give feedback, how they set objectives, who they involve in one-to-one discussions, and so on. It is not necessarily that someone may *actually* be being treated unfairly so much as that someone *feels* that he or she is not being treated the same as others. People who are doing well should not be ignored while those needing help are given all the attention. Similarly, people who are under-performing should not be ignored while resources and recognition are being given to the good performers.

Evenhandedness can have an influence over the psychological states of employees. **Job characteristics theory** (Chapter 16) suggests that managers can enhance the meaningfulness of a job by making sure that they discuss it in the same way they discuss other jobs. The example below illustrates how one manager got this wrong.

> The manager of a department which contained a filing team never referred to their successes when discussing the overall performance of the department. He also always referred to filing as a somewhat undesirable and not very important, job. When tasks were allocated, the manager made it clear he considered filing the worst job. Whenever a problem in the filing team was raised, he treated it as low-priority. Unsurprisingly, his filing team did not feel they were doing a meaningful job!

It is not recommended that equity is sought by ignoring all team members equally! Such action is likely to undermine confidence in the manager. **Hygiene theory** (see Chapter 14) warns that interpersonal relationships and supervision are factors that create dissatisfaction, and therefore demotivation, if they are considered poor. This theory suggests, however, that continuing to improve relationships with team members alone will not evoke corresponding increments in motivation. Managers have a key role in ensuring commitment and a lack of dissatisfaction, but they are unlikely to encourage more motivation simply by having the best possible relationship with their team.

This is not to say that managerial skills do not contribute to motivation – they certainly can. The motivating factors outlined by **Hygiene theory** (Chapter 14) – achievement, recognition, responsibility, advancement, and accomplishment in the work itself – are clearly influenced by the abilities of the manager. For example, the manager is likely to have a large influence over recognition – especially on an ongoing basis. Managers could also influence motivators, depending on the systems in place, such as promotions (advancement) and job design (responsibility and the work itself). Recognition may be one outcome of work an individual considers to be particularly valuable. **Expectancy theory** (Chapter 11) recognises the importance of having work outcomes that are valued by the individual. Managers should be aware that recognition does not have to be financial, and should implement other forms of recognition that appeal to different individuals' values.

Whereas recognition may provide an incentive for some, **Goal-setting theory** (see Chapter 12) provides a reminder of the importance of incentives that include praise and reproof, knowing the score, participation, competition, and so on. Again, these are things managers can build into ongoing performance management.

A careful balance is needed in relationship management to enable awareness of individuals' needs within and outside work without appearing to be nosy or intrusive. A manager may require some insights into each team member's domestic and social situation if he or she is to help individuals maintain motivation at work. **Existence-relatedness-growth theory** (Chapter 10) and **Hierarchy of needs theory** (see Chapter 13) can help managers think about why a person may be motivated in the first place. For example, if a person is focusing on meeting existence, physiological or safety needs, he or she is more likely to be motivated by extrinsic rewards. If this is the case, day-to-day performance management can link to these rewards by giving feedback on how well the person is performing in relation to bonuses, for example. However, detailed discussion of extrinsic rewards may be counter-productive for people focusing on growth or self-actualisation. In these circumstances, managers may be better off discussing progress against aspirations and development plans. At all times, managers should check out their assumptions to prevent their attempts to help from turning out to be quite the opposite.

The way a manager treats his or her staff affects how those

staff are likely to be motivated. A **Theory X** (see Chapter 19) management style is really only relevant where jobs are designed in a way that requires close supervision, detailed training, lots of direction, and so on. These conditions can also exist because of individuals' being new to a job or to a set of tasks. Either case may benefit from a Theory X approach in the short term, but the approach is likely to demotivate individuals once they feel competent and able to take responsibility for their work outputs. It is also a very resource-intensive management approach.

Theory Y (see Chapter 19) management requires the ongoing management of performance to be much more hands-off. Staff are motivated by being given responsibility, a degree of autonomy and empowerment – all features that are recommended in **Job characteristics theory** (see Chapter 16). However, this does not let the manager off the hook, for his or her role is imperative in ensuring that staff are able to take on their tasks and are given appropriate direction as and when needed. In many ways it is harder to motivate as a **Theory Y** manager than a **Theory X** manager (Chapter 19) because it involves the management of diversity – a much 'softer' approach where there are no hard-and-fast rules. Despite this, however, it is generally accepted that intrinsic motivation creates a more sustainable level of performance because it does not require others to keep cracking the whip!

Managing effective performance requires a manager to support individuals in achieving objectives – especially when these change. **Control theory** (Chapter 7) and **Goal-setting theory** (Chapter 12) work on the basis that there are clear standards. This was covered in the chapter on **Objective-setting** (Chapter 30), but managers should be aware of it when monitoring performance. If objectives change, then new standards should be agreed as soon as possible. If they are not, managers should not be surprised that individuals are either performing well – but against old objectives – or becoming frustrated about which objectives they are supposed to be working towards.

Key points

Motivation plays a key part in managing effective performance. The theories suggest that the key points below should be taken into account.

- [ ] Individuals need work to be meaningful and to know what is expected of them.
- [ ] People need to know how well they are doing toward goals and objectives.
- [ ] Feedback is essential but must be managed carefully.
- [ ] People need to feel responsibility for the outcome of their efforts.
- [ ] Managers should not expect an individual to be motivated equally by all of their objectives.
- [ ] Challenging but achievable objectives tend to be more motivating than easy objectives.
- [ ] Changes in an individual's activation levels could indicate a potential motivation issue.
- [ ] Individuals with a high need for achievement may believe they need only increase effort to achieve.
- [ ] Managers need to evaluate whether an individual can actually do what he or she is willing to agree to.
- [ ] People dislike inequity and may well do something to try to redress the situation.
- [ ] Where rewards are linked to objectives, the links should be made clearly visible.
- [ ] There are many forms of incentives. Not all appeal to everyone equally.
- [ ] Individuals' needs vary and influence what motivates them.
- [ ] Relationships with managers can impact on motivation.
- [ ] The design of jobs has an impact on motivation.

32 MANAGING UNDER-PERFORMERS

Introduction

This chapter is about motivation in the face of performance that falls short of required or expected standards. The standards may constitute specific levels in agreed objectives, acceptable behaviour, conformity with values, or any other benchmark used to measure performance. Poor performance may therefore manifest itself in many ways – for example, failure to achieve a goal, changes in the general attitude of an individual, or a drop in overall performance.

This chapter looks at how motivation theories could help managers explore the reasons why motivation to perform well may be lacking. We also use the theories to suggest ways in which such situations might be improved.

It is important to distinguish between performance that is falling short of required standards and performance that is falling short of the person's own previous standards. The former cannot usually be tolerated even for a short period of time. The latter might be tolerable, unless it also falls below an acceptable standard. However, it might become a significant problem if ignored for too long.

Application of theory

In all cases poor performance, if not addressed, may result in a downward spiral of motivation. The individual may well try to remedy the situation, but if he or she cannot, or does not believe he or she can do it within the organisation, he or she may consider leaving the situation to be the only solution.

However it reveals itself, poor performance could follow,

accompany or precede a drop in motivation. In the first of
these cases, motivation may be a cause of poor performance
and in the third case it may be a reaction to poor performance. Where a drop in motivation accompanies a drop in
performance, it may be a cause or an effect.

There are three key aspects of under-performance.

☐ a sudden drop in performance

☐ gradual under-performance

☐ consistent under-performance.

A sudden drop in performance

A sudden drop in performance is likely to reflect a sudden
change in the circumstances of the individual. The change
may or may not be known to the manager and may require
some tactful exploration. If a change has instead been identified within the job or workplace (promotion or a change in
objectives, standards, job design, organisational structure,
strategy, location, technology, etc), see the chapters on **Organisational change** (Chapter 26), **Job design** (Chapter 21) or
Objective-setting (Chapter 30).

If no obvious change has been made, managers need to
investigate possible changes with the individual. Exploring
motivational issues requires skill, tact and objectivity, and may
not necessarily be easy for either party. For example, it is not
easy for someone to tell their manager that he or she thinks
the manager is the cause of the poor performance! **Attribution theory** (see Chapter 5) also suggests that managers need to
be aware of the biases they or the team members have when
trying to identify causes for a change in performance and/or
motivation. This is illustrated in the example below.

Sally's management style is collaborative and consultative. One of her
team, Tim, was becoming increasingly frustrated by an important task
and asked Sally for advice. Sally approached the problem in her usual
way and asked Tim what he felt should be done in the situation. The
subsequent discussion did not go as well as Sally would have liked, so
she approached Tim the next day to find out whether she had actually
helped.

> It turned out that Tim simply did not know what to do – he did not have the experience Sally had and actually just wanted to be given some guidance. Sally's assumption that the issue was down to Tim's lack of confidence (and all she therefore needed to do was help him come up with an answer himself) was wrong.

Individual circumstances within the workplace that can suddenly affect motivation and performance include changes in relationships with an employee's colleagues and/or manager. **Hygiene theory** (see Chapter 14) suggests that a change of manager or in manager relationship can have a significant effect on motivation because poor relationships can be a major source of personal dissatisfaction. Where the manager has changed, it may just be a matter of time to establish a good working relationship. A change in relationship with an existing manager may be the result of a change in the manager's own motivations as much as a change in those of the individual.

One way of gauging whether hygiene factors are relevant is to observe whether the drop in performance applies to a whole group or just to an individual. Hygiene factors are more likely to affect a whole group rather than just one individual. An example illustrates this.

> An organisation changed its hot drinks machine arrangements. From being free all the time, the new arrangements meant that there were only two times of the day when drinks were free – the rest of the time they were 5p per cup. The result was that people made sure they had as many drinks as possible during the free times and, in some cases, people even used vacuum flasks to store the free drinks. Although the new system did not cause a massive drop in performance, it initially caused some disruption until people came to terms with it. Significantly, the change caused discontent that far outweighed the minimal 5p charge for coffee.

For a change in relationships with colleagues, managers should consider whether some form of perceived inequity may have occurred. **Equity theory** (see Chapter 9) suggests that the actions people may take to reduce a feeling of inequity may not be conducive to good performance. Inequity could be seen in terms of many factors, including promotion, demotion, sharing of information, workload, rewards, recognition, feedback, relocation, development opportunities, objectives, career discussions and work environment.

A sudden change in an individual's circumstances outside the workplace may often explain an equally sudden change in motivation and performance at work. In particular, changes in lower-order needs outlined in **Existence-relatedness-growth theory** (see Chapter 10) or **Hierarchy of needs theory** (see Chapter 13) – eg a sudden threat to financial security, relationship issues or concern over personal health – can significantly redirect an individual's priorities and thus his or her motivation. These theories suggest that when more basic needs are threatened, individuals may put more effort into protecting them and turn their attention away from higher-order needs such as additional activities for interest and/or self development. In these circumstances it may be possible to restore performance on key job objectives by deferring some of the developmental objectives or activities, provided they are not key to current job performance.

Other changes outside work may impact on an individual's activation levels. **Activation theory** (see Chapter 4) suggests that each person has an optimum level of stimulation. If activation rises significantly outside work, the individual may compensate by reducing his or her level of activation at work. Activation may be most affected by things that require more thinking, effort, emotional resolve or personal time. Examples of these are family illness, a new partner, a new child, legal proceedings, a house move, and so on. Increased activation outside work (eg taking on part-time study or part-time work) may also be due to higher-order needs – as outlined in **Existence-relatedness-growth theory** (Chapter 10) and **Hierarchy of needs theory** (Chapter 13) – not being met at work. In this situation the manager should establish what ought to change at work to re-engage the individual and prevent him or her from leaving.

In the face of many of these situations, the manager should be able to work with the individual to establish an estimate of how long it will take before things return to normal. Where activation levels outside work make it difficult for the individual to maintain previous activation levels at work, the manager may have to accept that motivation and performance will have to suffer in the short term. Alternatively, the manager may be able to work with the individual to speed up resolution of external activation demands – eg by providing time out for the individual to deal with the external demands, or by providing the resources for higher-order needs to be met.

Job characteristics theory (see Chapter 16) outlines a number of features of a job which, if not present, could cause demotivation. Issues relating to these job characteristics may arise because of an actual change or a belief that a change has occurred. The manager has a role in managing and correcting perceptions. Some changes may not be correctable within the existing job – eg a substantial reduction in the impact of a job may be a genuine sign that the job or some aspect of it is no longer needed. For the sake of job-holders and the organisation, this situation must be seen to be receiving urgent attention.

Gradual under-performance

As noted earlier, a drop in performance may be preceded, accompanied or followed by a drop in motivation. Managers need to monitor performance regularly if they are to spot a gradual drop in performance. If not addressed, such a drop in performance may become critical, and the individual may see no easy way out.

There is one situation where motivation may appear to increase despite dropping performance. This can occur in an individual with a high need for achievement (nAch). **Achievement theory** (see Chapter 3) suggests high-nAch individuals are likely to believe that achievement is simply an issue of effort and may well appear to increase in motivation as they increase their effort to achieve a particularly challenging objective. Only when their increased efforts fail to deliver are they likely to suffer a drop in motivation.

Achievement theory (Chapter 3) suggests that if performance has deteriorated, it could be that a task or job has lost its challenge. This might be rectified by increasing the challenge. It does not necessarily have to be achieved by making the task more difficult – perhaps a new dimension should be added instead. Clearly, the person has to have the necessary ability to undertake thc amended task, but this could be the challenge needed to increase his or her level of motivation. Consider how this issue was dealt with in one organisation outlined in the example below.

> Claire had become the most proficient person on the team – there was no more she could learn about the job. Her manager realised that this could result in Claire becoming demotivated because there were no further challenges within the job itself. To rectify this, the manager agreed that she could become the team trainer/coach. This gave Claire the challenge she needed to keep her motivated.

Sometimes a drop in performance may be accompanied by a noticeable change in behaviour, possibly resulting in disruptive or unacceptable behaviour. **Activation theory** (see Chapter 4) suggests that low performance could be the result of under- or over-stimulation. Some possible causes of under-stimulation at work were described earlier in our examination of a sudden drop in performance, and these could be explored here. However, a gradual drop in performance may indicate that the job itself is not providing sufficient stimulation. In these circumstances individuals may create ways in which they can increase activation to their preferred level. Daydreaming, seeking social interaction with colleagues and focusing on tasks the person finds interesting rather than job-critical tasks are possible efforts to increase activation levels. When an individual has an evident desire to increase activation levels, the manager where possible should seek productive ways to accommodate the individual's desire – eg with additional objectives or activities.

Of course this assumes that the individual can recognise the cause of his or her predicament and that added activation is possible. In some cases increased activation may not be possible, and it may be necessary to try to motivate the individual by reminding him or her of the instrumentality of achieving the agreed objectives as outlined in **Expectancy theory** (see Chapter 11) – ie what's in it for them if they achieve the objectives.

Expectancy may be at the root of the problem. If the individual does not value the possible rewards or does not believe they are available, such perceptions should be addressed. **Existence-relatedness-growth theory** (see Chapter 10) and **Hierarchy of needs theory** (see Chapter 13) suggest that the importance of a goal does not always remain the same. It could be that the instrumentality of the reward has been reduced (eg the car that the person wanted the bonus for has now been paid for via a windfall) or that the expectancy has changed (eg an organisational restructuring has removed the position the person was hoping hard work would put him or her in line for). The outcome itself may also no longer be desirable.

In the chapter on **Maintaining effective performance** (Chapter 31) we noted the importance of feedback and of informing job-holders of their progress toward their objectives. We also warned of the dangers of doing this poorly. **Cognitive evaluation theory** (see Chapter 6) suggests that how people perceive the feedback they get can be demotivating. If they consider the feedback is being used to try to control their efforts, they will be less intrinsically motivated. The manager could explore what feedback the person is getting and how he or she perceives it.

Control theory (see Chapter 7) suggests that people are motivated to achieve goals, and that feedback is key in helping them ascertain how near (or far) they are from the goal. An assumption here is that a person knows what to do in the event of negative feedback. The manager dealing with poor performance might do well to explore this. The person may correctly understand the performance required, and know that he or she is not meeting that standard. However, if he or she is unsure how to correct the situation, the poor performance may well continue and demotivation increase. It is not always easy for people to admit to not knowing how to deal with something – especially if they think that they *should* know. Take the man who has just come back from an off-the-job learning event – it cannot be easy for him to admit he has forgotten how to do something he was taught only a week ago.

Acceptable performance has to be reinforced to ensure that people know whether it is acceptable or not. Poor performance could simply be the result of 'guesswork' if there is no feedback to suggest what level of performance is required. **Reinforcement theories** (see Chapter 17) suggest that the most powerful confirmation is continuous reinforcement. The most influential reinforcer is a 'valid' individual. This explains why it is that some people will follow the crowd and the crowd's standards as the norm rather than the organisation's. The only hope of rectifying poor performance in such circumstances is if standards are clear and desired behaviours are reinforced across the group.

Comments about the crowd made above are supported by **Social learning theory** (see Chapter 18). If a manager ignores the poor performance, behaviour or values of others, he or she ought to be aware that new arrivals are likely to perceive them as being approved of and therefore acceptable.

One option for dealing with poor performance is to use extinction (as outlined in **Reinforcement theories**: Chapter 17) – in other words, simply ignore poor behaviour. We suggest that this is likely to work only if (a) there are clear standards of behaviour (and so people should know without being told they are not performing to standard), and (b) positive reinforcement is being used for behaviour conforming to standards. If these two conditions apply, a manager is basically relying on an individual's desire to conform to motivate them to 'toe the line'. The strategy may work – but managers should be prepared to abandon it early on if it has no effect.

If poor performance is the result of a required change of behaviour (eg an organisational restructuring that has caused people to be moved to new jobs, or a change in organisational standards) managers would do well to take note of **Drive theory** (see Chapter 8). This theory suggests that people find it very hard to change long-established habits and that they will only change habits if the new behaviour is reinforced (and if they know what the new behaviour is). There also has to be an incentive for people to change – and we would assume that most managers would prefer this to be a positive incentive rather than a threat.

Another possible reason, also highlighted by **Cognitive evaluation theory** (Chapter 6), for a lack of motivation (which may contribute to poor performance) is the attachment of extrinsic rewards to something the person finds/found intrinsically rewarding. The manager may wish to explore whether such an event has occurred prior to the downturn in performance. An example illustrates this.

> Lee was studying for a qualification at work. He took it up because he wanted to progress to the next level in management and felt that the qualification would help him to achieve this. He was also interested in the subject. Lee enjoyed studying and was intrinsically motivated.
>
> The organisation Lee worked for introduced a new promotion system that made the qualification Lee was studying for a *prerequisite* for promotion to the job he was aiming for. This extrinsic reward, attached to something Lee was happy to do anyway, took away some of the motivation he originally felt to undertake the course. The choice about whether to do the course or not had shifted away from being a free choice to one which was almost an obligation.

As noted earlier, poor performance may be the result of someone's shift in position along the continuum outlined in **Existence-relatedness-growth theory** (Chapter 10) or up the hierarchy of needs outlined in **Hierarchy of needs theory** (Chapter 13). For example, the person might have moved towards growth or self-actualisation needs while in a job he or she was initially motivated to do because of basic existence needs. If someone has received pay rises (with perhaps a corresponding reduction in expenditure), it might mean that he or she is now not so focused on the bills at home. These theories suggest that individuals in this position may at this point be looking for other things in their lives, in the relationship or growth areas. Such a person may be looking to expand his or her role or move into a role that seems more fulfilling.

At the other end of the spectrum, a need at the existence end of the Existence-relatedness-growth continuum may become more pressing, and performance may slacken as a result. For example, steeply rising expenses may gradually make a previously comfortable financial situation uncomfortable. The focus on growth- or relationship-type activities may diminish as the person concentrates on the more basic needs.

In both the circumstances described in the previous two paragraphs, the manager should explore the background reasons for the change in behaviour and be aware that either of these circumstances could have occurred so gradually that the person may not understand or be able to explain why his or her behaviour has changed.

Perceived unfairness in the way people are managed at work can be a source of dissatisfaction and lead to reduced performance. **Equity theory** (Chapter 9) states that most people are motivated to do something about dissonance. If individuals feel they are being treated more shabbily than others, they may deal with the dissonance by lowering their efforts, which could result in poor performance. Managers might explore with a poor performer whether he or she feels in some way hard done by. For example, has a colleague been promoted to a position the person felt was his or hers? Does he or she now think that a lot of hard work has thus gone to waste so there is no point in carrying on working so hard?

The point made in the introduction about poor performance against organisational standards as opposed to previous personal standards is particularly relevant here. An individual may still meet or exceed the required standards but his or her performance may have dropped from where it was previously. In this case the person may be doing enough to avoid discipline, but no more. It would be foolish to ignore such a change in performance – it is clearly a sign that all is not well. Even though the manager cannot complain about substandard performance, it is a problem that needs addressing positively, before the individual becomes so disillusioned and demotivated that he or she decides to leave the situation.

A gradual drop in performance could also result from someone taking on too much. **Achievement theory** (Chapter 3) suggests that people with high fear of failure (fF) may take on challenges that are too stretching. Perhaps the individual simply does not have the ability to fulfil the task. Managers should be wary not to confuse 'ability' with availability of resources to achieve the task. For example, there is a difference between people who are capable but just do not have the required resources (however hard they try, they will not succeed) and people who are able and *think* they do not have the resources (in which case they need to know how to access them). This point is illustrated further by **Internal–external control theory** (see Chapter 15), which suggests that people take different views on the extent to which they control their environment. The more internal control a person perceives, the more likely he or she is to consider success as due to effort rather than to circumstances.

During mergers and subsequent restructuring, extra tasks and responsibilities often get added into existing jobs. Initially this may result in small effects on motivation and performance that resolve themselves as job-holders come to terms with the changes. However, to ensure that performance and motivation are not likely to suffer in the long term, managers should try to ensure that additional tasks and responsibilities form a logical and coherent addition to the existing tasks and responsibilities within each job.

An individual's relationship with their supervisor or manager is identified within **Hygiene theory** (see Chapter 14) as a factor that would demotivate if it was considered poor. This can be a cause of gradually diminishing performance. A manager may be too close to the situation to notice or accept that his or her relationship with a team member has become a source of dissatisfaction and demotivation. Managers might look around to see if there are any signs of a relationship problem – signs such as increased absenteeism, reluctance on the part of individuals to attend meetings with the manager, a drop in casual communication, general impatience, comments from colleagues, coolness in meetings or discussions.

There are various ways in which a manager might cause a change in the relationship with his or her team, including changing the method by which he or she gives feedback on performance and recognition. A manager could undermine motivation by simply forgetting to do these. In addition, fairness, responsibility, challenge and intrinsic motivation can be undermined if a manager does not pay sufficient attention to monitoring and managing individual performance.

Another hygiene factor likely to have a detrimental effect on performance is lack of job security. Organisational changes can generate rumour and insecurity, usually unintended.

> Amy, a department manager in a retail chainstore, had noticed that the performance of her deputy, Lance, had been getting steadily worse over the past few months. Amy had been involved in a project team looking at how to implement some radical changes among the stores. This project required her to spend a lot of time away from the shop, and Amy needed Lance to be performing at his best. Amy decided to tackle this issue.
>
> At the meeting it transpired that Lance felt unsure about all the changes and was missing having Amy around for support. Amy usually worked closely with Lance and she had not realised that her absences, and the impending changes in the shop, were leaving Lance demotivated. They agreed to have weekly meetings to discuss issues relating to the store. This was enough for Lance to quickly revert back to his previous levels of performance.

This example illustrates how insecurity and a changing relationship can adversely effect motivation.

Consistent under-performance

Above we noted the importance of feedback. This applies in all cases of performance management. According to **Control theory** (see Chapter 7), feedback should show deviation (above or below) from a particular standard. If an individual's performance has never been good, the manager should explore (a) whether the person is aware of the standards required, (b) what feedback the person is receiving about his or her performance, and (c) whether he or she knows how to do the job. If the standards are not clear, the person can hardly be expected to meet them. It should also be obvious that if the person is getting no feedback on performance, he or she may find it hard actually to know whether the standards are being met or not. Likewise, even if the person knows the standards and is getting feedback, he or she may not be able to do the job.

Managers should be aware that just because a standard is written down does not mean that people know what it is. There are often external factors that are more 'real' than anything written down. Consider the example below.

> A call centre had set a customer service standard for answering the telephone within three rings. The reality was that most people answered the telephone as soon as they could – rarely within three rings. Managers never criticised the staff for this because they felt that staff were overstretched as it was.

The call centre, in reality, did not have a 'three ring standard' – despite the fact that it was published in the customer service standards.

When exploring the reasons for poor performance, it may be worth considering how much responsibility people are taking for their performance, and the reasons they are giving for why performance is poor (assuming that it is acknowledged in the first place). **Attribution theory** (see Chapter 5) and **Internal–external control theory** (see Chapter 15) suggest that people ascribe failure to factors inside or outside their control. Those with internal locus of control (see **Glossary**) are likely to ascribe failure to their own lack of effort. These individuals are likely to recognise that they are responsible for poor performance and be willing to make the effort to put it right. The manager should be careful to assure them that the extra effort alone will be sufficient, because these individuals may not perceive when skills need improving or real external restrictions are blocking achievement. It is important to recognise situations when people cannot achieve their objectives because of things outside their control which were not anticipated at the time the objectives were set. The manager should check out such possibilities before agreeing performance improvement plans.

Those with external locus of control are likely to attribute failure to factors outside their control. There may even be a denial that the problem exists. Managers in this situation should explore why the person is attributing failure to such external factors (because the attribution may be valid). If the attribution is not valid, the individual has to be helped to understand that the poor performance is his or her own responsibility.

Another reason for consistently poor performance may be the result of a low level of expectancy. **Expectancy theory** (see Chapter 11) states that people have to link worthwhile outcomes to their performance in order to be motivated to work towards them. If people cannot see that they will get anything worthwhile from their efforts, they are not likely to be motivated to perform well. Ideally, expectancy is to achieve positive things, so managers should preferably be discussing all the positive reasons why the outcome is desirable – this could be influenced by **Existence-relatedness-growth theory** (see Chapter 10) and **Hierarchy of needs theory** (see Chapter 13) in relation to outcomes individuals are likely to be seeking.

A desirable outcome for the individual could be the avoidance of a negative situation. It would be reasonable for a manager to point out that extra effort to succeed in an objective or task might avert disciplinary action, if a more positive approach is coming to nought. Managers would be wise to consider, in this latter case, why a person may not think his or her poor performance might lead to negative consequences. Has it been tolerated before? Many employment tribunal cases have been lost when employers 'suddenly' clamp down on behaviour which, although it may seem unreasonable to an outsider, has actually been standard for the individual over many years previously.

Continuous poor performance may also be the result of the low valence of outcomes, as outlined in **Expectancy theory** (Chapter 11). Similar comments could be made here as in the previous paragraph. Are there ways in which the required performance can be attached to outcomes important to the individual? For example, can they be linked to longer-term aspirations – skills being developed relevant to career goals, for example? Managers should make sure that there is real expectancy here or the person may become demotivated.

In terms of job performance, some form of objective, target or goal is essential. This is stated or implied in most motivational theories but it is perhaps most central to **Goal-setting theory** (see Chapter 12). Individuals can deliver what is expected of them only when they know what it is they are expected to deliver. Goals should be clear and challenging, and have defined standards. Poor performance may be because goals do not have these characteristics or because the person is simply incapable of delivering the specified goal without training and support. Managers should establish that individuals really do understand what is expected of them and that they have the necessary resources and support to be able to deliver it.

Behavioural intention is also key to **Goal-setting theory** (Chapter 12). Managers might question the purpose of the standard a person is falling short on. If a person accepted a particularly challenging goal because he or she had the intention of getting a sense of personal satisfaction out of the task, but the manager actually just wanted the job done quickly, there might be a clash of intentions. As with **Expectancy theory** (Chapter 11), the outcome must be considered valid by the person doing the work.

When examining gradual drops in performance we noted the importance of an individual's relationship with the supervisor or manager. This is identified within **Hygiene theory** (see Chapter 14) as a factor that would demotivate if it was considered poor. It can equally be the cause of consistently poor performance. A manager may be too close to the situation to notice or accept that his or her relationship with a team member is a source of dissatisfaction and demotivation. As with gradual decline in the relationship, clues to a poor relationship include absenteeism, reluctance to attend meetings with the manager, no casual communication, general impatience, comments from colleagues, coolness in meetings or discussions, and so on. The ways in which the manager may be responsible for a poor relationship with the team are much the same as those outlined in the section on how the relationship can cause a gradual decline in performance.

Hygiene theory (Chapter 14) provides a cautionary note in relation to dealing with poor work hygiene factors. The theory states that motivating factors are not the opposite of hygiene factors, and nor does one compensate for the other. So if poor performance is due to a hygiene factor, it will be difficult for an organisation to make up for it via a motivator.

The components of **Job characteristics theory** (see Chapter 16) give managers areas to explore in situations of poor performance. This theory suggests that people are motivated by jobs in which they experience meaningfulness, responsibility for outcomes and knowledge of the results of their work activities. Motivation issues may arise when feedback fails to provide job-holders with the knowledge they need or when feedback undermines individuals' sense of value and/or responsibility for their work. The manager has a role in influencing the perceptions of every job-holder.

Job characteristics theory (Chapter 16) also suggests that the complexity and challenge of a job should be matched to individuals and not assumed to be the same for all employees in a job. If poor performance is caused by poor job characteristics, then ideally the job should be redesigned for it to motivate. **Activation theory** (see Chapter 4) suggests that if it is only the processes around the work that are changed (eg rest periods), any increase in productivity will last only as long as the novelty of the change.

The characteristics of the job are defined by the design of the job itself, and the degree to which a manager can influence or change them varies from organisation to organisation. However, there are always elements of the job that managers can influence, and poor performance may be rectified without having to redesign the job.

Managers could also consider whether changes have occurred that undermine or devalue the job as a whole. For example, has autonomy been removed, actually or implicitly? This can happen if a manager interferes with or overrides decisions or agreements. It happened in the example below.

A company board agreed a strategy for sales and marketing. However, two senior directors pursued their own ideas for these areas with little or no discussion with the sales director who was responsible for delivery of the strategy. The result was confusion and significant demotivation, particularly of the sales director.

Theory X and Y (see Chapter 19) describes two broad approaches to management, but there can be no one 'right' way to manage performance. There is, however, a right way for a given individual in a given situation. A manager's preferences should not interfere with matching the needs of individuals to the needs of the organisation to achieve a worthwhile and mutually rewarding synergy. To do this, managers need to ensure that they keep in touch with their staff – enough to know what is going on with any individual at any given time – and keep up to date with what is happening in the organisation that might impact on the motivation and performance of different individuals. When necessary, the manager must then act to restore the conditions that keep people motivated toward their goals and objectives.

Key points

Many managers consider motivation to be a key issue when managing under-performers. Motivation theories can assist managers in dealing with such issues – and the key points are summarised below.

☐ Poor motivation can manifest itself through attitudes, behaviour and performance.

☐ A drop in performance could be preceded, accompanied or followed by a drop in motivation.

☐ Managers can undermine motivation through their actions.

☐ Organisational changes are likely to affect motivation.

☐ Some performance/motivation issues may just need time to resolve themselves.

☐ Individuals may not be able to attribute poor motivation to any particular cause.

☐ Changes in personal circumstances within or outside work may be causes of reduced motivation.

☐ Sometimes poor performance is accompanied by increased motivation.

☐ Managers should not assume that a person receiving feedback on poor performance knows what to do to correct it.

- [ ] People are usually motivated to address inequity, some-times resulting in poor performance.
- [ ] Expectations influence motivation and performance.
- [ ] Poor hygiene factors demotivate. Motivation factors do not necessarily compensate.
- [ ] Acceptable or desired behaviour should be reinforced.
- [ ] There is no one right way to manage motivation.

33 LEARNING

Introduction

This chapter is about the development of skills in relation to job learning. Development can be either of skills required to do the current job (job development) or of skills required to do the job, or type of job, a person aspires to (career development). We use the term 'learning programme' to discuss issues that relate to both job and career development. Although learning programmes often include formal learning events, this chapter does not cover the design or delivery of such events. The motivational issues relating to the design and delivery of learning events are covered in the chapters on **Learning for current jobs** (Chapter 24) and **Career development** (Chapter 25).

Application of theory

There arc many areas within a learning programme where motivation issues arise – three of the major ones are considered in this chapter:

- □ getting started
- □ applying new skills
- □ keeping focused on long-term goals.

Getting started

The main theme presented here is managing the attraction and selection of individuals for learning programmes. Motivation theories can help identify why individuals do not apply to join as well as what can be done to encourage them to do so. Implicit in the notion of individuals' being motivated to take part in a learning programme is the view that attendance or involvement will be voluntary. If involvement is not voluntary, individuals may resent being on a programme (even if it would be beneficial to them) and they may resist active participation. This is a view supported by the majority of motivation theories.

Most motivation theories emphasise the need to be clear about what individuals are working toward. This applies equally to learning programmes, where it is essential that potential participants know the purpose of the programme, what they need to do to join and succeed on it, and what they will get from it. **Control theory** (see Chapter 7) implies that a 'learning contract' should clearly specify standards and expectations for all involved in the programme. While clear and challenging goals need to be stated for the programme, **Goal-setting theory** (see Chapter 12) also points to the need to modify goals to account for personal differences, because 'challenging' is going to be different for different people. Interim goals could also be specified at the outset of the programme because these may help maintain short-term motivation on long-term programmes.

To be motivating, and therefore attractive, development programmes should be both challenging and worthwhile for potential participants. According to **Achievement theory** (see Chapter 3), these features should attract individuals with a high need for achievement (nAch) but may put off individuals with a high fear of failure (fF). The former are likely to give it their all if they consider the end result worthwhile. Managers should check that high-nAch individuals have the skills to succeed on the programme because they often see effort, not necessarily ability, as key to their success.

High-fF individuals may avoid getting involved in learning programmes in the first place. This may be frustrating for a manager who feels a person is wasting his or her talents, but must be sensitively explored to discover what it is that is making the individual avoid the programme. This is illustrated in the example below.

An organisation had developed an assessment-for-development event. This event was designed to highlight shortfalls in skills and behaviours required for middle management positions. The development plan that followed the event was largely self-driven and was designed to help staff get the initial experience required to be successful at the selection events for middle management positions.

The manager of Becky, a competent member of staff, felt she had potential to progress to a middle management position and encouraged her to attend the development event. Despite her manager's encouragement, Becky was reluctant to do so. When her manager asked why, Becky confessed that by attending the event she was publicly stating her intention to go for a promotion. Becky was not at all sure she was capable of taking on a more senior role and felt she would be setting herself up for failure by attending the development event.

In this example, Becky's manager could stress the benefits of the programme in general terms rather than specifically for a particular promotion. Alternatively, the manager could find out why Becky feels she would not succeed in getting a more senior position, and deal with that issue.

Attribution theory (see Chapter 5) and **Internal–external control theory** (see Chapter 15) suggest that people attribute their successes and failures to elements either largely within their control or largely outside it. This should be taken into account when reasons are being presented for not being able to attend a learning programme. People who fear failure are likely to present problems outside their control as reasons for not attending – because they do not imply any personal failure. Again, careful exploration is needed, and it may be necessary to sensitively challenge the arguments and reasons being put forward. Unless the individual can see that a threat of failure has been reduced and/or is manageable, he or she is likely to remain reluctant to join a programme. If he or she does join, it may be only to seek, or agree to, impossibly challenging goals. Once more, this is protection against failure because the person will be able to attribute any failure to the size of the goal rather than to personal inability to achieve it.

An individual may say he or she wants to join a learning programme but does not have the time or energy to do so. In this case the reluctance may be due to over-activation. **Activation theory** (see Chapter 4) suggests that an individual's

motivation to join a learning programme will partly depend
on how it contributes to his or her activation levels. These
levels apply to life overall – not just time at work. A learning
programme may thus appear stimulating and attractive to
people who feel they need more to do, and too much for those
who feel they already have enough to do – both regardless of
actual ability to develop. Managers should be aware that low
activation may attract individuals to a learning programme
for the wrong reason. If such a person's primary motivation
is for increased activation, then managers should check that
the development is also relevant. There are other ways of
increasing activation at work that might be more productive
for both the individual and the organisation.

As noted earlier, and expanded in **Expectancy theory** (see
Chapter 11), learning programmes should offer something the
individual wants, and there must be a realistic expectation
that it can be achieved. **Drive theory** (see Chapter 8) suggests that motivation is created by the dissatisfaction
between where a person is and where he or she wants to
be. This dissonance could be capitalised on when marketing
learning programmes, by pointing out opportunities and what
can be achieved by individuals who attend the programme.
Social learning theory (see Chapter 18) suggests that the
inclusion of real examples of success may strengthen the
motivation for joining the programme because people learn
from others as well as from personal experience. Of course,
these messages will only work if individuals recognise them
as genuine. **Reinforcement theories** (see Chapter 17) suggest
that messages are only reinforced if they have been observed
to be true. If a programme has established a poor reputation,
negative reinforcement and social learning may have to be
overcome before people can be expected to be motivated to
attend.

The worthiness of a programme can also influence an individual's intentions to join. **Equity theory** (see Chapter 9)
describes how people need to feel their opportunities to
develop are fair. Fairness is as perceived by the individual,
and is more than just 'Applications are welcomed from all
staff'-type statements. If a programme is presented as the
route to a particular type of position, but there are many

instances of this route being bypassed, then the programme is likely to be seen as part of an unfair process. Similarly, if a programme is seen to exclude individuals who could benefit from it, it will be seen as unfair despite an organisation's intentions.

The attractiveness of a learning programme may also vary depending on where an individual is in terms of his or her needs. **Existence-relatedness-growth theory** (see Chapter 10) and **Hierarchy of needs theory** (see Chapter 13) suggest that career development programmes are going to be particularly relevant to those interested in personal growth. They are the ones who are likely to be thinking in the longer term and feeling free from other anxieties that might otherwise stop them from undertaking extra work. However, managers should be aware that growth needs do not have to be met in work. A person who is on top of his or her job may be meeting growth needs via activities outside the workplace.

These theories also suggest that people who focus on lower-level basic-existence needs are going to be less likely to be motivated by career development programmes because their efforts are concentrated on satisfying those short-term needs. This is not to say that people with these needs should not be considered for career development programmes – rather that their motivation to attend career development programmes is likely to be extrinsic or not present at all.

Job development is probably less likely to be affected by a person's place along the continuum from existence to growth needs. What may be affected is *why* they are motivated. The person at the growth end may be motivated out of the intrinsic interest the learning can bring, and may respond to discussions about the content of the job itself and how learning will help him or her succeed in the future. The person at the existence end may be motivated by the extrinsic rewards and may respond to the attractiveness of the extrinsic rewards and some indication of how soon learning could help bring these rewards. Neither approach is right or wrong. But they do need to be managed differently.

Finally, it may help to provide learners with insights to actual programme content. If these 'tasters' are to be appetising to learners, they should reinforce the positive messages included in any marketing for the programme. In addition they need to show that the programme design is motivating in itself. Motivational design can be achieved by using **Hygiene theory** (see Chapter 14) and **Job characteristics theory** (see Chapter 16) and is covered in the chapters on **Learning for current jobs** (Chapter 24) and **Career development** (Chapter 25).

Applying new skills

Development initiatives sometimes fail because of a lack of follow-through from learning events into the workplace. The necessary follow-through is often left as the responsibility of individuals – ie they have to implement learning or undertake some form of practice or of further learning. However, effective follow-through usually requires support from other individuals in the workplace. Although the manager is usually the person to support the transfer of learning to the workplace, we recognise that this is not always the case. We therefore use the word 'supporter' as a catch-all term.

A person with a high need for achievement (nAch), as outlined in **Achievement theory** (see Chapter 3), is likely to be keen to apply his or her new-found skills or techniques. For these people the opportunity or situation in which to practise might also need to be seen as a challenge. The supporter should help to ensure that necessary resources are available, without taking responsibility away from the individual. However, this theory also suggests that people who do not value the goal may well do enough to avoid failure and no more – even if they naturally have high nAch. If circumstances surrounding the original goal have changed, it may be necessary for the supporter to help the individual focus on why the goal is still important.

Individuals who set extremely challenging development goals for themselves may have a fear of failure (fF). **Achievement theory** (Chapter 3) suggests that they may be setting themselves up to fail 'acceptably' so that they will be able to blame failure on the ridiculous goals. Careful support is needed to ensure that goals are not impossible at the outset. High fF may also cause an individual to resist follow-through from learning into practice, because it is in application that failure becomes real. It may help some individuals to be assured that their practice will not be made public knowledge.

If individuals feel they already have enough to do without learning more, **Activation theory** (see Chapter 4) suggests that they may have problems motivating themselves to add in new tasks or to take time to practise new skills. In these circumstances, the best support is to create space in 'the day job' to enable the new tasks or skills to be practised. Managers might consider ways of relieving the individuals of some of their daily workload – eg providing better support technology or an additional team member. Activation levels apply across a person's whole life, so suggesting that they practise new tasks or skills at home may not work.

Drive theory (see Chapter 8) suggests that motivation to apply or practise new techniques could come from an individual's desire to resolve a feeling of dissatisfaction in his or her current situation. An individual may thus be keen to try something in the belief that it will improve his or her current situation. If the practice is to maintain motivation, it needs to be set up in a way to ensure a positive outcome – even if not completely successful the individual needs to see that success is close at hand. Some sense of achievement is essential and is supported by theories such as **Hygiene theory** (see Chapter 14) and **Job characteristics theory** (see Chapter 16). These theories also emphasise the importance of recognition which can be part of feedback.

Recognition through extrinsic rewards should be delivered with care, because learning has to be largely driven by the individual since it is about practice. For example, a sports person can be taught the techniques (training) required for a sport, but it is the practice (development) that makes him or her good at it. **Cognitive evaluation theory** (see Chapter 6) suggests that if organisations attach extrinsic rewards to learning, it may detract from any intrinsic motivation, especially if the rewards are considered controlling (rather than informational). Supporters should think carefully about how they reward people for practical elements of learning programmes. Feedback and results should be seen as informational rather than controlling. If the programme has assessed elements – eg for practice or assignments – the marks should ideally be seen as information regarding progress rather than as objectives of the programme.

Attribution theory (see Chapter 5) and **Internal–external control theory** (see Chapter 15) suggest that people attribute their successes and failures when practising tasks or skills to factors within or outside their control. Consider the example below.

> Peter, was expected to compile a portfolio of evidence to support an assessment on an NVQ programme. Peter's manager met with him on a regular basis to give him support in doing this. It transpired during these meetings that Peter was not collecting enough information. When his manager discussed this with him, it turned out that Peter felt he was being asked to do too many other things to allow him the time to compile the portfolio. These extra duties often resulted directly from requests for Peter to take on extra duties. Peter felt he could not turn any of these requests down because he thought people would see him in an unfavourable light.

People with an external locus of control (see **Glossary**) may blame external factors as impediments to practising tasks and skills. In the above example, Peter felt he was not in control of his time, and this meant that he was restricted in the time available for learning. If the causes are actually within a person's control, the supporter may have to help the person perceive that he or she is responsible for the outcome and needs further practise and support. In the above example, Peter's manager could help him to understand that he can say 'No' to requests, and perhaps also assist by asking that all requests for extra duties for Peter go via the manager. People with an internal locus of control, and who are also high-nAch (**Achievement theory**: Chapter 3), may feel that failure to apply their new skills is simply a lack of effort on their part. The supporter may have to correct this view if it is not valid.

The preceding points introduce the need for feedback to help the individual apply new skills. **Control theory** (see Chapter 7) suggests that people have to know what the standards are and receive feedback to enable them to assess progress. Feedback on implementing learning clearly has a role here. The supporter needs to ensure that the individual knows what the standards are and how he or she is doing. It may be easy to assume that job development programmes do not require standards – after all, they should be obvious. However, it should not be *assumed* that people know what the standards are for their developing skills. It should be checked out. **Goal-setting theory** (see Chapter 12) suggests that clearly-stated goals and expectations are the most motivating – and this applies to learning goals as much as any other type of goal. Provided individuals understand and have bought into these goals, the relevance of feedback should be apparent to them.

Reinforcement theories (see Chapter 17) suggest that progress on learning programmes should be reinforced to be motivating, and feedback is one mechanism for this. However, on career development programmes that run alongside a current job it may be difficult to reinforce behaviours for a future job because those behaviours may not be appropriate to the current job. In these circumstances it will be necessary to establish a valid forum within which the learner can practise and obtain reinforcing feedback. Common ways to do this are the use of projects, placements or work-based assignments. As noted above, **Cognitive evaluation theory** (Chapter 6) suggests that feedback must be handled carefully to avoid undermining intrinsic motivation.

Reinforcement of learned skills or techniques can also be provided by role models, as described in **Social learning theory** (see Chapter 18). Provided the learned behaviours are demonstrated by significant others in the organisation and rewarded by the organisation, this can act as an incentive for the learner to seek opportunities to try out the new skills or techniques.

Keeping focused on long-term goals

Having been attracted onto an appropriate learning programme, individuals may experience difficulties in staying motivated. This is potentially most problematic when the goals individuals have agreed and set for themselves are a long way from the start-line. Particular distractions are going to be the challenges of day-to-day work and changes in individual circumstances.

At this point, it is assumed individuals are on programmes that have been well designed for relevance and motivation, and that they are working toward desirable learning objectives. In these circumstances, **Goal-setting theory** (see Chapter 12) suggests that a simple motivator is regular reminders of the learner's objectives and clear feedback on progress toward them. This might be easier to achieve if interim objectives are set along with interim development reviews. **Drive theory** (see Chapter 8) can also help if it is possible to show learners how their learning so far has made a difference in moving them nearer their goals.

It is easier to maintain an individual's interest in long-term learning goals if he or she is intrinsically motivated to pursue those goals. **Cognitive evaluation theory** (see Chapter 6) suggests that the organisation must be careful not to undermine this by shifting someone's motivation to learn from the individual to the organisation.

Anne attended a career development programme because she was interested in developing skills for possible promotion to a more senior role. Anne's development goal included developing eight new skill areas, and she quickly succeeded on three. When giving her feedback on this success, her manager said, 'I want to give you this promotion but I really want to see more progress. I tell you what – get the next two areas covered by next month, and I'll put in a good word for you.'

Not only did Anne's manager take over responsibility, and therefore a degree of control, of Anne's goals, he also, by offering to 'put a good word in', took away Anne's sense of responsibility for achieving a possible promotion.

Reminding individuals of their goals and progress toward them is important, and, as indicated, must be done carefully if it is to restore or maintain intrinsic motivation. However, there will be distractions from the day-to-day demands of the individual's current role which will also need addressing. Such pressing short-term goals may start to mean that motivation for longer-term goals diminishes. **Achievement theory** (see Chapter 3) suggests that people who do not value a goal may do enough to avoid failure and no more – even if they naturally have a high need for achievement (nAch).

Individuals with high nAch enjoy challenges, particularly ones they find rewarding and worthwhile. If the 'day job' offers more challenge and reward than the learning programme, then the job and the programme may be in competition for the individual's motivation. It may be that a supporter is needed to monitor the situation and work with the individual to maintain a balance of demands between job and learning programme. This may require adjustments to the job or programme content.

Adjustments to job content may also be necessary to ensure that an individual's activation levels remain optimum while trying to cover the demands of both the job and the learning programme. **Activation theory** (see Chapter 4) suggests that activation can be affected by increased or decreased demands outside work, and these have to be taken into account.

When individuals are concerned that they are not succeeding, and particularly those with a high fear of failure (fF), it may be tempting for them to seek reasons to give up. Those with high fF may take on goals that are too stretching – setting themselves up to fail early on. To keep going will in itself therefore be an achievement, for both the individual and the supporter. If the individual has a high external locus of control, as described in **Internal–external control theory** (see Chapter 15), it may be easy for him or her to attribute lack of motivation on a development programme to factors outside personal control – particularly if he or she is undertaking career development alongside the day job. As noted previously, short-term pulls on time may overtake longer-term needs of development. If lack of progress is actually to do with external factors, the supporter can help by securing the resources required for the learner to undertake his or her development (if it is being supported by the organisation). This includes making sure that time as well as physical resources, such as materials, are available.

People with an internal locus of control, and who have high nAch, may feel that any failure to progress on a programme is through a lack of effort. The supporter of such an individual may need to explore the reasons for this perception to check whether it is the case or not. There may be factors that are in the person's control but that are not simply a matter of effort. For example, perhaps the individual ought to learn how to manage time more effectively in order to make his or her efforts more productive.

Changes in the circumstance of an individual can include changes in the workplace and changes at home. In the workplace, changes are likely to include things that affect an individual's activation levels (as previously noted) or change the value he or she places on learning goals.

In some cases a change may make a learning objective redundant – eg promotion to a role that does not require the development provided by the current programme. **Drive theory** (see Chapter 8) explains that the resulting demotivation is because a source of dissatisfaction has been removed. The dissatisfaction a person may be seeking to resolve can also be resolved by some form of change to his or her existing role or an organisational change.

A less satisfying change to the value placed on learning objectives is one brought about by a sense of unfairness. **Equity theory** (see Chapter 9) contends that individuals, if they feel they are being treated unfairly, are motivated to address the unfairness. This may be by removing themselves from the apparently unfair situation. As noted previously, if a programme is presented as the only route to particular jobs, exceptions are likely to be perceived as unfair. The value of the learning programme and the value of the learning objectives are then brought into question. This point is illustrated by **Expectancy theory** (see Chapter 11). To maintain motivation toward a goal, individuals need to know, or at least believe, that their efforts will bring about the desired change. Instances of inequity can significantly undermine confidence in obtaining the desired outcomes. Organisational changes that reduce opportunities for achieving desired development outcomes may also have this effect.

Other changes to motivation for learning might be brought about by changes to an individual's needs. **Existence-relatedness-growth theory** (see Chapter 10) and **Hierarchy of needs**

theory (see Chapter 13) suggest that individuals who are pursuing higher-order needs, such as growth or self-actualisation, may shift their attention to protect basic needs if they feel these are under threat. Concerns about personal health or worries about finances may be such that an individual decides to defer learning objectives. Sometimes, frustration at not achieving growth needs can result in an individual seeking comfort from an area where some satisfaction is easier to obtain (frustration-regression, as outlined in Existence-relatedness-growth theory). In these instances individuals may seek satisfaction from relationships or from doing simple tasks that have clear rewards or where the outcomes are very easy to see.

Key points

Learning requires people to be motivated. Motivation theories can assist those who act to support the learners in establishing and maintaining motivation. The key points made in this chapter are listed below.

- Motivation for learning can be influenced before, during, and after a learning programme.
- Motivation to take part in learning programmes differs between people and can change for an individual over time.
- Individuals need to know that learning will be challenging and worthwhile to them.
- Individuals need to know what they are aiming at, and what the outcome will be.
- Motivation to take part in learning does not necessarily equate to ability to take part.
- Learning programmes must be seen to be fair to avoid being demotivating.
- Personal needs and drives change and affect motivation for learning.
- Ownership of learning is important and can be undermined by poor feedback.
- The 'day job' may compete with learning programmes for an individual's motivation.

☐ Lack of apparent motivation to take part may not be due to an inability to take part.

☐ Highly-activated people may not have time to learn.

☐ It is easier for an individual to keep going when learning because he or she wants to.

☐ Inappropriate rewards or recognition can undermine intrinsic motivation.

PART III

CONCLUSION

34 CONCLUSION

Most people are interested in motivation. For some it may be a passing interest in why they, or others, have behaved in a particular way. For some it is a quest to understand motivation so that they can create the circumstances in which it can flourish. For others the interest extends as far as experiments, and eventually theories, to try to explain the reasons for people's behaviour. *The Motivation Handbook* brings together the views of the theorists and applies those views to practical organisation settings.

Few motivation theories were developed specifically in work-related environments. Despite this, they can be used to help individuals understand human behaviour at work. Knowledge of the motivation theories, however, will not be enough to make a person a good manager. Motivation theories do not give definitive answers to motivation questions, but provide frameworks within which people can explore the specific situation in which they find themselves. It is thus the *application* of theories that help managers – not knowledge of the theories alone.

Bringing together theories and applications, a number of key points begin to emerge. These are explored below.

Why should organisations be interested in motivation?

Whatever the objectives of an organisation, it will require its employees to work to achieve these objectives – even if the 'employee' consists of the sole trader! The opportunity to influence the productivity of employees depends on the balance betwen technology, process and human effort in the production of goods and services – what we term the 'productivity equation'. The degree to which improvements to any part of the productivity equation makes a difference to the 'bottom line' is of interest to organisations. Improving motivation is often seen as being the way to improve the people element of the equation.

The productivity equation implies that all elements are important in the outputs of an organisation. Concentrating on improvements to one, without considering the others, may not have the desired results. Organisations who feel that they can improve their output by *only* looking at how to improve the motivation of its employees may thus have limited success for two reasons. Firstly, the production improvements gained by increased motivation may be limited by poor technology and/or processes. Secondly, people may have a limited effect on production, however motivated they are, if they are the smallest part of the equation.

We illustrate this point using two organisations – one a car manufacturer (where technology is the major part of the equation), the other a retail outlet (where people are the major part of equation). Both wish to improve profits. Despite both having antiquated technology and processes, they decide to concentrate time and effort into improving the motivation of employees. Both organisations' initiatives may successfully increase motivation. However, it is the retail outlet which is likely to see the best results in its profits – because the people element of their production equation is so much greater than that of the car manufacturer.

Motivation may also be of interest to an organisation because of its stated values. Although organisations are unlikely to choose values detrimental to their objectives, an organisation that publicly states that it values and respects the people in it may feel that it is better to set up an environment more likely to result in intrinsic motivation than extrinsic. Extrinsic motivation through inducements and threats may achieve results but is unlikely to be commensurate with a stated value of 'respecting the views and opinions of others'.

Whatever the reason, organisations have long striven to understand human behaviour. The very complexity of motivation means that most of them are still striving.

Creating a motivating environment

Because motivation is something personal to each individual, organisations and managers cannot *impose* it on others. The drive, or motivation, to behave in a particular way comes from within. However, managers *can* create incentives for others to behave in certain ways. For example, a manager who promises a pay rise or promotion is providing an incentive for those who wish for such things (or for what they bring) to perform to a particular standard. A manager who threatens staff with some punishment (showing them up at a meeting, a poor appraisal rating, or whatever) is also providing an incentive for those who wish to avoid such situations to perform in a certain way.

Organisations *can* provide the environment, resources and support to influence and affect others' motivation to behave in a particular way. For example, a promotions policy which has clear criteria and a well-supported, linked development programme is going some way to providing an environment likely to motivate some employees to behave in a particular way. A learning event that has no support from an individual's manager and that has no obvious link with what an individual sees happening in his or her job is unlikely to motivate employees to attend, or take any notice of, the learning event in question.

Although most of the motivation theories are not directed at work situations, we have shown through the practical sections that they can still apply. For example, **Cognitive evaluation theory** (Chapter 6) is used to challenge some of the assumptions about feedback and rewards. **Reinforcement theories** (Chapter 17), while not specifically about motivation, are used to illustrate the importance of actions over words. Those theories that are more directly related to work settings, such as **Hygiene theory** (Chapter 14) and **Job characteristics theory** (Chapter 16), offer many suggestions for creating motivating working environments and jobs.

The application of motivation theories to practical settings is more an exercise of encouraging readers to think 'How do I create an environment, and incentives, that encourage motivation?' than 'How do I change a person, or people, to make them motivated?'

Extrinsic v *intrinsic motivation*

Most recent views of motivation in the workplace seem to suggest that intrinsic motivation is 'good' and extrinsic motivation is 'bad'. Both achieve results, so why does it make a difference?

Herzberg describes extrinsic motivation as 'movement'. He states that 'the surest and least circumlocuted way of getting someone to do something is to administer a kick in the pants (KITA)' (Herzberg, 1968). However, the person being kicked is 'moving' – it is the kicker that is motivated. Even 'positive' KITA is still movement according to Herzberg. If an organisation provides incentives and rewards which result in action, all that is happening is that the kicker changes – 'the organisation does not have to kick you; you kick yourself' (*ibid.*). Both types of KITA require the kick (or the threat of a kick) to be administered for action. In other words, extrinsic motivation requires the inducements (or threats) that achieve results to be carefully managed and usually to be ever-present in order to continue to motivate.

Intrinsic motivation is usually seen as more effective because the impetus to 'move' is from within. People are acting because they feel satisfied or fulfilled by the activity they undertake. In a work setting this means that management is more about support than control.

It could be concluded that intrinsic motivation may result in an easy life for managers. However, in many ways, striving to create an environment in which intrinsic motivation is the preferred result of management practice and process is more complicated and challenging than setting up one in which extrinsic motivation is the result. Seeking to satisfy every member of staff's needs is a challenge when some degree of similarity in jobs and processes is required in order to organise the work. Even if everyone had the same needs, **Hierarchy of needs theory** (Chapter 13) and **Existence-relatedness-growth theory** (Chapter 10) suggest that people move on from needing to satisfy short-term basic needs to seeking to satisfy longer-term fulfilment needs. People will therefore want different things from a job depending on where they are in the hierarchy.

It could also be inferred that *any* extrinsic motivation is 'bad'. This is an unrealistic view. For example, all organisations using pay, bonuses, performance management processes and so on to encourage a particular standard of performance could be 'accused' of encouraging people to work for the incentive rather than for the satisfaction of the job itself. As outlined in **Cognitive evaluation theory** (Chapter 6), all such rewards are likely to have some detrimental effect on intrinsic motivation.

It is probably unrealistic to hope that all aspects of a job will satisfy the intrinsic needs of those that undertake it. **Job characteristics theory** (Chapter 16) suggests that a more realistic approach for organisations seeking to encourage intrinsic motivation is to ensure that the basics are right (pay, working conditions, policy, etc) and then spend most energy on those factors that appeal to intrinsic motivation (autonomy, feedback, skill variety, etc).

Extrinsic motivation is therefore part and parcel of modern working life. It is not a 'bad' thing, but to encourage it to the exclusion of intrinsic motivation requires much management control, precisely-written job descriptions, and constantly-enforced management systems and processes. Because this is contrary to many current people management policies we suggest that most organisations would not want to work this way.

Perception is key

A core feature of many motivation theories is that the perception of the individual is key. Whatever managers or colleagues may think, if an individual perceives a situation in a particular way, that is his or her reality. For example, in **Equity theory** (Chapter 9) the concept of fairness is defined in terms of the individual's perception, not in terms of what other people deem 'fair' to be. In **Attribution theory** (Chapter 5) a person's control over his or her environment is described in terms of the degree to which an individual perceives external factors influence his or her behaviour, not in terms of how much others perceive those factors to be influential.

What we have aimed to achieve with *The Motivation*

Handbook is to outline the key motivation theories and suggest ways in which they apply in practice. We hope that our readers have gained the insights they were seeking.

References

HERZBERG F. A. (1987) 'One more time: how do you motivate employees?'. *Harvard Business Review*. Vol. 46. pp109–20. (Note: This article includes a reprint of an article that appeared in *Harvard Business Review* in Jan–Feb 1968).

GLOSSARY

A few of the terms (mostly psychological jargon) we use in the book may not be familiar to some readers.

affect The conscious aspect of an emotional state; the awareness of motivation behind personal feelings.

cognitive Involving knowing/knowledge (eg through sensation or perception) as distinct from involving emotion or impulse. A cognitive process is therefore one in which a person applies his or her knowledge.

consonance A state of agreement or harmony.

contingent Dependent on something else. For example, an organisation's performance is contingent on the performance of its staff.

cybernetics The science of communication and automatic control systems in both machines and living things.

dissonance A state of discord or disagreement.

expectancy An attitude that centres on anticipation of a particular event.

extrinsic motivation Motivation that is based on factors external to the individual. Any inner satisfaction is usually considered secondary.

extrinsic reward A reward (not necessarily financial) that is bestowed on an individual by someone else, or an external factor.

ibid. The reference is to the one cited immediately before.

intrinsic Motivation that is based on factors internal

motivation	to the individual rather than on an extrinsic reward.
intrinsic rewards	Rewards felt by the individual that are effectively also bestowed by the individual. For example, feelings of self-satisfaction and fulfilment.
locus of causality/control	The source of the control a person perceives he or she has over his or her behaviour.
mystery shopper audits	Audits conducted by auditors posing as customers to assess levels of the services provided by an organisation.
neurophysiology	The study of the relationship between the nervous system (especially the brain and spinal cord) and the processes of life.
physiological	Of the science of the processes of life.
piece rate pay	Pay per unit of work produced.
prepotency	Something taking precedence over something else in its effect.
teleworking	Working from a location other than the organisation's premises (usually at home) but connected to the organisation's base via modem and telephone.
valence	The predicted value of an object, event, goal, or equivalent.
validity	The degree to which a theory is true in a particular setting.
work ethic	The attitude of a society or group which places a high moral value on hard work.

References

Definitions in the above Glossary are based on those given in:

Chambers English Dictionary. 7th edition (1990). Edinburgh, W. and R. Chambers Ltd.

REBER A. S. (1985) *The Penguin Dictionary of Psychology*. Middlesex, Penguin Books Ltd.

CHARACTER PROFILES

Throughout the book we have used four fictional characters to bring to life various theories and points about behaviour. Each character's background is outlined below.

Rachel

Financial status: Has just purchased her first home and is finding money a bit tight.

Job: Personnel clerk for a large bank. This is Rachel's first job after leaving college.

Short-/medium-term aspirations: Finishing her professional qualification with the aim of becoming a personnel officer in her department.

Long-term aspirations: Rachel would like to work her way up in the bank to become a personnel manager and maybe do some further studies.

Interests: Currently mostly interested in furnishing her new house.

Relationships: Rachel is feeling a bit lonely socially because the flat she has just bought is in a new area for her. Generally, Rachel gets on well with people at work, especially those in her department where she has worked for two years. She is keen to be a popular member of the team and likes others to see her as sociable and approachable. She is single.

Character: Rachel sees herself as a bit of a 'victim'. She feels that the things that happen to her in life happen due to luck, chance or fate. She has lately felt that she is perhaps too fatalistic, and that she ought perhaps to take more control of her life. Recently she attended an assertiveness training course to try to help.

Neil

Financial status: Has just become a father for the third time and is finding money a bit tight. His partner is planning to go back to work, but child care and household bills will obviously increase.

Job: Sales manager for a mail order company.

Short-/medium-term aspirations: Because he is fairly new in the job, Neil would like to spend a couple of years getting to grips with it and achieving high sales figures in his department. Bonuses are closely tied in with sales in Neil's company.

Long-term aspirations: Would like to become a sales director either within his current firm or somewhere else.

Interests: Mostly family-related. He is a good artist and likes to spend his rare moments of spare time painting.

Relationships: Neil and his partner are finding the new baby and their financial worries a strain on their relationship. Neil's focus on getting the job done well means that he is sometimes seen as aggressive and uncaring. He likes others to think of him as successful, and personal presentation (how he dresses, what car he drives, and so on) is very important to him.

Character: Neil is a firm believer in working hard to achieve what you want. Generally he thinks that if you want something enough, and if you work hard enough at it, you will get it. He dislikes working with people who do not share this belief.

Mandy

Financial status: Is comfortable, and although would not turn down the opportunity to earn more money, feels that she has enough to support her lifestyle.

Job: Management consultant in a small partnership.

Short-/medium-term aspirations: Would like to specialise in management development and do most of her work in this area over the next few years.

Long-term aspirations: Mandy would like to become recognised as a specialist in her field not only through her work but through published articles, speaking at conferences and perhaps even writing a book.

Interests: She very much enjoys her field of work and spends a lot of her spare time reading up about – or attending meetings and conferences on – management development.

Relationships: Mandy likes to be thought of as knowledgeable and professional in her line of work. She is not concerned about being liked, and more interested in being good at what she does. Mandy finds that she does not have close friends at work, mostly because of the nature of her job. However, she has a good network of contacts, most of whom she considers she gets on well with. Mandy is married to Fred, who has retired from his job. They have a very stable and mutually supportive relationship.

Character: Mandy feels that she is very much in control of her destiny and situation. Sometimes this means that she takes responsibility for situations that are actually for others to deal with.

Frank

Financial status: Is very comfortably off having paid off his mortgage five years ago. His eldest child is just about to finish university, so Frank considers his major financial commitments to be at an end.

Job: Human resources director for a major insurance company.

Short-/medium-term aspirations: The organisation that Frank works for is introducing a new pay and grading structure. Frank's short-term ambition is to get this introduced and working well. He is heading up the pay and grading project, which is considered key to helping the organisation improve its performance.

Long-term aspirations: Frank is two years away from retirement. He likes to keep fit and wants to build up his fitness so that he can run a marathon during his first year of retirement. He is planning a six-month tour of Europe with his wife soon after he retires.

Interests: Frank spends a lot of his spare time running, cycling or swimming. He is also keen on history and enjoys visiting old churches, castles and stately homes – particularly those dating from the sixteenth and seventeenth centuries.

Relationships: Frank likes to be thought of as a firm but fair professional man who is good at his job. He considers it important not to be a distant boss with no interest in his team, so he makes a point of celebrating such key events with his team as birthdays, weddings and the like. Frank's wife Sally has been very supportive of him and is looking forward to his retirement and their trip around Europe.

Character: Frank feels that life is generally a mix between events that one can control and events that one cannot. He has worked hard to achieve his successes, but also admits that some things – good as well as bad – have been beyond his control.

INDEX

hierarchy of needs theory 156, 158
hygiene theory 107, 110–11, 156
reinforcement theories 154–5
theory X and Y 154
see also job characteristics theory
job design theory *see* job characteristics
   theory
job diagnostic survey 122, 124
job dissatisfaction 103–4, 105, 108, 109
job satisfaction
   hygiene theory 103–7, 108–11
   and instrumentality 78, 80
   relationship with performance 81
job security
   hygiene factors 104
   organisational change 190, 246
   safety needs 95
   temporary team members 207–8

Kanfer, R. 2–3, 6
Kelly, H. H. 31
Klein, H. J. 48, 50
Koopman-Iwema, A. M. 5–6, 21, 82,
   109, 115–16

labour turnover 79, 106, 121–2
latent learning 60
Lawler, E. E. 80, 81
learned helplessness 32
learned responses, drive theory 56–8, 61
learning contracts 254
learning events
   delivery 178–80
   design 175–8
learning needs 176–7, 180–81
learning policies 174–5, 180
learning programmes 253–66
   attraction and selection of
      participants 253–8
   long-term goals 261–5
   transfer of learning 258–61
Leventhal, G. S. 67
Locke, E. A. 52–3, 84, 85, 86, 87, 88, 91
locus of causality/control cognitive
   evaluation theory 37–8, 44
   definition of term x
   internal-external control theory 33,
      34, 112–14, 115–16
   and learning programmes 260, 263–4
   and organisational change 192–3
   and poor performance 247–8
   and selection processes 198
Lord, R. G. 48

low activation 25–7, 28
lower-order goals 50–51, 52
lower-order needs 94–5, 97, 100
luck 32, 34, 112, 163

Manderlink, G. 46
Mandy (case example)
   achievement theory 19
   character profile xiii–xiv
   drive theory 58
   equity theory 65
   existence-relatedness-growth theory
      73
   expectancy theory 79
   job characteristics theory 122
   reinforcement theories 130
   social learning theory 137–8
manipulation, resistance to 113–14,
   115
Martinko, M. J. 35
Maslow, A. H. 94, 95, 96, 97, 98,
   100
McClelland, D. C. 15, 17–18, 20
McGregor, D. M. 142
mental health 106
Miller, G. A. 48
minority groups, equity theory 67
motivating potential score (MPS) of jobs
   120, 121, 124
motivation
   definitions of 2–3
   hidden nature of 3
   relevance to organisations 269–70
   role of organisations and managers 7,
      271
motivation theory
   classifications of 6
   definition and nature of 5–6
   practical value of 7–9, 271
   see also names of individual theories
motivator-hygiene theory *see* hygiene
   theory
motivators, described by Herzberg
   104–5
'movement', distinguished from
   motivation 103, 108, 109, 272

nAch *see* need for achievement (nAch)
nAff *see* need for affiliation (nAff)
need for achievement (nAch)
   applications 205, 211, 215, 219, 220,
      223, 229, 239, 254, 258
   theory 16–17, 20, 21–2